Britain's Conservative Right since 1945

Kevin Hickson

Britain's Conservative Right since 1945

Traditional Toryism in a Cold Climate

Kevin Hickson
Department of Politics
University of Liverpool
Liverpool, UK

ISBN 978-3-030-27696-6   ISBN 978-3-030-27697-3   (eBook)
https://doi.org/10.1007/978-3-030-27697-3

Cover credit: Sven Hansche/EyeEm/Getty Images

This Palgrave Macmillan imprint is published by the registered company Springer Nature Switzerland AG
The registered company address is: Gewerbestrasse 11, 6330 Cham, Switzerland

FOREWORD

This is an excellent and wide-ranging book—excellent, at least in part, because it is so wide-ranging.

Anyone who fondly imagines that the political Right is somehow synonymous with a Thatcherite attachment to the unfettered workings of the free market will soon be disabused by Dr. Kevin Hickson's patient unravelling of the many different strands of conservative right-wing thought. Indeed, although there was much that was genuinely conservative about Thatcherism—notably, its patriotism and moral traditionalism—circumstances dictated that it would be seen, above all, as the resurrection of nineteenth-century liberalism.

Hickson's discussion in some ways resembles an archaeological dig. For he has unearthed specimens of conservative ideology (including my own) which, without his work of excavation, would perhaps not have come to light after their initial, fleeting appearance. Still, if in the aftermath of Brexit, Conservatives are ever again to adopt a coherent public philosophy, they may find it profitable to sift through the material here presented in such a thoroughly rigorous, academic fashion. If nothing else, Hickson's book should remind us all that there is (or at any rate should be) more to Conservatism than keeping the CBI happy or appearing nice rather than nasty.

Among the many interesting questions arising from the book is this: what distinguishes the Conservative Right from your average or mainstream Conservative politician, who incidentally lives in terror of being labelled right-wing for fear he will be shunned by polite society as well as, in all likelihood, his own party.

Actually, without the Conservative Right to nourish it, the Conservative Party would have precious little to offer beyond a thin gruel of bromides: the gospel of getting on, aka (materialist) aspiration; equality of opportunity; and, of course, economic liberalism extending, more and more these days, to social liberalism, with both doctrines enshrining freedom of choice as their most sacred dogma.

To liberal-minded conservatives, then, society is a contract between freely consenting, self-interested individuals who, if left more or less to themselves, will (so it is claimed) produce a natural harmony. Granted, a minimal legal framework, buttressed by a 'night-watchman state', are both needed to prevent people harming one another (as John Stuart Mill famously said); but otherwise laissez-faire is the best policy.

It is little wonder that those Conservative politicians who subscribe to this self-denying ordinance seldom have anything of consequence to say. They don't really believe in politics. Indeed, if truth be told, they have no political vocation. For them, all too often, politics collapses into economics. The business of politics is, well, business.

To compound this low view of government, many Conservatives, whether explicitly or not, endorse a state which is neutral towards rival conceptions of the good life, all of which are deemed to deserve equal respect. Judgementalism is the one sin decent, godless folk, and their representatives, cannot abide. Legislators must not permit their private ethical concerns to affect their public policies, which should be addressed purely to the satisfaction of people's desires and the protection of their interests, whatever these happen to be.

The Conservative Right takes an altogether less sanguine view of the anything goes, all lifestyles are equal, culture of liberal modernity. And for this reason, it takes a more elevated—high Tory, one might say—view of government and what it can or should do. The 'what Lola wants, Lola gets' credo may be appropriate for the marketplace where the consumer's sovereign wants cannot be gainsaid. But the notion is destructive of what Edmund Burke called the 'little platoons' of society, namely those intermediary institutions—intermediary, that is, between the individual and the state—which are not governed, wholly or at all, by the promptings of self-interest.

Of these, the most important is the family. The experience of the last fifty years or more (confirmed by countless pieces of research) has taught that when this institution disintegrates, the effects, particularly on children—and by extension, on society—are dire: educational under-attainment, increasing resort to drink and drugs, unemployment and crime. Modernising Conservatives (David Cameron's name springs to mind) like to say they are 'relaxed' about the different forms families now take, thereby revealing a lazy acquiescence in the idea that whatever the process of change brings is necessarily beneficent or progressive.

The failure of conservative politicians and policy-makers to edit or judge social change is apparent in other areas, for example in the pathetic reluctance to enforce our drug laws on the grounds (not readily admitted) that the demand for illegal substances is such that decriminalisation is an inevitable consequence. Similarly, a woman's 'right to choose' seems so in tune with the prevailing ethos of consumerism that most Conservatives dare not even listen to arguments about lowering the time limits at which abortions should take place.

Needless to say, the Conservative Right is far from hostile to a market economy. But it does not believe in a market society, in which man as a moral and ethical creature is eclipsed by economic man. Citizens are not simply consumers and customers. How could they be when by definition privatised individuals are not citizens? Hollowed out by free-market dogmatists as they may have been in recent years, many institutions— one thinks especially of those belonging to the legal and medical professions—nonetheless resist to this day crass attempts to turn them into businesses. Sadly, it seems to be too late for the Universities.

Hickson has done his readers a valuable service in reminding them of conservative voices which have continued to echo Burke in asserting that:

> The state ought not to be considered as nothing better than a partnership agreement in a trade of pepper and coffee, calico, or tobacco, or some such low concern... It is to be looked upon with other reverence, because it is not a partnership in things subservient only to the gross animal existence of a temporary and perishable nature. It is a partnership in all science; a partnership in all art; a partnership in every virtue and in all perfection. As the ends of such a partnership cannot be obtained in many generations, it becomes a partnership not only between those who are living, but between those who are living, those who are dead, and those who are yet to be born.

Child Okeford, UK   Ian Crowther
June 2019

ACKNOWLEDGEMENTS

This book would not have been possible without the cooperation of numerous people. I am very grateful to all those who gave up their time to be interviewed. The book has taken longer than anticipated, not least because of the substantial number of interviews which I secured, far more than I initially thought likely. The interviewees listed in the bibliography all welcomed the chance to discuss their ideas with me. Numerous librarians and archivists have assisted me at various stages. I am personally grateful to Sir Adrian Fitzgerald for allowing me access to his papers on the Monday Club.

A special word of thanks must go to Ian Crowther for writing the Foreword. Ian has made a sustained, distinctive and thoughtful contribution to the political thought of the Conservative Right, firstly as a regular contributor to *Monday World* and then as Literary Editor of *The Salisbury Review* for a number of years.

I am also grateful to the publisher for supporting this project, especially to Anne-Kathrin Birchley-Brun for her encouragement and practical support, and to the publisher's anonymous reviewer for his/her helpful comments on the draft.

I wish to put on record my appreciation to family and friends. Matt Beech and Jasper Miles, in particular, had to hear more about my thinking on the Conservative Right than they ever would have wished and there were times when I should have been more attentive to the needs of my family when I was instead locked in my study.

Wistaston   Dr. Kevin Hickson
July 2019

CONTENTS

Contents

CHAPTER 1

Introduction

This is a study of the Conservative Right since 1945: its major ideas, policy positions, organisations and personalities. It is written in the immediate context of Brexit, where the Conservative Right has gained greater significance. With the Government lacking a majority, the influence of factions within the Conservative Party increases. The need for such a study is therefore most timely. With the Conservative Right in a position of ascendance, it is necessary to trace its development historically. In order to do this, the study makes use of relevant archives and extensive interviews with key figures associated with the Conservative Right. It provides a distinctive and rigorous academic study of the Conservative Right, while adding to a growing body of literature which takes ideas and ideology importantly when studying the Conservative Party.[1]

The aim is to describe, to analyse and to evaluate. The book is not a polemic, but an academic study of a distinctive tradition, one which has arguably received insufficient scholarly attention.[2] It follows a hermeneutical methodology, seeking to recover the meaning of concepts, arguments and ideas in their historical context. Rather than following a chronological framework, the book instead approaches the Conservative Right in a thematic way, examining the key ideas within its political thought. A thematic, rather than chronological, framework allows for a clearer understanding of the Conservative Right. The ideas, concepts and issues which are held to be core to the political thought of the Conservative Right since 1945 are: Empire, immigration, Europe, the constitution, the Union, political economy, welfare and social morality.

© The Author(s) 2020
K. Hickson, *Britain's Conservative Right since 1945*,
https://doi.org/10.1007/978-3-030-27697-3_1

The study begins in 1945 for the obvious reason that it marks a watershed moment in British politics with the end of the Second World War and the election of the first majority Labour Government which embarked on a programme of what—by British standards at least—can be regarded as a radical reforming agenda. These reforms—social and economic—led to a new policy consensus up until the 1970s and those on the Right of the Conservative Party were to argue that mounting social and economic problems of that era were the direct consequence of the post-1945 settlement. It was also apparent that the United Kingdom had come out of the War weakened though victorious against the threat of Nazism and Fascism. However, Britain was to continue its decline after 1945—both relatively in terms of its economy and absolutely as a geopolitical power. The British Empire ceased to exist as the majority of its overseas territories were granted independence. The emerging Commonwealth led to dilemmas over how to handle rising non-white immigration. The emergence of European integration also posed a major challenge to the British system of government. Moreover, there were a number of challenges to the British constitution throughout this period, notably political violence in Northern Ireland and the rise of nationalism in Scotland and in Wales. The stresses and strains within the old order were apparent to those who wished to see it, and those who claimed to see it most clearly were the Conservative Right who saw themselves as not only the keepers of the Conservative conscience but also as defenders of the nation state.

THE IDEOLOGY OF THE CONSERVATIVE RIGHT

Definition, if not quite everything in scholarly writing, is certainly of fundamental importance. Hence, we need to define what is meant by Conservative Right much more precisely.

One way of doing this is through the identification of core values and principles of an ideology. Inevitably, such an exercise is somewhat arbitrary and always open to challenge. The book will demonstrate that the set of core values identified here are recurring themes within the Conservative Right historically and contemporaneously. Another issue that needs to be discussed is whether it is possible to identify a single tradition we can term the Conservative Right or whether there are in fact multiple traditions, each underpinned by different value judgements and relevant at different times and for different reasons.

A key distinction here is between Conservatism and conservatism. While the latter concerns a more general tendency or disposition to resist change and preserve the familiar or could be understood as a wider tradition of philosophy, the former is concerned with the ideas and practices of the Conservative Party. The two may be interlinked, indeed it is one argument of this book that the traditional Conservative Right is the point at which the two most clearly intersect, but they can be—and usually are—distinct entities. The extent to which the Conservative Party is genuinely conservative can, and has been, questioned throughout the party's history. The party's desire to remain a credible electoral force has often seen it adopt the colours of its ideological (and sometimes) party rivals. In the late 1970s and early 1980s a dispute erupted within the party between opponents and supporters of Margaret Thatcher, with both sides claiming to be 'genuinely' conservative. On the pro-Thatcher side of the debate, Keith Joseph argued that he always thought he was a conservative but realised at the fall of the Heath Government in 1974 that he was not.[3] By this he meant he had been insufficiently free market. However, among the opponents of Thatcher and the rapidly emerging 'Thatcherism', Ian Gilmour spoke for them when he said that the free market had nothing to do with conservatism.[4] A third possible interpretation—one with which this book generally concurs—is that neither were conservative, but rather liberal in essence. Joseph was liberal in an economic sense, while Gilmour was liberal in a social and cultural sense.[5]

This dispute between Gilmour and Joseph leads on to the need to distinguish the terms Right and Left. Though dating back to the French Revolution, the usefulness of the terms has been disputed for almost as long. While the original use of the terms referred to those who sought to defend the status quo (Right) from those who sought radical change (Left), the terms have not always meant this. Indeed, in the era of Thatcherism, the terms appear to have been upended with the Right seeking radical change and the Left often defending the status quo. Indeed, as this study will show, there were those on the Right who also critiqued Thatcherism for its pace and extent of reform. It is now typical to argue that the terms should be rejected completely. However, this study uses the term for two reasons. Firstly, that many of the figures we examine self-identified as being on the Right. In the extensive interviews conducted for this study, few objected to being deemed to be on the Right of the political spectrum or the Right of the Conservative Party. Secondly, the terms Left and Right are used as convenient shorthand labels in political conversation and so could be reasonably considered to have meaning to those participating in the conversation.

This, in turn, leads on to a further distinction. Thatcherism was synonymous with the New Right. However, for there to be a New Right there also has to be an 'Old Right'. While the former has been studied at considerable length, this study seeks to discover more precisely what the 'Old Right' was and how it both related to and differed from the New Right. The distinction is arbitrary to the extent that some individuals and organisations explored in this volume moved, with varying degrees of enthusiasm, from the Old to the New Right. The New Right should not be seen as a distinct ideological position. Instead there was some evolution from the Old Right to the New Right due to changing political context, in particular growing concerns over the decline of the British economy which led some to embrace the then fashionable idea of economic liberalism. Some went along with more conviction, others believed that there was really no alternative whereas some opposed the free-market emphasis which they believed was destructive of the traditions they were seeking to uphold.

It is also necessary to distinguish the Conservative Right from the One Nation tradition. The Conservative Right would distinguish itself from the moderate, or One Nation, wing of the Conservative Party which it would see as essentially liberal in character. Whereas the moderate wing would be willing to make the compromises necessary to get into power, the Right would see itself as defending the conscience of the party. For this reason the Conservative Right is frequently antagonistic towards currents in society and critical of the Conservative Party for being too willing to follow those currents.

Throughout the book we refer to the terms Tory, Toryism and Traditional Toryism. The term is related to but not synonymous with Conservatism. Enoch Powell said that he was born a Tory and would die a Tory.[6] John Biggs-Davison said that Toryism was something which was unique to the English: it 'is not a name for foreign intimation... Toryism is not for export'.[7] Although they disagreed over several issues as this book will explore, these two politicians were central to the development of the Conservative Right. For Biggs-Davison there were two strands of the Conservative Right the traditional which he represented and the popular, which was articulated by Powell.[8] Norton and Aughey distinguish between Whig and Tory strands of Conservatism. While the former was rationalistic, the latter was anti-rational, being concerned with instincts rather than programmes.[9] The theme of Traditional Toryism is then explored by Aughey,[10] in general, and by the current author in terms of several of its key thinkers in particular.[11]

Several analysts of the Conservative Party, especially those who may be deemed more sympathetic to its Right wing would deny that the Party is ideological, or indeed that ideology matters. The influential Tory historian Maurice Cowling formulated a historical approach which treated ideas as if they were largely unimportant.[12] Instead, in the sphere of what he called 'high politics' what mattered was the pursuit of power by individual politicians within the political elite. Outcomes of such things as the struggle to extend the franchise to sections of the male working class in the 1860s, the rise of the Labour Party in the years after the First World War and the events which led up to the outbreak of World War Two can all be interpreted in this way. Building on this approach, Jim Bulpitt argued that ideas were irrelevant to serious politicians as they were concerned with statecraft, the pursuit and exercise of power.[13] Hence, to look for an ideology of the Conservative Right would be foolhardy from this perspective. However, it is possible to identify certain core ideas or recurring themes in the historical evolution of the Conservative Party more generally and its right-wing in particular.

Michael Freeden describes political ideologies as clusters of social concepts, each interpreted in different ways and consistently being reformulated.[14] He identifies core, adjacent and peripheral values. The core values are at the essence of any ideology, for instance freedom is essential to liberalism and equality to socialism. However, these concepts are essentially contested. They are open to a range of possible interpretations. Liberty can be described as either positive (freedom to) or negative (freedom from); equality as either outcome or opportunity. Adjacent values are those which have a semi-permanence and peripheral concepts are those which come and go over time as issues ebb and flow. Applying this model to conservatism (I deliberately use lower case here to signify a wider philosophical position) we could identify certain core values without the presence of which it would be possible to argue that an ideology is not conservative. Such concepts would include tradition, authority, social order and nationhood. Each of these concepts is itself contested so that there emerge different strands of conservatism. So too in the Conservative Party. To give two examples. Social order is normally interpreted by the Party's right-wing as concerned with the defence of traditional (Christian) morality and the rule of law. However, while not necessarily opposing those things, more progressive (or One Nation) Conservatives would normally place more emphasis on social order as the preservation of social unity through measures designed to alleviate class antagonisms. Similarly, when we look at the concept of the nation, more right-wing elements within the Conservative Party would tend to see their country as being under threat from internal and external challenges. In contrast, One Nation Conservatives have often defined nationhood as something which is best expressed and enhanced through international cooperation. For instance, that membership of the European Union extends, rather than limits, national sovereignty.

Hence we can identify certain interpretations of key concepts which are central to any understanding of the Conservative Right. These concepts, or values, can be simply listed as: a pessimistic view of human nature, preservation of social order, promotion of the authority of the state, nationalism and inequality. As will be discussed in the next section listing of values for any ideology is problematic since there will always be tensions within any given ideological tradition. Ideologies are evolving traditions of thought and practice. However, we will list them here and enter qualifications later. These views are held instinctively by those on the Conservative Right. As Jonathan Aitken put it, 'a true conservative feels things from the heart and doesn't intellectually rationalise them'.[15]

Pessimism

Most ideologies would tend to start with a conception of human nature. For liberals and for most socialists, human nature is best understood in positive terms. Human beings, following Enlightenment philosophy, are imbued with reason and rationality. They should therefore be free to pursue their own version of the good. Social reform is only justified where existing structures are deemed to corrupt 'true' human nature. In contrast, traditional conservatism held to a much more pessimistic view of human nature. As John Hayes put it, 'we appreciate that man is fallen, frail and faulted'.[16] Hayes argues that the only option, therefore, is to 'make the best of an imperfect world'.[17] Normally, the justification for this came from Scripture, with the act of original sin being committed in the Garden of Eden. Since we are all descended from Adam and Eve, as the first humans, then we all inherited that sin. For some, Biblical reference was explicit. For John Biggs-Davison: 'The Tory believes in the doctrine of original sin... His opinion of human nature and human beings is humbler and more cautious than that of the liberal or social-ist'.[18] Lord Blake warned that optimistic social reformers were bound to be disappointed since, 'cruel and evil people exist at all times in all forms of society'.[19] For others they derived their sense of pessimism from empirical observation, if human beings are rational then why should there be so much sin in the world?

Hence philosophic conservatives would tend to a much more negative view of human nature. Rather than seeing the extension of human freedom as inherently a good thing, therefore, greater emphasis was placed on the need for social order and respect for established tradition, custom and practice. Lord Sudeley argued that, 'our nature is so corrupt that laws are necessary to impose the code of conduct which rests a little above ourselves'.[20] The conservative view of human nature leads traditionalists on to emphasising responsibilities rather than rights. According to Alan Smith, writing in a Monday Club pamphlet at the end of the 'permissive' 1960s, 'man is an individual but an individual with duties as well as rights'.[21] It was this focus on duties which distinguished conservatism from its major ideological rivals liberalism and socialism.

One example of this was the Seventeenth Century philosopher Thomas Hobbes who argued that human beings were driven by selfish instincts who would inevitably conflict with other individuals pursuing their self interest. In a state of nature—that is a social condition without the existence of a sovereign power to uphold the rule of law—life of man would be 'poor, nasty, solitary, brutish and short'.[22] Individuals, realising that the only way they could live in peace and security would forgo their unlimited freedom by signing it away in the form of a social contract to a sovereign power, which would be charged with the sole responsibility of maintaining the social order.

In contrast to Hobbes' reliance on the theoretical construct of a social contract, Edmund Burke emphasised the need for individuals to respect tradition.[23] The idea that individuals chose which polity they belonged to was nonsense since people were born into a pre-existing social order. They had no right other than to plead allegiance to its rule over them. The established political system had evolved over centuries and had developed its own character over time. Individuals could not possibly know more than the accumulated wisdom of tradition and so any attempt to overthrow it, as was happening in France at the time he wrote, would be bound to end in tyranny.

At the end of the Nineteenth Century, Lord Salisbury served as Prime Minister. His premiership is one of the longest in British history yet is known for having few striking achievements. As Andrew Roberts says, it is barely remembered at all.[24] Modern governments would seek to find their place in history, a lasting legacy, some major act of social change for which they would be remembered. Salisbury, in contrast, believed that the role of government was to do very little other than to preserve social order and protect the nation from external enemies. Although he believed that certain forces at work at the time he was alive would lead to social disintegration there was nothing one could ultimately do to stop them. The wise statesman would delay. Government would need to be ever vigilant but ultimately was bound to fail. The frailties of human nature would ensure that all that was good in society would decay.[25] The traditionalist Conservative therefore would resist change, and would only see it as justified where it is designed to avert more radical reform by remedying a recognised and accepted defect in the present arrangement of things.

The primary aim of the Conservative statesman should therefore be to maintain the status quo, only allowing limited change where necessary. As Kenneth Pickthorn stated, 'a Conservative is a man who believes that in politics the onus of proof is on the proposer of change, that the umpire when in doubt should give it for the batsman'.[26] Such a bias towards limited change was based on a recognition of the frailties of the human intellect. As Gillian Peele put it: 'for the Conservative, ordinary men and women and their imperfect and perhaps regrettable wants and emotions have to be seen as the starting-point of political debate and not as the raw material from which a new and radically different sort of society might be moulded'.[27] Whereas the 'progressive' reformer would welcome radical change where it furthered their principles, the conservative would regard this as the arrogant dismissal of accumulated wisdom. In place of progress, conservatives recognised that all that may be achieved is to go 'round and round very much on the same spot'.[28] As the current Lord Salisbury put it, 'proper Tories don't really believe in –isms because they don't really believe in the perfectibility of man and if you don't believe in the perfectibility of man you know that things are going to go wrong'.[29]

Although followers of the Victorian Salisbury would maintain he was correct they would accept that a political party in the democratic era would be hard pressed to echo his pessimism publicly. A party exclaiming at a General Election that it could ultimately not do anything to halt the forces of decay would not attract much support. Therefore, even the most pessimistic of Tories have been keen to demonstrate their support for any Conservative Leader they think capable of fighting the good fight, even if they ultimately thought they would lose the battle against the forces of 'progress'.[30]

However, to leave this discussion of the Tory view of human nature there would be mistaken. Traditional Conservatives have also stressed the virtues of human character.[31] Michael Oakeshott talked of the individual as someone possessing character, a character of self-help and individual responsibility. In contrast, there was the individual manqué, a person who lacked the essential characteristics of the upright individual.[32] Although such people exist in any society they were particularly prevalent in Britain after the Second World War since the welfare state had created a culture of dependency. Margaret Thatcher stated that she wished to reverse this process and restore what she termed the Victorian values, or what one of her closest academic supporters termed, the vigorous virtues.[33] Hence, although humans would ultimately remain sinners—meaning that there will always be some level of social coercion—they were also capable of acting responsibly. Writing in 2005, Edward Leigh still believed that there was grounds for optimism.

> in poll after poll, the majority of the British show themselves...obstinately attached to common sense. They still believe, for the most part, in "small c" conservative values – law and order, patriotism, marriage, family, parental discipline, and so on.[34]

Lord Coleraine believed that authentic conservative philosophy combined both Tory and Whig elements in its understanding of the human condition. The Tory tradition recognised that human nature contained 'dark and frightening propensities', whereas the Whig appreciated that the individual is a 'uniquely valuable being'. The two strands were complimentary, holding each other in bounds.[35]

Such a view of human nature leads traditionalist Conservatives to adopt one of two positions. The first is the importance of experience in contrast to radicals, who stress the importance of youthful idealism and who embrace youth culture and counter culture. This was seen most vividly in the 1960s, but also frequently among those who argue for the lowering of the voting age and other reforms designed to foster a greater sense of political activism in the young. In contrast, conservatives have argued that politics is a skilled activity requiring the application of judgement based on experience. Such arguments for the value of experience were also used to justify the refusal to extend the franchise to working-class men and to women. Peregrine Worsthorne was unashamedly elitist when he argues that this is the virtue of a political system based on aristocratic rule.[36]

However, another tendency within the Conservative Right has led it to embrace more populist arguments, trusting the instincts of the masses against the elites. Biggs-Davison thought it a virtue that the British people had 'been shrewdly resistant' to intellectuals.[37] Sir Cyril Osborne argued that the character of the people is to be found in the rural areas:

> Village life retains much of England's traditional virtues – self reliance and self respect, and a willingness to work... You country people have a natural gentility, dignity, and decency.[38]

In contrast, the metropolitan elites hold to a different set of values to the majority of the population. This has been seen most vividly in recent years in relation to Brexit, where the wishes of the electorate are deemed to be being thwarted by the elite. Michael Gove's comment that Britain no longer trusts experts can be seen in this context.[39] Writing in 1944, Christopher Hollis stated his belief that, 'there is no form of inequality more generally galling than the superiority over the average man claimed by the intellectual'.[40] Against the development of a professional political elite, charted by commentators such as Peter Oborne,[41] traditionalists prefer the well-intentioned amateur. Politics is ultimately about principles rather than facts, and the amateur is closer to the political instincts of the mass. In 1979, Margaret Thatcher captured the Tory mood when she spoke of 'another Britain which may not make the daily news (of) thoughtful people, oh, tantalisingly slow to act yet marvellously determined when they do'.[42] The values of liberals and socialists are alien to the instinctive positions of the mass of the population, for whom Tories claim to speak. William Cash stated that 'Conservatism is not anti-establishment for the sake of it, but should be willing to take it on when it is doing things which are not in the interests of the people I represent and not in the interests of the country at large'.[43]

Social Order

Following on from this conception of human nature, traditionalists would therefore argue that the central objective of public policy must be the preservation of social order. Moral order must be defended, for otherwise, as Ian Crowther puts it, 'people left to their own devices... are people left to their own vices'.[44] Throughout this study we will see that the Conservative Right placed great emphasis on the preservation of the rule of law. To cite Lord Salisbury again, the state needed not only to possess strong coercive powers but to demonstrate them. Hence, he believed that it was wrong to abolish public executions in England since this sent out the clearest symbol of all regarding the duties the citizen had to follow the laws of the land. A particular strength of the English (not British) system of law according to Roger Scruton is the evolutionary nature of judge-made law in the form of Common Law, which is a distinctly English tradition. However, the failure of the English themselves to recognise this has placed it in jeopardy.[45]

Each generation of the Conservative Right has sought to dismiss claims by those of more 'progressive' opinions that law and order needed humane reform. According to Biggs-Davison, liberals neglected the importance of individual responsibility: 'men can be made better, the "progressives" insist by Act of Parliament. Nor is man wholly responsible or culpable. He is the product of his environment and that can be transformed'.[46] This approach dehumanises by reducing, if not eliminating the importance of punishment. For Scruton, punishment concerns retaliation for breaking the law. Rehabilitation fails to deal with an evil which has been perpetrated. 'It is a retribution, an institutionalised revenge, the desert of the criminal as much as the right of his victim'.[47] We see this in the attempts to refute arguments in favour of abolition of the death penalty in the 1960s, of corporal punishment in schools, in prison reform and in the apparent 'softness' of rehabilitation schemes. It is not that traditionalists seek to dismiss the role of rehabilitation in penal policy, since what would be the point of a criminal law which did not lead to reduced rates of recidivism? However, they would argue that a policy which prioritises rehabilitation over all else is incorrect since it negates the victim. Instead, penal policy should have a strong deterrent effect—like Lord Salisbury's defence of public executions—and prioritise punishment of wrongdoers.

Social conservatives have been repeatedly concerned about what they see as the erosion of traditional moral precepts, again drawing on their own interpretation of the Bible. This reached its peak in the 1960s with the passing of so-called 'permissive' legislation including abolition of the death penalty, relaxation of divorce law, legalisation of homosexuality and abortion, and loosening laws on censorship. Advocates of such reforms would argue that these measures were 'civilising'. However, traditionalist critics argued that they were giving licence to immoral acts and storing up future social problems. By the 1970s and 1980s, the Conservative Right believed that their warnings of the previous decade were coming true. Writing in 1982 John Heydon Stokes argued that progress had been exclusively material, with 'a marked rise in living standards and an appalling fall in moral standards'.[48] Whether one was the cause of the other, however, was largely ignored in these commentaries. The matter split the conservative right in the 1980s, with defenders of Thatcherism, such as Shirley Letwin, arguing that Thatcher was restoring the 'vigorous virtues' whereas dissenters such as Peregrine Worsthorne believed that all she was doing was fuelling bourgeois materialism.[49] More recently, socially conservative commentators have argued that further social liberalisation and political correctness have only exacerbated such issues. Despite 18 years of Conservative Government in the intervening period, Hayes sounded a similar note to earlier warnings when he said that, 'the liberal orthodoxy is failing Britain'.[50] For some, the Thatcher years had not really been socially conservative at all.[51] Indeed, although social conservatism is not limited to the right of the Conservative Party it is certainly something which exercises the Conservative Right including—as we will see later in the book— criticising the Conservative Party itself for being too influenced by social liberalism.

Authority and Sovereignty

The Conservative Right would also uphold the virtues of a strong but limited state, possessing both authority and sovereignty.

As T. E. Utley has argued, the primary responsibility of the state is the defence of the nation and the preservation of social order.[52] This is the essence of political activity, contrary to more idealised notions of the political. It must therefore be imbued with significant powers including a monopoly of legitimate coercive power. It must also be able to apply this power to all parts of the territory which it governs. As Lord Salisbury said, the role of the government is like that of the policeman. If there were no criminals there would be no need for the policeman. Similarly, if there were no threats to the social order there would be no need for the government. Utley argued in the period after 1945 that government had lost sight of this essential function and had started to develop other interests which at the same time increased the powers of the state but also weakened it as its attention was diverted from its core functions.[53] Similarly, Oakeshott argued that the British state had moved decisively away from being a 'civil association' concerned with upholding the rule of law towards an 'enterprise association' which had a project within which individuals ceased to be free actors and instead became resources for the attainment of some specific purpose.[54] Such projects included social justice and higher rates of economic growth. The post-1945 policy settlement was a clear instance of an enterprise association. Supporters and detractors of Thatcherism would argue over whether her governments marked a new type of enterprise association or a return to a pre-1945 era of civil association.

For traditionalists, society is comprised of several institutions which provide sources of authority. These include the church and the family. Unfortunately, they maintain, these institutions have been consistently undermined. Church attendance was high in Victorian and Edwardian Britain, but declined from the end of the First World War onwards. This decline has become sharper in more recent years. Factors such as the spread of secular humanism and of other faiths as Britain became more multicultural are significant, but so too have been the growth of liberalism within the churches and especially the Established Church. For some, a key aim is the need to show reverence for the traditional prayer book.[55] While the Church of England remains important to some such as Roger Scruton,[56] precisely because it is the established church and imbued with English cultural influences, others have moved to either the Catholic faith or evangelical churches because they have remained less open to the forces of religious liberalism. The family, too, has been in decline due to the increased numbers of children born out of wedlock and changes to the law which make divorce and abortion easier. Hence, Edward Leigh argues that 'traditional sources of authority, including religion and the family, have been challenged by liberal ideas that assert the primacy of individual choice in all political considerations'.[57] Once again, the threat is not deemed to be socialism but rather liberalism, in this case secular liberalism.

Traditionalist Conservatives have sought to defend sovereignty against what it perceives as threats to it. Such challenges can be external or internal to the nation state. Examples of such internal challenges would include political violence in Northern Ireland. Irish republicanism was seen as a direct threat to the sovereignty of the United Kingdom state since the IRA sought to achieve Irish reunification through violence. The real threat of the IRA was not so much direct since with the right policies it could be defeated, but rather through successive British governments seeking to compromise with the IRA and with the government of the Irish Republic. Hence, even when there was an overtly right-wing Conservative Government in the 1980s the Party's right wing—along with the Unionist parties of Northern Ireland—roundly rejected the Anglo-Irish Agreement. The Union was also perceived to be under threat from the rise of Scottish and Welsh nationalism from the 1960s onwards. Sovereignty was understood by the Conservative Right as an absolute, or indivisible concept. Sovereignty could not be shared between Westminster and another centre of power, be it Dublin, Cardiff or Edinburgh.

Similarly, this absolutist conception of sovereignty led to traditionalist Conservatives largely—but not, as we will see, exclusively—opposing the process of European integration. While it was valid to be a part of international organisations such as the United Nations which professed no intention of being a supranational body, equally the European Economic Community (EEC)/European Union (EU) was not compatible with the defence of national sovereignty since it had intentions of operating above the level of the nation state. While pro-Europeans would see no derogation of sovereignty in joining the EEC, indeed they would claim that the UK would gain more effective power by being part of a larger political entity, nationalistic Conservatives would point to the ways in which the Westminster Parliament could no longer take decisions by itself.

Nationhood

A further concept associated with the Conservative Right is that of the nation, indeed a commitment to a nationalistic form of politics is central to the thought of those who hold such an ideological position. For conservatives, the community cannot be maintained purely or for very long by coercion, with patriotism being the force which sustains communities. As Pickthorn said, 'order can be maintained most easily and with the least coercion among men who have most in common… common memories, sentiments, aversions, hopes and principles'.[58] Conservative nationalism is essentially defensive rather than aggressive. The nation state is under threat and has to be defended.

For Angus Maude and Enoch Powell, 'there is no objective definition of what constitutes a nation. It is that which thinks it is a nation'.[59] Although nations may be defined by characteristics such as language and ethnicity they argue that nations are defined above all else by a collective self-consciousness consisting of two aspects: 'one looking inwards, the other outwards; one the sense of unity, the other the sense of difference'.[60] By 1968, Powell was notoriously to argue that the sense of unity was being undermined by the arrival of people with a different skin colour.

For the Conservative Right nationalism was exclusive in the sense that it belonging to some and not to others, not everyone could share in a specific nationality. 'It is a very great privilege to be an Englishman' stated Christopher Hollis.[61] However, this did not mean that nationalism was aggressive or expansionary. By highlighting that which made a person of one nationality different to others did not mean that other nationalities were inferior or to be attacked, but it was something worth defending from it enemies. Powell made this clear in the course of the 1970 General Election when he claimed that 'Britain at this moment is under attack'[62] not from outside enemies as in the case of the two world wars but from the internal enemy.

It was to be a rhetorical phrase used again by Margaret Thatcher throughout the 1980s when she sought to defend the nation from the 'enemy within' and the 'enemy without'.[63] The enemy within was predominantly the trade unions but also left-wing councils, civil liberties organisations and the anti-nuclear lobby. Such concern with taking on and defeating the enemy within led to open battles with the trade unions, especially the National Union of Mineworkers in 1984–1985, the abolition of the Greater London Council and the, according to her opponents at least, erosion of civil liberties. The enemy without variously being the Argentinian junta, the Soviet Union and, finally, the European Economic Community which Thatcher had initially supported but then moved increasingly against from the late 1980s with her Bruges speech of 1988 followed by vocal opposition to her successor's stated aim of being at 'the heart of Europe'. At first, commentators on the Conservative Right were sceptical of Thatcher, who they believed to be little more than a Nineteenth Century liberal. Roger Scruton penned *The Meaning of Conservatism* as a corrective.[64] However, with Thatcher's stance over the Argentinian invasion of the Falkland Islands, Powell commented that she had proven her strength. Stokes argued that 'the nation has suddenly found itself over the Falklands Crisis'[65] after years of political timidity and national decline following the Suez Crisis. Later, however, some criticised Thatcher for diluting national sovereignty by signing the Anglo-Irish Agreement.

For many on the Conservative Right in the 1940s and 1950s the nation was very much bound up with Empire. Britain had been struggling to maintain its colonial commitments in the interwar years with India and Burma being granted greater independence. Joseph Chamberlain had called in the early years of the last century for the closer integration of the UK and her colonies through a system of preferential trade but this had split the Party between its imperial and free-trade wings. It was only in the 1930s that preferential trade was accepted. For its supporters this was too little, too late. The moment to save the empire had passed. The imperialism of the post-1945 era was, therefore, also defensive in tone and content, seeking to slow down the rate of decolonisation and stressing the importance of the colonies and former colonies in the emerging Commonwealth. This in turn also led supporters of the Commonwealth such as Julian Amery and John Biggs-Davison to advocate closer European integration believing that the two were mutually reinforcing rather than antagonistic. However, for others the disintegration of the British Empire, though painful, was fact and the interests of the nation involved recognising this reality and adjusting accordingly. Powell was of this view which led him from being an arch-imperialist to arguing against both the Commonwealth and the EEC.

These stresses and strains over the winding up of the Empire also clouded the postwar Right's view of America. For them, whether imperial diehards or 'little Englanders' America was viewed with suspicion. In this the views of the Conservative Right echoed those of the Labour Left, albeit for different reasons. America was to be distrusted. The idea of a 'special relationship' between the UK and the USA was a myth. America had actively sought to force the UK into a position where it had to wind up its Empire so that the US could become the dominant superpower. They had also intervened, and continued to do so, in the politics of Ireland in the interests of Britain's enemy.

Very much at the heart of this nationalism was the Tory belief in exceptionalism. Britain had a unique history, one marked by peaceful evolution compared to the violent revolutions on continental Europe. The evolution to the industrial society and to mass democracy had been handled skilfully. The aristocracy were respected and admired in the UK as they had been able to adapt pragmatically to changing times, unlike on the continent where they had shown themselves to be reactionary leading to events of which the French Revolution of 1789 was the most dramatic. Britain had also stood alone in Europe in 1940 against the Nazi threat, or if not completely alone then with the support of its loyal Commonwealth and Empire which had generally been a force for good in civilising and developing the continent of Africa in particular and other backward countries more generally. Whereas other European powers had lost their Empires or had tried to maintain them through force, the close ties between the former colonies and the UK was evidenced by the Commonwealth. Britain had emerged victorious through two world wars. Moreover, Britain was distinguished by its island mentality and seafaring ways.

While in the postwar period the major threat to the nation was from communism, in more recent times the Conservative Right has seen liberalism as a major threat. According to Leigh, 'patriotism of all but the most subdued kind is regarded by the liberal establishment as at best vulgar, at worst sinister... Liberals are only too happy to see a decline in debate about the nation state'.[66] The essential task of the conservative in such conditions is the preservation of the nation. For Crowther national loyalties and differences remained a natural part of political life.

> Only someone leading an especially sheltered life – dare one say, a liberal intellectual, or perhaps a globe-trotting businessman – could seriously believe that from the spread of free markets and democratic regimes will come a new form of humanity, unencumbered by national, cultural or ethnic differences... A sense of nationhood... is not something that can be relegated to the realm of folk dancing and kept alive only as a tourist attraction.[67]

Intellectuals, as George Orwell stated, were inclined to be dismissive of English identity.[68] Traditional conservatives, seeing themselves as being more in tune with the instincts of the masses, see their task as the defence of England even if it means battling against the elites. Brexit being a prime example.

But if the political association was of the United Kingdom of Great Britain and Northern Ireland then the cultural reference point was to England.[69] The Union was defensible as long as it was predominantly English. Welsh and Scottish identity could be maintained as long as they did not threaten the Union. Englishness did not need to be demonstrated as it was synonymous with Britishness. Two problems emerged later from this. The first was that once the pressures for separation—politically and culturally—began to show there was little sense of what Englishness was. One of the challenges for the Conservative Right was to forge a clearer sense of English identity when the future of the Union looked doubtful. The second was the presence of a community in the North of Ireland which was more expressively British, than the rest of the UK.

Inequality

A final characteristic of the Conservative Right, and one which led it to reject socialism, was a belief in the inevitability and desirability of the hierarchical society.[70] For the Conservative Right this was not only inevitable but was desirable precisely because it was natural. Maurice Cowling said that inequalities were not just sought by those who would 'benefit from inequality of wealth, rank and education but also by enormous numbers who, while not partaking in the benefits, recognise that inequalities exist and, in some obscure sense, assume that they ought to.' They assume this because, 'they are accustomed to inequalities, inequalities are things they associate with a properly functioning society and they do not need an ideological proclamation in order to accept them'.[71] In pre-industrial times such inequality was manifest in rural communities where the local squire took a paternalistic concern over the lives of his servants and tenants. This had, they claimed, survived after the Industrial Revolution in the countryside up until the early part of the last century. Aristocracy was also an ideal, as Peregrine Worsthorne maintained: 'English aristocracy is best understood as a particular manner of exercising power – a uniquely domesticated and civilised manner of exercising power, which in turn encouraged and made possible an equally civilised manner of exercising powerlessness'.[72]

However, postwar political, social and economic developments had undermined the ideal of aristocratic government. Both socialism and the economic liberalism of Thatcher had, in their own ways, damaged the traditional ruling class.[73] Socialism required a ruling class to implement its policies but at the same time preached an egalitarianism which eroded its authority. Thatcherism had unleashed selfishness and materialism which had eroded the authority of the ruling class by undermining public service. Hence, 'matters were made only worse by the arrival in the 1980s of Mrs Thatcher – a force as destructive of gentlemanliness as any in the 1960s'.[74] The result was a new rich of 'vulgar, loud-mouthed, drunken yobboes, scarcely better, if at all, than football holigans'.[75] The legacy of Thatcherism was to destroy the value of public service, which the old order promoted. The economic policies, and the alliances which were necessary in order to implement them, may have been necessary, but they brought with them great costs. Hence, by 2004 Worsthorne was lamenting the loss of the old order: 'when I say that aristocracy is missed, I do not mean... that dukes and earls are missed; rather that the aristocratic idea, of which they used to be an embodiment, is what is missed'.[76] Writing years before, Hollis had made the same defence of the aristocracy: 'the truth is that it has been one of the greatest of national strengths that the moneyed men in this country, to an extent far greater than in any other country, have been willing to give up their time and energy to unpaid public service'.[77]

The most common way for the Conservative Right to defend the notion of inequality against its socialist rivals in recent decades is to promote the idea of meritocracy. The problem with the post-1945 welfare state is that it had reduced incentives to work and created a dependency culture. According to Christie Davies, this misplaced emphasis on equality amounted to destroying 'the old order of thrift, knowledge, culture and respectability in order to confer equality on the thriftless, the ignorant and the feckless'.[78] Instead, Thatcher and her governments sought to reduce taxes on the rich in order to encourage entrepreneurship while also attaching more conditions to the receipt of welfare. The result was that inequality increased over the course of the 1980s and 1990s. According to advocates of the 'New Right' such inequality was desirable since it would create more wealth overall and some of this would 'trickle down' to the less fortunate thus raising all ships. Although Thatcher presented this in the language of freedom, for some it was not freedom which was the true aim of Conservatism but inequality.[79]

STRESSES AND STRAINS

The above fivefold categorisation of the ideology of the Conservative Right is inevitably an abstraction, the ideal type. In reality political ideas evolve, sometimes rapidly, as politicians respond to developments and seek other objectives such as raising their own profiles or courting public support. Individual politicians who we will look at experienced significant adaptations to their own ideas and also held opposing ideas to their contemporaries who may otherwise be deemed to be on the same ideological page. For instance, Powell originally favoured membership of the EEC at the first attempt at joining in the early 1960s but later came to be an arch opponent of entry even to the point of encouraging people to vote Labour in 1974 on the basis that they promised the prospect of leaving the EEC through a referendum. Not everyone we will examine in this study held consistently to socially conservative viewpoints. Thatcher, for instance, believed in the restoration of the death penalty—although her long premiership did not see its revival—but had a much more liberal viewpoint on divorce, no doubt because of her husband's experience.

There were three main fault lines within the Conservative Right in the period under consideration which will be explored in later chapters.

The first concerns the response to the absolute decline of the British Empire. Although the empire had been in decline for many years prior to the outbreak of war in 1939, the period after the restoration of peace in Europe showed a marked decline in Britain's imperial commitments. For some, the decline of the empire may not have been inevitable, and certainly did not need encouragement from the Conservative Party. This led them to embrace rearguard actions against the more moderate wing of the party which openly embraced decolonisation. This was particularly so in the early 1960s when Harold Macmillan called for the 'winds of change' to sweep across the continent of Africa.[80] The Monday Club was established to resist, or at least delay, decolonisation. In contrast, others—notably Enoch Powell—argued that the Empire had long ceased to be a reality by this point and urged the party to adopt a more overtly nationalist position. Debates erupted on the Right between 'late imperialists' and 'little Englander' nationalists over issues such as immigration and European integration.

The second set of tensions relate to constitutional issues. For traditionalists, the constitution represented the gradual evolution of political wisdom. It should therefore be reformed as little as possible, with major reforms likely to result in untold damage to the body politic.

However, for some the decline of Empire, and other deleterious changes which had taken place in Britain since the end of the War, led them to believe that the constitution wasn't working. Moreover, the system had failed—indeed had appeared to facilitate—the rise of socialism. Some on the Conservative Right therefore embraced radical or reactionary postures on the constitution. The same pattern could be detected in terms of the Union, where some argued—especially post-devolution—that alternatives to the status quo needed to be found.

The third was domestic and concerned the economy. The values we have sketched out, with the possible exception of inequality, are not primarily about economics. Most ideological positions do take economics as their central concern. Certainly the major disagreements within the Labour Party concern the management of the economy—such as the balance of public and private ownership in the 1950s—alongside non-economic issues such as the retention of nuclear weapons. Similarly, the tensions between Thatcher and her One Nation critics in the early 1980s were principally ones about economic management. However, the traditional right of the Conservative Party was less concerned with economics. This reflects the fact that it has a pre-democratic lineage. Tories are non-rational, or anti-rational, and therefore concerned with concepts such as those mentioned above. In contrast, Whigs take a more programmatic approach to politics and are therefore either economically liberal or more collective in their approach to the economy. As the franchise expanded economics became more important as a political issue. Manifestoes took on greater importance and economic competence became a key test of a party's ability to win an election. Certainly from the 1970s onwards the Conservative Right, first under the influence of Powell and then Thatcher has been committed to the free market. Economic liberalism has had a massive impact on the Conservative Right. However, this was not always the case and there were alternatives in the 1970s and beyond including the maintenance of a more protected national economy or a more distributist economy based on the ideas of G. K. Chesterton and Hilaire Belloc where the class divide is overcome through economic partnership and cooperation. These ideas will be explored and the extent to which the traditional aims of the Conservative Right have been helped or hindered by the pursuit of economic liberalism will be assessed, not only in terms of economic policy but also the impact of economic liberal ideas on the welfare state and wider social change.

STRUCTURE OF THE BOOK

In addition to this Introduction and the Conclusion, the book has eight main chapters. Each of these chapters is based around a key theme. A thematic approach was preferred to a strictly chronological framework for clarity in demonstrating how the ideas of the Conservative Right have evolved.

Chapter 1 discusses the Empire since many of the subsequent themes and debates can only be understood in the context of the disintegration of the British Empire which challenged views of national identity and economic and social change. It looks at how the Empire was disestablished after 1945 and how this reflected Britain's diminishing world role. Events such as the Suez Crisis of 1956 and Harold Macmillan's 'winds of change' speech in 1960 will be explored. This is very much wrapped up in the notion of British decline and the extent to which Thatcher reversed national decline through events such as the Falklands War will also be explored.

The end of empire led on to two specific issues which will be explored in Chapters 3 and 4. The first is the phenomenon of Commonwealth immigration and debates over national identity and multiculturalism. The second is the emergence of closer European integration and the nature of Britain's involvement in the process, charting the attitudes of the Conservative Right to entry, membership and finally leaving the EU.

The following two chapters will examine constitutional issues as these are very much concerned with the authority of the state and the nation as a political entity. The first issue relates to constitutional conservatism and the defence of the Westminster Model and the traditional institutions of the nation state as they faced growing demands for reform. The second issue is the territorial integrity of the Union in response to armed violence in Northern Ireland and separatist movements in Scotland and Wales alongside growing demands for political and cultural articulations of Englishness.

Chapter 7 will examine economic policy. In particular it will look at the spread of economic liberal thinking within the Conservative Party. Three positions can be identified here. Those who embraced economic liberalism with enthusiasm, those who became more sceptical and those who opposed it more fundamentally. Alternatives such as distributism and national protectionism will be explored.

The next chapter will explore Conservative Right attitudes to the welfare state, examining why it largely opposed the extended provision of welfare services by the state after 1945 and how its arguments have evolved over time. It will show that the Right had limited impact in the era of the so-called postwar consensus but was closer to the policy agenda implemented after 1979.

The final substantive chapter will explore Conservative Right attitudes to wider social change such as punishment, divorce, censorship and homosexuality. Not surprisingly the social conservatives opposed the 'permissive' reforms of the 1960s, but were also critical of subsequent Conservative Governments including that of Margaret Thatcher, who purported to be reviving social conservatism.

The concluding chapter will evaluate the impact of the Conservative Right since 1945 and how it has sought to come to terms with changes it has not liked.

NOTES

1. It thus builds on my own previous scholarship, notably K. Hickson (ed.), *The Political Thought of the Conservative Party Since 1945* (Basingstoke: Palgrave, 2005); M. Garnett and K. Hickson, *Conservative Thinkers: The Key Contributors to the Political Thought of the Modern Conservative Party* (Manchester: Manchester University Press, 2009).

2. There have been serious academic studies before, of course. In addition to my own initial works cited above numerous others are relevant. The Right has either been analysed as part of wider studies of the Conservative Party which have stressed the importance of ideas. Such accounts would include A. Gamble, *The Conservative Nation* (London: Routledge, 1974); A. Gamble, *The Free Economy and the Strong State* (Basingstoke: Macmillan 1988 and 1994). Other studies take a more chronological approach, notably classic texts such as R. Blake, *The Conservative Party from Peel to Major* (London: Heinemann, 1997). A recent study which has examined the Conservative Right is, *The Conservative Party and the Extreme Right, 1945–75* (Manchester: Manchester University Press, 2013) by Mark Pitchford. This is an excellent study, but differs from this one in the sense that this study is primarily about ideas rather than organisations and doesn't seek to address the issue of the connections between the Conservative Right and the extreme Right. It is a study of the 'inside Right' rather than the 'outside Right' in this sense.

3. See the relevant chapter in Garnett and Hickson, *Conservative Thinkers*.
4. See I. Gilmour, *Inside Right* (London: Quartet, 1977).
5. Garnett and Hickson, *Conservative Thinkers*—'The Traditionalists'.
6. See S. Heffer, *Like the Roman* (London: Weidenfeld and Nicolson, 1998).
7. J. Biggs-Davison, *Tory Lives* (London: Putnam, 1952), p. 5.
8. John Biggs-Davison papers, Parliamentary Archives, BD/1/864.
9. P. Norton and A. Aughey, *Conservatives and Conservatism* (London: Temple Smith, 1981).
10. A. Aughey, 'Traditional Toryism', in Hickson (ed.) *The Political Thought of the Conservative Party Since 1945*.
11. Garnett and Hickson, *Conservative Thinkers*—'The Traditionalists'.
12. See, in particular, M. Cowling, *1867: Disraeli, Gladstone and Revolution: The Passing of the Second Reform Bill* (Cambridge: Cambridge University Press, 1967); *The Impact of Labour* (Cambridge: Cambridge University Press, 1971); and *The Impact of Hitler* (Cambridge: Cambridge University Press, 1975).
13. J. Bulpitt, 'The European Question', in D. Marquand and A. Seldon (eds.) *The Ideas That Shaped Postwar Britain* (London: Fontana, 1996).
14. M. Freeden, *Ideologies and Political Theory* (Oxford: Oxford University Press, 1998).
15. Interview with Jonathan Aitken, London, 6 February 2017.
16. J. Hayes, 'Being Conservative', in Cornerstone Group, *Being Conservative: A Cornerstone of Policies to Revive Tory Britain* (London: Cornerstone Group, 2005).
17. Interview with John Hayes, London, 4 July 2017.
18. J. Biggs-Davison, *Look to the Foundations: A Tory Restatement* (1949).
19. Lord Blake, 'A Changed Climate', in Lord Blake and J. Patten (eds.) *The Conservative Opportunity* (London: Macmillan, 1976), p. 11.
20. Lord Sudeley, 'The Role of Heredity in Politics', *Monday World*, Winter 1971/72.
21. A. Smith, *No Mean City* (London: Monday Club, 1969).
22. T. Hobbes, *Leviathan* (Harmondsworth: Penguin, 2016, originally published in 1651).
23. E. Burke, *Reflections on the Revolution in France* (Harmondsworth: Penguin, 2003, first published in 1790).
24. A. Roberts, *Salisbury: Victorian Titan* (London: Orion, 1999).
25. P. Smith (ed.) *Lord Salisbury on Politics* (Cambridge: Cambridge University Press, 1972).
26. K. Pickthorn, *Principles or Prejudices* (London: Signpost Booklets, 1943).
27. G. Peele, 'The Conservative Dilemma', in Blake and Patten (eds.) *The Conservative Opportunity*, p. 14.
28. A. Jones, *The Pendulum of Politics* (London: Faber, 1946), p. 13.

29. Interview with Lord Salisbury, London, 12 October 2016.
30. C. Moore, *Margaret Thatcher: The Authorised Biography, Volume 1: Not for Turning* (London: Allen Lane, 2013).
31. Aughey, 'Traditional Toryism', pp. 14–18.
32. M. Oakeshott, 'The Masses in Representative Democracy', in T. Fuller (ed.) *Rationalism in Politics and Other Essays* (Indianapolis: Liberty, 1991).
33. S. Letwin, *The Anatomy of Thatcherism* (London: Fontana, 1992).
34. E. Leigh, *The Strange Desertion of Tory England* (London: Cornerstone Group, 2005), p. 9.
35. Lord Coleraine, *For Conservatives Only* (London: Tom Stacey, 1970), pp. 21–22. See also, K. Hickson, 'Lord Coleraine: The Neglected Prophet of the New Right', *Journal of Political Ideologies*, 14/2 (2009), pp. 173–187.
36. P. Worsthorne, *In Defence of Aristocracy* (London: HarperCollins, 2013).
37. J. Biggs-Davison, *The Centre Cannot Hold: Or Mao, Marcuse and All That Marx* (London: Monday Club, 1969).
38. Quoted in Gamble, *The Conservative Nation*, p. 113.
39. H. Mance, 'Britain Has Had Enough of Experts, Says Gove', *Financial Times*, 3 June 2016, available at https://www.ft.com/content/3be49734-29cb-11e6-83e4-abc22d5d108c, accessed 30 April 2019.
40. C. Hollis, *Quality or Equality?* (London: Signpost Booklets, 1944), p. 16.
41. P. Oborne, *The Triumph of the Political Class* (London: Pocket Books, 2008).
42. Moore, *Margaret Thatcher*, p. 414.
43. Interview with Sir William Cash, London, 13 October 2016.
44. I. Crowther, 'Conservatism', in W. Outhwaite (ed.) *The Blackwell Dictionary of Modern Social Thought* (Oxford: Blackwell, 2002), p. 111.
45. R. Scruton, *England: An Elegy* (London: Continuum, 2006).
46. J. Biggs-Davison, *The Centre Cannot Hold*, p. 5
47. R. Scruton, *The Meaning of Conservatism* (Basingstoke: Palgrave, 2001, 3rd edition), p. 77.
48. J. Stokes, 'The State of the Nations', *Primrose League Gazette*, 86/2 (April 1982), p. 5.
49. P. Worsthorne, *The Politics of Manners and the Uses of Inequality* (London: Centre for Policy Studies, 1988).
50. Hayes, 'Being Conservative', p. 3.
51. P. Hitchens, *The Abolition of Britain* (London: Quartet, 1999).
52. T. E. Utley, *Essays in Conservatism* (London: Conservative Political Centre, 1949).

53. T. E. Utley, 'A Comparison of Parties', in P. Dean, J. Douglas and T. E. Utley (ed.) *Conservative Points of View* (London: Conservative Political Centre, 1964).

54. Oakeshott, *On Human Conduct* (Oxford: Clarendon, 1975).

55. Lord Sudeley, 'The Church Militants', *The Salisbury Review*, 5/3 (April 1987).

56. R. Scruton, *Our Church: A Personal History of the Church of England* (London: Atlantic, 2012).

57. Leigh, *The Strange Desertion of Tory England*, p. 23.

58. Pickthorn, *Principles or Prejudices*, p. 6.

59. A. Maude and E. Powell, *Biography of a Nation* (London: Pitman, 1955).

60. Ibid.

61. Hollis, *Quality or Equality?* p. 8.

62. E. Powell, 'The Enemy Within' speech, Birmingham 13 June 1970, reprinted in J. Wood (ed.) *Powell and the 1970 Election* (Kingswood: Elliot Right Way Books, 1970).

63. See Gamble, *The Free Economy and the Strong State* (1994), pp. 61–68.

64. R. Scruton, *The Meaning of Conservatism* (Basingstoke: Palgrave, 2001, 3rd edition).

65. J. Stokes, *Primrose League Gazette*, 86/3 (May–June 1982), p. 3.

66. Leigh, *The Strange Desertion of Tory England*, p. 48.

67. I. Crowther, 'Is Nothing Sacred?' in *The Salisbury Review*, 9/2 (December 1990), pp. 11–12.

68. G. Orwell, *The Lion and the Unicorn: Socialism and the English Genius* (Harmondsworth: Penguin, 2018, originally published 1941).

69. A. Aughey, *The Politics of Englishness* (Manchester: Manchester University Press, 2007).

70. P. Dorey, *British Conservatism: The Politics and Philosophy of Inequality* (London: Tauris, 2010).

71. M. Cowling, 'The Present Position', in M. Cowling (ed.) *Conservative Essays* (London: Cassell, 1978), pp. 9–10.

72. P. Worsthorne, *In Defence of Aristocracy*.

73. Ibid.

74. Ibid., p. 103.

75. Worsthorne, *The Politics of Manners*, p. 9.

76. P. Worsthorne, *In Defence of Aristocracy*, p. 94.

77. Hollis, *Quality or Equality?* p. 10.

78. C. Davies, 'The Three Inflations' *The Salisbury Review*, 20/3 (Spring 2002), p. 6.

79. Cowling, 'The Present Position'.

80. H. Macmillan, 'Winds of Change' speech available at https://www.youtube.com/watch?v=c07MiYfpOMw, accessed 30 April 2019.

CHAPTER 2

Empire

As the Conservative Party came to terms with the realities of democratic politics with the gradual extension of the franchise in the Nineteenth Century it presented itself as the party of the nation, rather than one associated with narrow class appeal.[1] By the second half of the Nineteenth Century the British nation was an Imperial nation, indeed the largest of the world's empires. The Conservative Party then was an imperialist party. Benjamin Disraeli had sought to capitalise on this by extending the franchise to sections of the male working class and crowning Queen Victoria as the Empress of India. However, even by the start of the Twentieth Century the cracks were beginning to show in the British Empire and Joseph Chamberlain sought to strengthen the ties that bound the Tory Party, the working class and the empire together through preferential trade. This split the Party between its imperialist and free-trade wings. The mounting economic problems in the 1920s and 1930s, together with the growth in support for the Labour Party did lead to the acceptance of such protectionist policies at the Ottawa Conference of 1932.

Despite this the stresses and strains of the British empire continued to show with growing calls for independence in the major colonies. Although the Commonwealth continued to support the UK during the Second World War it did not stop demands for self-determination culminating in the granting of independence to India and Pakistan in 1947, and Burma (Myanmar) early the following year. The Commonwealth was established in 1949 with all members able to leave at their will. The, at

© The Author(s) 2020
K. Hickson, *Britain's Conservative Right since 1945*,
https://doi.org/10.1007/978-3-030-27697-3_2

one time easy, appeal the Conservative Party could make to the Empire was no more.

This chapter will explore the attitudes of the Conservative Right to the Empire in the post-1945 era. It will begin by looking at the initial opposition to the process of decolonisation from 1945 onwards. It will explore the attitudes of key individuals associated with the Conservative Right who sought to defend the virtues of the British empire, not least against those who favoured more rapid decolonisation within the Conservative Party and those, notably Enoch Powell, who sought to formulate a post-imperial British nationalism.[2] It will also explore key developments such as the Suez Crisis in 1956, Harold Macmillan's Winds of Change speech in 1960 and the Falklands War of 1982 which for some at least marked the revival of British patriotism. It will also examine the role of key groups on the Conservative Right such as the Suez Group and the Monday Club. Although often adopting an assertive nationalism we will see that the position is better described as defensive on the matter of the empire, seeking to defend the empire from those who sought its demise.

THE IMPERIAL DIEHARDS

The case for continuing Britain's colonial commitments was made vociferously by Leo Amery who expressed strong doubts over the capacity of colonials to become self-governing.[3] His reason for doubting the capacity of Africans in particular to achieve self-government was not, he said, because of a lack of intelligence. However, self-government required more than this. It required: 'a widely diffused social conscience and sense of responsibility both in the electorate and in its would be leaders.'[4] The absence of such a social conscience would lead to the elites exploiting the unwitting 'countrymen for purely selfish and mischievous purposes'.[5] However, for those hopeful of decolonisation in the near future, Amery warned that it would take a long time given this lack of social conscience, for 'to change it in a community is a matter, not of a few years, but of generations.'[6] Amery went on: 'the future emergence of the dependent Empire into the higher status of equal free partnership, if not rejected altogether, was at any rate relegated to a dim and remote future.'[7] Britain's responsibility was to encourage this sense of social consciousness and responsible government. Although the intention of the imperialists had always been to foster this, there was still much to do before independence could be granted to the least developed colonies. W. W. Astor said that, 'while we can claim that British rule has led to political, economic, social and moral progress in the Colonial Empire compared with the situation in those countries before we went to them, and compared with comparable countries under other regimes, we must be first to acknowledge the vast progress that still remains to be made.'[8]

The Conservative electoral defeat in 1945 meant that the Party was initially impotent in the face of decolonisation. However, had they been in power it is unlikely that they could have done anything different. Andrew Gamble had described the position of the Imperialists, rightly, as diehards. There may have been an emotional opposition to the ending of the empire but in reality there was little choice.[9]

Whether there was a viable alternative is very much debatable. Maurice Cowling has argued that the decision of Britain to go to war in 1939 was mistaken:

> It was wrong to assume that a dominant Germany would have been more intolerable to Britain than the Soviet Union was to become, or that British statesman had a duty to risk British lives to prevent Hitler behaving intolerably to Germans and others.[10]

Given that the War was neither justified in terms of national interest or international morality then it was avoidable. Cowling goes on: 'these are harsh judgements which will be offensive to persons of goodwill who believe, and will doubtless continue to believe, that the war dead died in a particular righteous cause.'[11]

The outbreak of war furthered the interests of, and was later justified by, the progressive forces of British politics:

> Conventional wisdom will say that Hitler was evil, that, in willing his destruction, Britain was doing her duty, and that it was a providential blessing that the Empire had to be converted into the Commonwealth from 1947 onwards. It will also say that the war lanced social abscesses, broke down class bathers, and made Britain a better place to live in.[12]

However, from the vantage point at which Cowling was writing in 1991, it was possible to see that 'the war was debilitating politically and intellectually, and it took the British a very long time to recover from it.'[13] It followed that, 'moral indignation in virtuous causes was a dangerous luxury for a precarious Empire'.[14] The costs from entering the war turned out to be 'worse for Britain than German domination of Europe might have been.'[15] The empire could have been saved if Britain had only taken a different course of action.

Such a view was certainly one that did not chime with those on the Right of the Party who supported Churchill and certainly the attitude after the War, inevitably, was one which proclaimed him as very much on the right side of politics in the 1930s even if he had lost the 1945 General Election. Imperialists therefore had to adopt a different position which was defensive, seeking to promote the continuing benefits of empire as they saw it—both for the UK and the colonies. Certainly when Powell suggested that India could be reconquered by force he was dismissed as an eccentric by Churchill.[16] Powell professed a deep sense of loss, on a par with the loss of a close family relative, when India was granted independence. He had walked the streets all night 'trying to digest it. One's whole world had been altered.'[17] He had fallen in love with the country during wartime service and possibly had visions of one day being a senior colonial governor.

The return of the Conservative Party to government in 1951 may have given imperialists some hope. However, any belief that the party would maintain imperial commitments were dashed over the Suez affair.[18] The Suez canal played an important strategic role within the British Empire. It had first become a British responsibility in 1878 and was seen as vital to the route to India. However, in the 1950s the Egyptian government under Nasser sought to take control over the canal zone. Some were unconcerned about this, seeing it as unessential in modern times and that an agreement with Egypt would be secured meaning that it didn't matter who owned the canal.

However, the Conservative Right was concerned about the apparent willingness of the British state to comply with Egyptian demands. Prominent among them was Julian Amery, who had met Charles Waterhouse in Cape Town in January 1953.[19] They expressed concern over Anthony Eden's apparent willingness to surrender control over the Suez Canal. Back in the UK, they started to meet with like-minded Conservatives at Amery's home. The Suez Group thus came into being. Waterhouse, as a former Minister and longstanding MP, took the Chairmanship of the group, with Amery being a key figure. Other members included the more established Ralph Assheton, John Morrison and Christopher Holland-Martin, along with younger MPs including

John Biggs-Davison, Fitzroy Maclean, Enoch Powell and Angus Maude. According to Sue Onslow this was a group comprised of a 'motley collection of colourful, marginal, political eccentrics.'[20] However, it also included at least tacit support from Winston Churchill.[21] In total there were 50–60 MPs involved according to Amery. The Group also had the benefit of the diplomatic connections which the Amery family (father and son) possessed.

The aims of the Group were, firstly, to avoid the 'sell out' and to maintain a military base. However, Eden decided to grant control over the canal to Nasser with the Anglo-Egyptian Agreement in 1954. The policy was fiercely opposed by the group who organised a rebellion at the Llandudno party conference that July. According to Amery, Eden's 'decision to withdraw was a catastrophic gamble.'[22] The aim then became one of taking military action to retake control of the canal. On this there was disagreement within the group. Powell came back from the summer recess in 1954 and opposed military action. For him the key decision had already been taken when the troops were withdrawn. It was now too late to act, the moment had already passed. The majority, as Amery put it, 'remained convinced that we had been right in our assessment of the consequences of abandoning the base and believed that it would still be possible to retrieve the ground that had been lost.'[23]

The Group pressured Eden into taking military action. In a secret agreement between the UK, France and Israel military action was taken. However, the US strongly opposed military action. Using diplomatic and economic channels they forced Britain and France into an embarrassing retreat. The Bank of England and the City feared the economic repercussions of the Suez adventure and applied pressure on Eden. He was criticised for not having consulted America before taking military action. However, for Amery, Eden was right not to have done so for 'there is not much sense in consulting even with your friends if you know that they will advise against what you propose to do.'[24] The extent of anti-Americanism on the Conservative Right at this point led to communication with the Soviet Union. As Amery put it: 'we tried to persuade Moscow that a British and French presence in the Middle East or North Africa was preferable to an American takeover of these areas.'[25] Amery went on, 'I was never able to see any justification for the cease fire. Another 48 hours and we would, in my judgement, have toppled Nasser.'[26] Britain and France could have secured a decisive military victory in what should have been a 'relatively minor effort of gunboat diplomacy'.[27]

The defeat had numerous consequences, Amery said.[28] Firstly a loss of British and French prestige in the region. Public opinion in the two countries suffered a loss of confidence. The entente between Britain and France was also undermined. If the intervention had been a success then the two countries could have gone on to lead a closer European alliance. Moreover, Egypt resumed hostilities with Israel and the process of African decolonisation was accelerated. In sum, 'the consequences of our failure at Suez were tragic for Europe, for the Middle East, for Black Africa, and indeed for the world international order... In both Britain and France our defeat produced a collapse of the will to rule.'[29] Although America had desired to be the dominant power, it failed to exercise its responsibilities. For instance, the landing of US troops in the Lebanon in 1958 'scarcely got beyond the beaches, hardly even to the brothel quarter.'[30] After the withdrawal, America cancelled a summit and the Egyptians charged for use of the canal. Harold Macmillan, who had strongly supported the action, accepted this humiliation. It was the start of the end of a long friendship with the 5th Marquess of Salisbury, who initially supported the post-crisis diplomacy which Macmillan had initiated but came to the view that Macmillan had backed down too much.[31]

For Peregrine Worsthorne the effects of the Suez Crisis were severe, though misunderstood.[32] British power had declined significantly but the outward appearance remained. 'Because, in short, John Bull still looks so astonishingly unchanged, it is assumed that he is basically the same as he always was.'[33] Britain was keeping up appearances until 1956 and Macmillan's adroit handling of the post-Suez situation had restored appearances. But the mask temporarily slipped in 1956 and revealed the real nature of Britain. 'I cannot... forget the glimpse of Britain which Suez momentarily revealed.'[34]

> The classical aims were there, all right. So too were the traditional actors. Etonians were in the Cabinet; Sandhurst-trained generals at the War Office; the gentlemen of England rallied to the cause, as, by and large, did the rank and file. The intellectuals complained, but even that was nothing new. Yet somehow the body politic refused to function.[35]

The reason for this was the changing class structure which postwar domestic reforms had brought about. 'The fruits of ten years of social revolution were revealed.'[36] Toryism had been destroyed without creating socialism. Britain was in a state of stalemate.

The opposition of America to military action in Suez only confirmed what many on the Conservative Right felt at this time of the Americans. Years later Powell, when asked why he did not like America, was to remark 'de gustibus est nil disputandum'.[37] In fact, the Conservative Right did not like America because they believed, with considerable justification that she had sought to push Britain into abandoning its empire. At the Yalta Conference at the end of the Second World War, Roosevelt had sought to ensure that the Empire was no longer viable after the restoration of peace. Churchill retorted: 'I have not become the King's first minister to preside over the liquidation of his Empire.'[38] Later, Roosevelt's senior advisor, Harry Hopkins, would say that it was indeed an essential aim of American policy at this time to avoid supporting the British policy of maintaining an empire.[39] American policy of successive Presidents had been to push a reluctant Britain into winding down its imperial commitments. That the Conservative Right correctly understood the motives of the US was of little comfort. There was simply no alternative strategy open to the British state. It was characteristic of the Right at this time to make similar remarks concerning America as the Labour left, albeit for different reasons. John Biggs-Davison called America *An Uncertain Ally*[40] one that could not be relied on and one that sometimes worked directly against British interests. However, in a review of his book, Christopher Johnson argued that although Biggs-Davison had produced a well-evidenced analysis he had failed to come up with a viable alternative policy simply because there was not one.[41] Maintaining the pretence of the 'special relationship' had a more long-lasting impact according to Biggs-Davison for it 'inhibited Britain from taking the European lead that had been hers for the asking.'[42] Julian Amery came to a similar conclusion, 'Well before the Suez Crisis two World Wars had greatly weakened the strength of Europe. A Franco-British victory at Suez might just have begun to reverse the trend. As it was our defeat finally marked the end of Europe as the arbiter of international affairs'[43] and established the dominance of America: 'Suez was indeed Europe's Waterloo'.[44] Lord Lambton went further in arguing that 'the Anglo-American relationship has always been a myth.'[45]

It was this attitude to America which distinguished this generation of the Conservative Right from later figures such as Margaret Thatcher, who certainly regarded the US as the key ally in the fight against the Soviet Union. For Thatcher, Nasser's political victory in 1956 had been 'the cause of a great deal of the ensuing trouble in the Middle East'.[46] Two lessons were to be learned from this episode. The first was that 'the British political class... went from believing that Britain could do anything to an almost neurotic belief that Britain could do nothing.'[47] The second was that in the future Britain would need to secure the support of America before it could act.[48]

A further challenge for the imperialistic wing of the Conservative Party came in its stance towards Cyprus. Cyprus had been administered by the UK since 1878 and was, like Suez, seen as a strategically important point in the Empire. However, Britain faced growing Greek resistance from the mid-1950s as they sought to take control over the island. EOKA, led by the controversial figure of Archbishop Makarios waged violent action against British military personnel. Amery, who had reluctantly accepted the Suez outcome and gone in to Macmillan's Government, entered long negotiations with Makarios and an agreement was eventually reached which allowed Britain to retain its military bases.[49] However, Salisbury regarded this as a further abandonment of imperial commitments by the British state. Salisbury's departure from the Government followed. Macmillan clearly felt pleased that this Cabinet critic of his policy had gone. 'All through history the Cecils, when any friend or colleague has been in real trouble, have stabbed him in the back—attributing the crime to qualms of conscience.'[50]

WINDS OF CHANGE

The decisive action of the Prime Minister, Harold Macmillan in appointing the liberal-leaning Conservative Iain Macleod as Secretary of State for the Colonies in October 1959 in place of the more conservative Alan Lennox-Boyd meant that he wished to speed up the process of decolonisation, particularly in Africa. This was confirmed by his Winds of Change speech in Cape Town in 1960.[51] Amery had been asked to contribute to the speech, but his contribution was a statement of the positive contribution the Afrikaners had made. This was subsequently 'pencilled out'.[52] The speech was to set a new, liberal approach to Africa.

While the speech was warmly welcomed by those of a more liberal disposition, who wished to speed up the process of decolonisation, the Conservative Right were deeply suspicious of the new approach.

The result was the establishment of the Monday Club in 1961.[53] The founders were a group of younger, more right-wing Conservatives who were opposed not only to the new liberal agenda in international affairs but also to Macmillan's economic policy, which had taken on a much more overtly collectivist approach. Paul Bristol was to become its first Chairman. Bristol had established the Monday Club in response to the Bow Group, which he regarded as an essentially liberal organisation that with its 'airy fairy nonsense is not representative of the party.'[54] Bristol enlisted Lord Salisbury as its Patron along with Lennox-Boyd, following his replacement as Colonial Secretary. The Club had a small, carefully selected membership at first and the focus of its early pamphlets was to oppose the rapid decolonisation of Africa. For Bristol the aim was not to resist independence for the colonies indefinitely, still less to reverse what had already happened, but rather to have a managed decline of the remaining empire.[55] The association of Salisbury with the group was important for its establishment. Without it the founders would have struggled to make the group a success. Salisbury developed a distinctive approach to empire at this time, one certainly opposed to the policy of Macmillan. For Salisbury the focus on freedom and independence was wrong and instead the approach of government policy should be responsibility. The UK had a position of trusteeship in relation to her colonies. 'A policy of partnership between black and white... rests the only hope both for a peaceful and prosperous future for Africa' Salisbury said.[56] However, that future would be destroyed by 'handing over the reins of government to militant African leaders'. The result would be 'chaos and terrorism and cruelty and economic disaster.'[57] Writing in 1970, Lord Coleraine spoke to the frustrations the imperialist wing of the Party felt:

> Looking out on a world in which British power had faded and shrunk, a Conservative government made no effort to restore it. It could do no more than bend suppliant before the wind of change, which it had done so much itself to conjure up.[58]

Nevertheless the granting of independence to the colonies was indeed accelerated in accordance with the wishes of Macmillan and Macleod. As Bernard Porter states, 'in the 1950s the Sudan, the Gold Coast (Ghana) and Malaya had been the only colonies to escape. In the 1960s it quite suddenly became a stampede'.[59] However, subsequent unrest following independence seemed to justify the earlier assessments by Salisbury and others as far as those on the Conservative Right were concerned. Patrick Wall stated in 1969 that, 'Black Africa is likely to remain in a state of internal crisis throughout the decade.'[60] Such a position meant that Britain should maintain its earlier sense of trusteeship rather than furthering decolonisation. However, by then much of former colonial Africa had been granted independence.

The Unilateral Declaration of Independence by Rhodesia in 1965 created a new issue for the imperialists to get behind. The UDI was condemned by the Labour Government and sanctions were introduced, and then retained by subsequent governments. This was condemned by the Conservative Right who felt a natural loyalty to the white settlers. For Salisbury, Rhodesian settlers were British irrespective of there country of origin.[61] Others felt that the sanctions were foolish, they were not going to have the desired effect: 'what are sanctions for?' Amery asked, 'they cannot bring down nor are they the bargaining chip which can help negotiations.'[62] John Biggs-Davison put a motion forward to the Monday Club in 1965 opposing sanctions, which was carried unanimously.[63] In a 1973 Monday Club pamphlet, Patrick Wall argued that the sanctions needed to be lifted.[64] Instead, they were alienating the white government of Ian Smith, which they felt promised a hope of peace. The black leaders were unable to run an effective government. Wall wrote in 1970 that: 'I do not like what is going on... equally I do not like what is going on in many other independent African states who show an equal or greater disregard for human rights and have virtually eliminated all forms of democracy.'[65] Some feared that the Soviet Union was backing black nationalism in order to strengthen the position of communism on the continent of Africa. Hence, for numerous reasons, the Conservative Right sought to defend the new government in Rhodesia. For Worsthorne this meant that, 'it seems self-evident to me that the whites in southern Africa have every right to sustain their rule, for all its faults, by whatever degree of force is deemed to be necessary.'[66] This also extended to South Africa: 'better apartheid than black revolution.'[67] For Jonathan Guinness, writing in 1971, the correct policy was to continue selling arms to South Africa. It was in Britain's economic and strategic interests to maintain good links with the regime there. Moreover, many opponents of apartheid supported communism, and the Soviet Union was seeking to exploit the blacks for their own interests. Racial inequality was inevitable in South Africa, otherwise the white minority could not survive.[68]

The election of the first Thatcher Government in 1979 did not help those backing the Smith regime. She embarked on a new diplomatic initiative which resulted in the granting of the franchise to the black population and the election of Robert Mugabe. Amery responded to this in the House of Commons, 'Mr Mugabe's victory represents a major defeat for the West'.[69] Thatcher's response to the Rhodesia saga may have been a pragmatic one, but it marked a defeat for the imperialist Conservative Right in their defence of Smith's regime.

POST-IMPERIALISM

For Richard Body, writing in 2001, all of this had been but an 'imperial interlude'—a temporary period in the country's much longer history.[70] He was echoing the view which Enoch Powell had made over 40 years before. A key policy split on the Conservative Right emerged with Powell's quest for a post-imperial national identity. As already mentioned he had distanced himself from the rest of the Suez Group, of which he had hitherto been a very active supporter, in the summer of 1954. This coincided with a speech to the Conservative Party summer school in which he first argued that the Empire had been but a temporary phenomena in British history.[71] The Commonwealth was a beguiling organisation which was acutely damaging to British institutions. Underpinning Powell's nationalism was a belief both in the necessity of absolute sovereignty and a romantic, indeed mythical, appeal to the nation. This reached its fullest expression in his speech to the Royal Society of St George in 1961.[72] Powell set out to find the essence of Englishness. It did not, after all, rest with the empire, which had been only a brief phenomenon in the nation's long history. 'Perhaps after all we know most of England "who only England know"'.[73]

> Tell us what it is that binds us together; show us the clue that leads through a thousand years; whisper to us the secret of this charmed life of England, that we in our time may know how to hold it fast.[74]

The answer lay in stripping away the relics of empire and going back in time to the medieval kingship, the 'unlimited supremacy of Crown in Parliament' and the historical continuity 'which has brought this unity and this homogeneity about by the slow alchemy of centuries.'[75] The nation is English 'for all the leeks and thistles and shamrocks... The parent stem of England and its royal talisman'.[76]

Powell's formulation of post-imperial nationalism led him to adopt distinctive policy positions some of which were not shared by many on the traditional imperialistic Right. Several of these will be explored in later chapters. In addition, he believed that the Soviet Union was not as great a threat as was widely perceived, but America was a direct threat to British interests. He believed that maintenance of the Commonwealth was fundamentally against the national interest. He also developed a distinctive policy on defence. He was given this Opposition brief by Edward Heath. If Heath thought this would keep Powell out of more controversial areas he was wrong as Powell articulated his reservations over the refusal of others to accept that Britain was no longer an imperial power. For him Britain was, 'a nation with a split personality, rent between illusion and reality, withdrawing ever and again like the schizophrenic into a dream existence peculiar to ourselves.'[77] For Julian Amery, it all 'sounded like a sort of British Gaullism.'[78] Powellism, as far as the imperialists were concerned, amounted to an inward-looking—or 'Little Englander'—nationalism.

Against this those of more conventional Conservative Right views continued to believe that Britain should maintain its historic military commitments. For some, including Amery, Britain could never be a great power while it continued to depend on US nuclear weapons and should develop its own capacity.[79] By October 1965, the *Guardian* was reporting that Amery had emerged as the main leadership hopeful of the Right of the Conservative Party due to the different course being taken by Powell.[80] Amery stood for the traditional imperialistic wing, arguing that Britain and France should seek to maintain their nuclear capacity and that European powers including Britain should be maintaining, if not enhancing, their conventional forces too. There was no trade off between conventional and nuclear forces.[81]

Hence, two distinct positions had emerged by the late 1960s on the Conservative Right—a nationalist one represented by Powell and the older imperialist one which was still being defended by Amery. This split manifested itself in terms of three specific issues above others. Two—immigration and European integration—will be explored in the following two chapters. The third was the approach to the Commonwealth. For the imperialists, the Commonwealth was a 'good thing', an evolution of the empire, which demonstrated the willingness of the former colonies to remain close to the old imperial power. The empire was thus vindicated by the way in which it was brought to an end—which contrasted starkly with other European colonial powers who presided over a much more violent and costly end to their empires. However, for the nationalists the Commonwealth was a fiction, one which was costly to Britain, allowed for the continuation of the myth that the UK was still a world power and stopped it from taking the necessary steps to being a more modern and dynamic economic order. Powell was frequently scathing of the Commonwealth. Another was Rhodes Boyson, who argued that, 'the empire is now gone for good and the sooner we get it straight in our mind and out of our system the better.'[82] However, this did not mean that Britain had to be apologetic for its imperial past especially when others also had empires, for 'why should we apologise for being the most virile and successful of them?'[83] The fault lay with the Left: 'the destructive Left and the guilt-ridden self-flagellators had got to work on our memory of empire... One way to destroy a man is to destroy his memory of who he is. The way to destroy a people is to make them ashamed of their memory as a people.'[84] But it did mean that Britain no longer had duties towards its former colonies: 'alas no detached observer can say that the humble African is as well off economically or in the terms of the rule of law as if the empire had remained, but the way these countries are run is now their own problem.'[85]

LATE IMPERIALISM

Following the Suez Crisis governments of both parties had not sought to stop or even slow down the path towards colonial independence. However, Margaret Thatcher believed that the shadow cast by Suez had lasted too long. Her governments would not be cowed in the same way. The issue which brought this to a head was the Falkland Islands.

During the 1970s the then Labour Government had been willing to enter into negotiations with Argentina over the future of the islands. The possibility of some form of lease back with the UK retaining ultimate sovereignty was one possibility. Margaret Thatcher opposed all such attempts to give the Argentine's a greater say over the islands. For her the people there were British and wished to remain so. The history and geography of the islands was irrelevant compared to this basic matter of self-determination. However, the Foreign Office continued to support the option of giving the Falkland Islands back to the Argentines and Thatcher called on Amery to speak from the backbenches: 'it is almost always a great mistake to get rid of real estate for nothing' he said.[86]

However, following the 1979 General Election victory, Thatcher embarked on her agenda of cutting public expenditure. This included the decision to remove the presence of HMS Endurance from the South

Atlantic. Indeed, there were more substantial cuts in the budgets of the armed services, leading to ministerial resignation.[87] The Argentines saw an opportunity for landing troops on the islands. A declaration of war followed as Thatcher ignored the opinion held by some within her Cabinet and sections of the armed forces that the islands were too far away and that the UK could not retake the islands by force. There were also attempts made by the Americans and others to persuade Britain to reach a diplomatic solution, including an aborted Peruvian peace plan.

Thatcher would have no truck with such plans and determined to retake the Falklands by force, whatever the cost. A critical moment, which according to some was designed to scupper the Peruvian initiative, was to order the sinking of the Belgrano.[88] This was later to be the source of conspiracy theory, especially as the Government was found to be telling parliamentary untruths when questioned over a sustained period of time by the maverick Labour MP Tam Dalyell. It transpired that the Belgrano had been sailing outside the naval exclusion zone and possibly back towards port. The rights and wrongs of the action, which led to considerable loss of life both in sinking the Belgrano and retaliation on HMS Sheffield was lost in the surge of patriotism felt at this time. As Alan Clark said it didn't matter where the Belgrano was when it was sunk as far as the public were concerned watching the news on their television screens: 'so what does it matter where it was when it was hit? We could have sunk it if it'd been tied up on the quayside in a neutral port and everyone would still have been delighted.' These things happened in war.[89]

With the exception of the radical left of the Labour Party the opinion of Parliament was overwhelmingly supportive of military action in response to an aggressive act by a foreign power on what was British territory. Powell said that Thatcher had been given the sobriquet 'the iron lady' by the Russians. He was unsure from what metal she was made from until the Falklands but it was now clear to see that the Russians had rightly identified it.[90] However, America had once again shown itself to have a fundamentally different outlook from the UK: 'their ideas are not our ideas, their thoughts are not our thoughts, their view of the world is not our view of the world, their purposes are not our purposes, and their interests, except by occasional coincidence, are not our interests.'[91]

The military action lasted a matter of weeks as the weaknesses of the Argentine army and navy were exposed and Thatcher determined that she was to take the salute at the homecoming parades rather than the

Monarch. Peregrine Worsthorne spoke of the patriotism which swept the nation: 'during the Falklands crisis many people felt better than is their normal lot.'[92] For him it showed the limited appeal of the liberal intellectuals—who had disparaged patriotism since 1945—to the ordinary person: 'no wonder the spirit of the Falklands came as such a surprise. Who would have expected that the British bulldog, fed for so long on a diet of slops, with never even a sniff of red meat, should have survived so fighting fit?'[93] Or, as John Heydon Stokes put it, 'the nation has suddenly found itself over the Falklands Crisis.'[94] This further outpouring of patriotism encouraged her to call a snap General Election which she won with a much increased majority. However, on reflection what can be demonstrated from this experience is not how strong Britain's international role was but perhaps how far it had shrunk from its imperial heyday.

Nonetheless, there were still those who believed in the possibilities of colonial intervention. Worsthorne expressed a view that the experience of civil wars and humanitarian disasters on the continent of Africa demonstrated that Britain still had a colonial role to play, if not in terms of militarism then as a civilising force on the continent. If state aid was to work then corrupt governments needed to be overcome. 'Last time colonialism was born out of western greed. This time it could be that charity will bring about the same result.'[95] Worsthorne could easily be dismissed as a maverick commentator, certainly few followed him in making such claims. By now the Empire was of historic interest only. Conservative historians of the Empire including Niall Ferguson sought to defend it from left-wing critics who had denigrated it.[96] This is not the place to evaluate those competing historiographical debates, rather we must look at how the Conservative Right responded to two challenges which sprung directly from the decline of the Empire: namely, Commonwealth immigration and European integration.

NOTES

1. A. Gamble, *The Conservative Nation* (London: Routledge & Kegan Paul, 1974).
2. See C. Schofield, *Enoch Powell and the Making of Postcolonial Britain* (Cambridge: Cambridge University Press, 2013).
3. B. Porter, *The Lion's Share: A Short History of British Imperialism, 1850–1983* (London: Longman, 1984, 2nd edition), p. 290.
4. Quoted in ibid., p. 290.

5. Ibid.
6. Ibid.
7. Ibid.
8. W. W. Astor, *Our Imperial Future* (London: Signpost, 1943), p. 3.
9. A. Gamble, *The Conservative Nation* (London: Routledge & Kegan Paul, 1974).
10. M. Cowling, 'The Case Against Going to War', *Finest Hour*, 70, 1991.
11. Ibid.
12. Ibid.
13. Ibid.
14. Ibid.
15. Ibid.
16. S. Heffer, *Like the Roman* (London: Weidenfeld & Nicolson, 1998).
17. Quoted in Porter, *The Lion's Share*, p. 315.
18. For the Suez Crisis, see R. Brandon, *Suez: Splitting of a Nation* (London: Collins, 1973); S. Troen and M. Shemesh (eds.) *The Suez-Sinai Crisis, 1956: Retrospective and Reappraisal* (London: Cass, 1990); and S. Onslow, 'Unreconstructed Nationalists and a Minor Gunboat Operation: Julian Amery, Neil McLean and the Suez Crisis', *Contemporary British History*, 20/1 (2006), pp. 73–99.
19. J. Amery, 'The Suez Group: A Retrospective on Suez', in Troen and Shemesh (eds.) *The Suez-Sinai Crisis, 1956*, p. 84.
20. S. Onslow, 'Julian Amery and the Suez Operation', in S. Smith (ed.) *Reassessing Suez 1956: New Perspectives on the Crisis and Its Aftermath* (Aldershot: Ashgate, 2008), p. 71.
21. R. Bassett, *Last Imperialist: A Portrait of Julian Amery* (Settrington: Stone Trough, 2015), p. 148.
22. Amery, 'The Suez Group', p. 88.
23. Ibid., p. 85.
24. Ibid., p. 90.
25. Ibid.
26. Ibid., p. 91.
27. Ibid., p. 93.
28. Ibid.
29. Ibid., p. 94.
30. Quoted in Bassett, *Last Imperialist*, p. 155.
31. Ball, *The Guardsmen*, p. 332.
32. P. Worsthorne, 'Class and Conflict in British Foreign Policy', *Foreign Affairs*, 37/3 (1959), pp. 419–431.
33. Ibid., p. 422.
34. Ibid.
35. Ibid.

36. Ibid., p. 423.
37. Heffer, *Like the Roman*.
38. Quoted in Brandon, *Suez*, p. 27.
39. Ibid., p. 27.
40. J. Biggs-Davison, *An Uncertain Ally* (London: Johnson, 1957).
41. BD/1/117, John Biggs-Davison papers, Parliamentary Archives, London.
42. J. Biggs-Davison, 'The Special Relationship', *Salisbury Review*, 6/2 (December 1987), p. 61.
43. Amery, *The Suez* Group, p. 95.
44. Ibid.
45. Quoted in Brandon, *Suez*, p. 11.
46. C. Moore, *Margaret Thatcher: The Authorised Biography, Volume 1: Not for Turning* (London: Allen Lane, 2013), p. 130.
47. Ibid.
48. Ibid.
49. Bassett, *Last Imperialist*, p. 176.
50. Quoted in Ball, p. 337.
51. Available at https://www.youtube.com/watch?v=c07MiYfpOMw, accessed 5 May 2019.
52. Bassett, *Last Imperialist*, p. 175.
53. See M. Pitchford, *The Conservative Party and the Extreme Right, 1945–75* (Manchester: Manchester University Press, 2013) for a fuller description of the Monday Club's origins and early years.
54. Bristol, quoted in *Sunday Telegraph*, 28 January 1962, Monday Club papers in private possession of Sir Adrian Fitzgerald.
55. Interview with Paul Bristol, London, 3 May 2017.
56. Ball, *The Guardsmen*, p. 346.
57. Ibid.
58. Lord Coleraine, *For Conservatives Only* (London: Tom Stacey, 1970), p. 57.
59. Porter, *The Lion's* Share, p. 335.
60. P. Wall, *British Defence Policy in the 1970s* (London: Monday Club, 1969), p. 1.
61. Ball, *The Guardsmen*, p. 346.
62. Bassett, *Last Imperialist*, p. 229.
63. Monday Club papers in private possession of Sir Adrian Fitzgerald.
64. P. Wall, *The Soviet Maritime Threat* (London: Monday Club, 1973).
65. Quoted in P. Major, 'Patrick Wall and South Africa', *South African Historical Journal*, 52/1 (2005), pp. 102–118, 109.
66. P. Worsthorne, *Peregrinations* (London: Weidenfeld & Nicolson, 1980), p. 261.
67. P. Worsthorne, *By the Right* (Dublin: Brophy, 1987), p. 83.

68. J. Guinness, *Arms for South Africa: The Moral Issue* (London: Monday Club, 1971).
69. Bassett, *Last Imperialist*, p. 231.
70. R. Body, *England for the English* (London: New European Publications, 2001).
71. E. Powell, 'The Empire and England', in A. Maude (ed.) *Tradition and Change* (London: Conservative Political Centre, 1954).
72. In, J. Wood (ed.) *Freedom and Reality* (Kingswood: Elliot, 1969).
73. Ibid., p. 338.
74. Ibid., p. 339.
75. Ibid., p. 340.
76. Ibid.
77. S. Heffer, *Like The Roman*, p. 431.
78. Quoted in I. Yates, 'Brighton Notebook', *Observer*, 17 October 1965, Monday Club papers in private possession of Sir Adrian Fitzgerald.
79. Bassett, *Last Imperialist*, pp. 160–161.
80. *Guardian*, 16 October 1965, Monday Club papers in private possession of Sir Adrian Fitzgerald.
81. J. Amery, 'Notes on Party Policy', Amery papers, Churchill College, Cambridge.
82. Boyson, *Centre Forward: A Radical Conservative Programme* (London: Temple Smith, 1978), p. 139.
83. Ibid., p. 138.
84. Ibid.
85. Ibid., p. 139.
86. Bassett, *Last Imperialist*, p. 232.
87. K. Speed, *Sea Change* (London: Ashgrove, 1982).
88. M. Rossiter, *Sink the Belgrano* (London: Batam, 2007).
89. A. Clark, *Diaries* (London: Weidenfeld and Nicolson, 1993), p. 5.
90. Heffer, *Like the Roman*.
91. E. Powell, 'Britain and the Alliance', *Salisbury Review*, p. 29.
92. Worsthorne, *By the Right*, p. 165.
93. Ibid., p. 171.
94. *Primrose League Gazette*, 86/3 (May–June 1982), p. 3.
95. Worsthorne, *By the Right*, p. 180.
96. N. Ferguson, *Empire* (London: Allen Lane, 2003).

CHAPTER 3

Immigration

Few issues in British politics have attracted as much controversy, and few have alarmed the Conservative Right, as much as immigration. The arrival of the first generation of Commonwealth immigrants on the Empire Windrush in Tilbury on 22nd June 1948 marked the start of a process which was to lead to a strong public reaction in the years to follow. By the mid-1950s prominent voices on the Conservative Right were to speak out against the immigration then taking place and by 1968, with the intervention of Enoch Powell, it was to become an explosive issue. This chapter explores the oppositionist stance taken by the Conservative Right on the issue, looking at why they felt it was so important and the impact which they had on the development of public policy.

THE EARLY YEARS

To many politicians in the aftermath of the Second World War there was a predominant sentiment that the UK owed a debt to the residents of the colonies and former colonies. A growing sense of imperial guilt and a recognition of what the colonial subjects had done as an ally against the Nazi threat—combined with the fact that the colonies were becoming too costly to hang on to in the face of independence movements—led to mounting pressures for independence, starting with India and Pakistan in 1948 along with the granting of full citizenship rights to all colonial subjects. The emergence of the Commonwealth further encouraged such sentiments.[1]

© The Author(s) 2020
K. Hickson, *Britain's Conservative Right since 1945*,
https://doi.org/10.1007/978-3-030-27697-3_3

There was therefore little control on 'coloured' migration—as it was then termed—from the Empire and Commonwealth after the War. Commonwealth immigrants were welcomed and began to settle in particular parts of the UK, especially inner city areas in England. At first these settlers were peaceful, feeling a sense of gratitude for being allowed to enter the UK. However, the subjection of these residents to extremely poor quality housing and employment, the emergence of communal identities and the growing resentment of locals to their new immigrant neighbours created a more fraught situation with open unrest erupting.

Additional pressure on the Conservative Right came from far Right organisations including the League of Empire Loyalists (LEL) which was founded in 1954 under the leadership of A. K. Chesterton.[2] The LEL sought to disrupt Conservative Party meetings as part of its wider campaigns to restrict immigration and oppose decolonisation. Meanwhile Oswald Mosley had come back into British politics—albeit with much less success than he had had before the War. His Union Movement campaigned on similar issues to the LEL but with a pro-European stance and deep personal rivalry by this stage with his former acolyte, Chesterton.[3]

Attacks on immigrants had been increasing and the tensions erupted into rioting in Notting Hill in late August and early September, 1958. Local Afro-Caribbean's complained of the lack of police activity in response to their reports of intimidation and violence. Tough sentences were imposed on those who had perpetrated the acts and a carnival was established the following year. There had been unrest in other areas too. The response of figures on the Conservative Right was to argue that the lack of immigration controls was the cause of the unrest and called for a tougher immigration policy. Prominent amongst them was Cyril Osborne MP.[4] In 1958 he had sought, unsuccessfully, to bring in a new bill which would restrict immigration with Norman Pannell. In 1963, Osborne wrote in the *Spectator* that, 'if unlimited immigration were allowed, we should ultimately become a chocolate-coloured, Afro-Asian mixed society. That I do not want.'[5] In March 1965, he presented a bill which would allow for greater quantitative controls on migration. Although the bill failed to pass through the Commons, being rejected in its initial stages, Osborne called later that year for the Labour Government to restrict all immigration other than for students and professionals who would only be permitted to stay for limited periods of time.

From 1957, Normal Pannell MP had also spoken out on the issue calling for tighter controls on Commonwealth immigration. After disturbances in Nottingham in August 1958 he also called for more general immigration control. Although his proposals got nowhere in Parliament, he did attract support amidst the grassroots Conservatives, gaining support for a conference motion in 1958. In 1960, he sought to persuade the Home Secretary, R. A. Butler, of the need to impose health checks on newly arrived immigrants amid fears that they were carriers of disease. For Pannell, 'unrestricted immigration' was linked to illness, unemployment and crime. As Andrew Gamble comments, the issue of immigration gave the Conservatives 'one of their cruellest ideological dilemmas' since the belief in empire meant that all colonial peoples were British.[6] Immigration control therefore challenged this, replacing the ideal of empire with one of nation. At the 1961 party conference, 40 motions on immigration were submitted, of which 38 called for tougher controls. A range of social issues including lack of affordable housing and crime were seen as being caused, or at least exacerbated, by immigration which was also deemed to be responsible for fuelling racial unrest. The Government acted by passing the Commonwealth Immigrants Act (1962) which sought to impose restrictions. However, the Conservative Right did not believe that this went far enough.

Another prominent campaigner from the House of Lords on the issue of immigration was Lord Elton, who argued that the current level of non-white immigration couldn't continue.[7] It was not that opponents of current immigration policy were racist, the issue was purely about numbers. Immigration was an important issue, Elton said, 'for it is certainly the gravest social problem of this century, and may well prove to be the gravest social problem which we have ever encountered'.[8] However, the political establishment always felt uncomfortable when discussing it. The reason for this was that it always seemed as if the matter was substantially one of race, but in fact it was about the current levels of migration.[9] If the rate of change was too fast then it would always cause social resentment, irrespective of the type of people coming in. To substantiate this argument, Elton argued that:

> If it were known in my home village that the most reverend Primate the Lord Archbishop of Canterbury were coming to live there, we should undoubtedly ring a peal of the church bells. If it were known that five Archbishops were coming I should still expect to see my neighbours exchanging excited congratulations at the street corners. But if it were known that fifty Archbishops were coming there would be a riot.[10]

Having made this point, though, Elton then goes on to state that the problem was also a cultural one. It was not only the immediate issue that there were the new immigrants to deal with, but the higher birth rates among those communities and their unwillingness to integrate into mainstream society were creating more long-term problems. There was little prospect of absorbing peoples of a different culture:

> I ask: do we really believe that these Asians—and I emphasise the word "Asians"—can be absorbed? After all, they have their own religions, their own ancient cultures, their own deep-rooted traditions, which they have made it very clear they have no desire to change for ours—and who that reads our daily Press can blame them for that?[11]

However, it was in 1964 that the issue was to attract more national attention. Standing for Smethwick against Shadow Foreign Secretary Patrick Gordon-Walker, Peter Griffiths had used the issue of non-white immigration and the failure of those immigrants to integrate within society as an election issue. The election attracted campaigners from the far right and overtly racist messages were displayed on election leaflets and posters. Particularly notorious was the comment on posters placed around the constituency that 'if you want a nigger for a neighbour, vote Liberal or Labour.' However, Griffiths claimed that he was not responsible for these posters and was simply campaigning on issues which had been prominent in the area for a number of years.[12] There had been large-scale immigration and a failure to integrate these new settlers who had effectively lived separate lives. The political establishment, including his Labour opponent Patrick Gordon Walker, had failed to understand the anger and frustration which had built up. However, some pointed to the local residents' associations which had been infiltrated by the far right and which were fuelling local tensions.[13] Griffiths won the contest with a swing of 2.3%, in a national election which saw a swing to Labour. The nature of the campaign had clearly played a decisive role in the result. Wilson labelled him the 'parliamentary leper' and he was very much marginalised in that Parliament. He was to lose his seat in 1966 but re-emerged as an MP in 1979, winning Portsmouth North from Labour. Griffiths remained largely silent on the issue during his single term as the local MP, upsetting some of the far right who had been attracted to him.

ENTER ENOCH

Up until this stage Enoch Powell, who very much came to define the issue, was largely silent. He had made occasional remarks which would be a foretaste of what he was later to say. For instance he had written to the Bishop of Lichfield on 26th February 1955 stating that there needed to be greater immigration control and greater levels of integration for immigrants who were already here. This was in response to a strike by bus drivers in West Bromwich over the appointment of immigrant labour. He said that, 'however wrong headedly and gropingly, I believe the strikers in West Bromwich to have apprehended the dangers for this country of any appreciable coloured population becoming domiciled here.'[14] It was not a religious matter and therefore of no concern to the Bishop. To see him as changing his mind completely on the issue for reasons of political expediency are therefore misplaced, but it did certainly become a more important issue for him personally.[15] This may be because of his failure to make inroads in the 1965 Conservative leadership contest, the first where MPs were balloted and in which he obtained only 15 votes against his old adversary Edward Heath and Reginald Maudling. He had also seen the impact which the issue had on the neighbouring seat of Smethwick in 1964, where he had declined to campaign in the General Election. But he would maintain that seeing the effects of immigration and the increased concern the matter was getting from his constituency mail meant that he had to speak out. However, a mix of personal ambition and shifting ideological opinion was to lead to the explosive 'rivers of blood' speech in 1968. He had initially refused to comment on immigration saying that he would 'set his face like flint' against playing the race card.[16]

Following the Conservative election defeat and the ensuing leadership contest, he then began to articulate a range of new policies, largely economic in nature to which we return in a later chapter. However, his impact was still limited and he began to outline other issues including that of race and immigration.

His initial statements had been cautious but these failed to have much impact. He consciously sought to change his oratorical approach, taking advice from his friend and Editor of his local newspaper, the *Wolverhampton Express and Star*, Clement Jones, on how to raise his profile in the media.[17] He had developed a certain rhetorical approach in terms of his immigration statements, using what purported to be letters from local constituents. All of this was to reach its zenith at the so-called 'Rivers of Blood' speech on 20th April 1968. Powell had told Jones that the speech would explode like a rocket, but the effects would be long lasting.[18] The scene was the relatively inauspicious party meeting in Birmingham. However, Powell had seemingly only given the Party short notice of what he was going to say. He had also tipped off the press and handed out advanced copies. His later claim that he was surprised at the furore which the speech created rings untrue, especially as he admitted in the speech that he could 'already hear the chorus of execration. How dare I say such horrible things? How dare I stir up trouble and inflame feelings... The answer is that I do not have a right not to do so.'[19]

He begins by relating a story of a man he met—a working-class man—who said that he wished to leave the country. The reason being the rate of current immigration and the race relations legislation which was making it unlawful to discriminate. 'In this country in fifteen to twenty years time the black man will have the whip hand over the white man,' this man claimed. Powell believed he was right. Firstly, because current immigration was too high, especially when immigrants set-tled in particular areas which had transformed them. These immigrant communities had failed to integrate—a message which very much ech-oed the campaign message of Griffiths in 1964. Such lack of integra-tion was alluded to in Powell's second anecdote of a white woman—the only white woman—left in a particular street and who was seemingly subjected to racial abuse for she had refused to rent out her rooms to blacks. Her street was 'taken over' and the quality of the area deterio-rated meaning she could no longer find tenants. She was forced to go to claim benefits and 'was seen by a young girl' who suggested she rent out rooms. On explaining that she could only find 'negroes' the bene-fits officer said 'racial prejudice won't get you anywhere in this country'. She was subjected to further abuse from the immigrants in her street: 'she is becoming afraid to go out. Windows are broken. She finds excreta pushed through her letterbox. When she goes to the shops, she is fol-lowed by children, charming wide-grinning piccaninnies'.

Here all of Powell's rhetorical devices are used.[20] He sees it as nec-essary to retell these stories as the 'authentic' voice of those facing the brunt of immigration, people who the political establishment refuse to hear. He is not being racist, these are not his words, but he has a duty to retell them. The accuracy of the letter was questioned. The street which has only one white resident is not identified. A similar story which

Powell told in a different speech of a single white child in a class also proved difficult to identify and was only true because of particular circumstances. The woman is presented as hardworking, but struggling and the civil servant as ignorant based on her age. The immigrant community is seen as unable or unwilling to integrate, seeking to take over the area and bringing with them crime and anti-social behaviour. The official statistics are questioned to reinforce the argument that white working-class people are being ignored or deceived by the state. The current position, he went on, would result in civil unrest. He had recently been to America for the first time and had witnessed social tensions which existed between different racial groups and believed that the same would happen in the UK, despite the very different histories of the two countries:

> Those whom the gods wish to destroy, they first make mad. We must be mad, literally mad, as a nation to be permitting the annual inflow of some 50,000 dependents, who are for the most part the material of the future growth of the immigrant-descended population. It is like watching a nation busily engaged in heaping up its own funeral pyre.[21]

The speech finished with dire warnings over the future of the country: 'as I look ahead, I am filled with much foreboding. Like the Roman, I seem to see "the River Tiber foaming with much blood."'[22]

All of the populist buttons are pressed in the speech, which resulted in the inevitable uproar. Powell was dismissed from the Shadow Cabinet, and was subjected to widespread criticism from fellow politicians. However, he also saw organised support, including marches, and his popularity increased. He continued to defend his speech, both his right to make it and his claims. The statistical projections which Powell made were disputed. However, he continued to make further statements. In a speech in Eastbourne later the same year, Powell said that there was 'a deep and dangerous gulf in the nation'.[23] This was not between whites and immigrants, for the latter were among those who sought greater control over future immigration, but instead:

> between the overwhelming majority of people throughout the country on the one side, and on the other side a tiny minority, with almost a monopoly hold upon the channels of communication, who seem determined not to know the facts and not to face the realities and who will resort to any device or extremity to blind both themselves and others.[24]

The speech followed the same pattern in that it then used a letter from a GP telling Powell of things which were happening to his patients who were experiencing high levels of immigration. Powell went on to defend his statistical claims and to restate his case against anti-discrimination laws, which in practice empowered one community over another in his view.[25]

In the 1970 election, Powell made a number of speeches which his supporters claimed were responsible for securing the Conservative victory. He again argued that the statistical claims he makes were correct and that the Labour Government had been deceiving the voters. He repeated his claims that this would result in social unrest. Finally, he set out the policy which was needed to deal with this. Firstly, 'the cessation of further immigration'. But by itself this would be insufficient and so a 'major re-emigration or re-patriation is essential.'[26] He continued to make similar claims in speeches throughout the 1970s.[27]

DEVELOPMENTS ON THE RIGHT

Margaret Thatcher was firmly in the minority when she tried to caution Heath against inflaming the situation by sacking Powell. She maintained links with Powell thereafter.[28] The moderates within the Shadow Cabinet, notably Lord Hailsham and Edward Boyle, called for his resignation. Heath needed no encouragement to remove his old adversary.

Those on the Conservative Right were largely sympathetic to Powell. Lord Elton wrote to the *Telegraph* praising the Eastbourne speech against Powell's critics.[29] Ronald Bell MP echoed Powell's statements when speaking at a rally on race laws and freedom in 1968: 'the humiliation of the proud British has hitherto only been accomplished abroad. Now it can be brought to exultant fulfilment at home.'[30] In the first biography to be published within weeks of Powell's speech, the right-wing journalist T. E. Utley wrote that Powell's changing position on the immigration issue was part of the evolution in his wider thinking in his attempts to fashion a post-imperial British nationalism.[31]

However, not everyone on the Right was supportive. John Biffen believed that Powell had great gifts of intellect and oratory and so had no need to use the kind of language which he did.[32] In doing so he also made it harder to speak on the immigration issue. On the far right, Mosely and Chesterton were critical, believing that Powell had come to the issue too late. The National Front were also sceptical of Powell's statements.[33] There was no doubt concern that their distinctiveness on the far right was being lost as Powell was the first prominent mainstream politician to raise the immigration issue. Others from the older, imperialist, Right of the party were also suspicious.

The Monday Club became divided on the issue, thus demonstrating the tensions between the nationalist and imperialist Right.[34] Its membership had initially been small with people being invited to join by a tightly controlled national executive. However, a decision to expand the membership by setting up local branches and allowing people to apply directly transformed the organisation. By the early 1970s it was at its peak with numerous MPs and Peers openly supporting it and having an active branch structure. The older establishment of the Monday Club remained very cautious of Powell. Sir Adrian Fitzgerald wrote to Julian Amery in an effort to get him to be the Chairman.[35] Amery had impeccable credentials as an imperialist, as seen in the last chapter, and was an establishment rather than a populist figure. However, the Editorial of *Monday World* declared support for Powell, who had 'sharpened the political wits of the electorate'.[36] The newer members were much more supportive. G. K. Young, who the establishment found rather mysterious, significantly took increased control of the Club's finances and wrote a pamphlet supportive of Powell and calling for an immigration freeze. For Young, the problem lay with the forces of 'liberal humanitarians', to which the Conservative Party leadership had fallen prey.[37] Liberals had argued that the native population ought to accept the strictures of 'civilised tolerance' rather than placing the onus on the immigrants to integrate.[38] However, radical ethnic leaders would never integrate. Moreover, immigration brought a panoply of social issues including crime, anti-social behaviour, educational under-attainment and pressures on the welfare state.[39] There was growing opposition to liberal opinion 'among those who had to pay the price' of immigration.[40] Against this, liberalism has 'degenerated into a mindless orthodoxy which can only scream "evil" when its vacuity is exposed.'[41] If policy change was going to emerge on the issue it would have to come from the grassroots rather than the leadership, which was complicit in the liberal approach to immigration. But if the party did change it would gain electoral support for:

> A Conservative Party which confronted the problems of race and human diversity with courage and honesty would not only have the backing of the people but would help to restore Britain's own pride and sense of historical identity.[42]

It was around this time that far right entryism of the Club occurred, especially some local branches.[43] One such was that of Essex, where local Club secretary Len Lambert had clear links with the far right. Another activist with far right connections was Bea Carthew who was elected on to the national executive committee. In September 1972 the Club held a 'Halt Immigration Now' campaign which attracted considerable support. Speakers included Ronald Bell MP, John Biggs-Davison MP, Harold Soref MP and John Heydon Stokes MP. The Monday Club had become firmly associated with the immigration issue.

It was at this stage that the old guard began to fight back when Jonathan Guinness was challenged for the Chairmanship in 1973. His rival was Richard Body. While Body had views widely considered more moderate than Guinness on other matters he was closer to Powell and championed the immigration issue. Although Guinness won the contest it was something of a pyrrhic victory with the Club going into seemingly permanent decline. By the early 1980s Alan Clark, commented that the Club was very much a shadow of what it had once been: 'I really cannot bear the Monday Club. They are all mad, quite different from its heyday... Now they are a prickly residue in the body politic, a nasty sort of gallstone.'[44]

The decline of the Monday Club led to the establishment of alternative organisations on the Right. One such organisation was the Salisbury Group with its founding members including the historian Maurice Cowling and Roger Scruton, who went on to edit the organisation's main outlet, *The Salisbury Review*. The *Review* was seen as an explicitly more intellectual output of Conservative Right thought, but was itself to become embroiled in the immigration issue on at least two separate occasions. Powell's preferred policy of voluntary repatriation begged the question, what if the non-white immigrants did not wish to return to their country of origin? In the first edition of the *Review*, Cambridge academic John Casey discussed the issue of immigration. He repeated the familiar theme that immigration and the more multicultural society which would result lacked popular support, being something imposed from above by liberal-minded reformers. He said that, 'I believe that the great majority of people are actually or potentially hostile to the multi-racial society which all decent persons are supposed to accept.'[45] Given that he doubted that Powell's preferred policy of voluntary repatriation could work, he advocated compulsory repatriation: 'I believe that the only radical policy that would stand some chance of success is repatriation'.[46]

Peregrine Worsthorne had been a long-standing opponent of liberal immigration laws:

> The great mass of the public…do not want a multiracial society. The prospect fills them with disquiet. An influx of black and brown faces into their neighbourhood is found unsettling and jarring. Of course it is.[47]

However, he remained critical of Powell's speeches arguing that they were too negative in their focus on repatriation rather than integration and had surrendered ground to the left. 'In Tory hands the race relations industry could have become an agency dedicated to the propagation of patriotism.'[48] The articulation of a strong British patriotism could have led to successful integration. However, now that there has been a large-scale immigration a solution had to be reached, and compulsory repatriation was not it.

Later *The Salisbury Review* was to achieve further notoriety when it carried an article by Ray Honeyford questioning the extent to which children of immigrants effectively integrated into mainstream society and the problems of teaching children of different cultural and linguistic capabilities.[49] Honeyford was a Headmaster at a school in Bradford and had already published letters in the local and national press and an article in *Times Educational Supplement* in 1982, but it was his piece in *The Salisbury Review* which was to attract most attention. He argued that immigration and a multi-ethnic society was causing educational under attainment. Some cultures did not value education and did not seek to integrate with the indigenous population. Rather than seeking to address these problems, the 'growing bureaucracy of race in local authorities' sought to promote their own ideological agenda and to dismiss anyone who opposed it as prejudiced. He maintained this view, later arguing that the Race Relations (Amendment) Act (2000) was damaging and the result of the then Home Secretary's pandering to the Commission on Racial Equality.[50] The theme has been a recurring one in *The Salisbury Review*. In 2019 Paul Weston wrote that there is now racial inequality with disadvantaged and under-achieving white boys in the education system being ignored by the race relations lobby who see them as possessing white and male 'privilege'.[51]

Meanwhile, the election of the new Leader in 1975 led the party to adopt more robust policies, including on immigration. In an interview for *World in Action* in 1978 Thatcher made the comment that people feel rather 'swamped' by immigration and that this was creating a potentially explosive situation.

> I think it means that people are really rather afraid that this country might be rather swamped by people with a different culture and, you know, the British character has done so much for democracy, for law and done so much throughout the world that if there is any fear that it might be swamped people are going to react and be rather hostile to those coming in.[52]

She was criticised by her senior colleagues—still mostly moderates at this stage—and never revived that language again. However, she did put in to the 1979 manifesto a number of commitments to further strengthen immigration controls, although ruling out repatriation.[53] The effect of this was to bring many of those who were considering voting for the National Front into the Tory fold and give her a secure majority.

Writing in 1981, T. E. Utley argued that:

> Today there are many more that two nations within our midst. The sudden and colossal immigration into this country which followed the dissolution of the British Empire confronts us with the most formidable challenge which has faced us perhaps for many centuries.[54]

So it seemed to the Conservative Right when riots broke out in the early 1980s. In 1981 there were riots in areas of the country's major cities Toxteth, Brixton and Moss Side. Each of these areas were economically deprived and had immigrant communities. Subsequently the Scarman Report—the Commission which had been set up to investigate the underlying causes of the unrest in Brixton and propose policy recommendations—pointed to the levels of poverty, funding cuts and the strained relationship between non-white communities and the police. However, for the Conservative Right the phenomenon of rioting proved their claims that immigration rules had been too loose (and also a wider decline in individual responsibility, which is the subject of Chapter 9). To Worsthorne, this was very much a report by the liberal establishment designed to further their own ideological agenda. The rioters in Brixton were West Indian and Powell had been right to warn of the forthcoming social upheaval.[55] For Powell, despite his dire warnings the lessons of postwar policy had yet to be learned: 'the passionate attachment of post-war Britain to the myth of a continuing Commonwealth has to be grasped in all its fullness if the disaster of the 1950s is to be understood.'[56] In *The Salisbury Review* E. J. Mishan argued that positive discrimination was misguided because it was unfair to whites and treated minorities as inferior and thus in need of extra help, both of which maintained social division.[57] Similarly, David Dale argued in the same publication that, 'anti-racism is a pernicious doctrine. Its methods are those of intimidation, censorship and the suppression of truth, and its ideology a totalitarian one which defines as racist any view which falls short of total commitment.'[58] What links these diverse comments is a rejection of the 'liberal approach' and a defence of a more resolutely conservative approach to race relations and immigration.

IMMIGRATION IN CONTEMPORARY BRITISH POLITICS

More recently concern over immigration has been bound up with Euroscepticism. The single market created a situation where there was free movement of labour, alongside goods and capital. While the original notion of the single market had been devised when the EEC/EU was relatively small this policy was not especially controversial. However, with enlargement of the EU to include the countries of Eastern Europe immigration increased significantly. East European migrants, moving westwards to take advantage of relatively higher paid jobs created new tensions. Under the Labour Government of 1997–2010 the foreign-born population increased by 3.6 million with roughly a third of this being due to the accession of East European counties according to Migration Watch UK.[59] On this issue, critics claimed, New Labour was extremely relaxed. Indeed, they argued that New Labour had desired the increase in order to encourage a more diverse society. This attitude, they argued, was confirmed when Gordon Brown was accidentally recorded saying that a Labour activist was 'bigoted woman'.[60] Not only was this an embarrassing gaffe but also showed the cultural divide which separated the metropolitan liberal elites from the working class. Nicholas Winterton spoke for the Conservative Right when he said that 'Labour's programme is wholly damaging to the UK and the unique British way of life.'[61] In reality, the Government had been advised that allowing free movement of citizens from the new members of the EU would only add a few thousand per year to net immigration levels. This was a serious miscalculation.

The immigration issue which precipitated the Brexit referendum and was one of the most significant issues for those voting Leave—with one poll showing roughly a third of Leave voters did so on the basis of immigration—alongside a more general but related sentiment of wanting to 'take back control'.[62] Elements of the Leave campaign stressed immigration, with posters depicting large-scale immigration from Turkey, which they claimed would be joining shortly after the referendum. For Leave campaigners such as Boris Johnson, the annual net level of immigration, which in 2015 was 333,000, was unsustainable and promises to reduce the level could not be achieved without Brexit.[63]

In opposition the Conservatives had criticised strongly the Labour Party's record on immigration. They had refused to impose transitional arrangements when Eastern European countries joined which led to large-scale immigration, especially as other existing members did impose such restraints. They pledged to reduce immigration to 'tens of thousands'. In government David Cameron occasionally pushed this message, including a poster campaign designed to encourage immigrants to 'go home'. However, whilst there was no control over EU migration under a system of free movement this meant that the primary focus had to be on non-EU migration. The 'Windrush scandal' led to the questioning of such an approach. Public reaction was to be highly critical. While it seems that there is a persistent public demand for more immigration controls there is also a deep-seated sense of fairness which manifests itself in the form of allowing those seeking asylum and respect for those who have been accepted. Tougher demands by those on the Conservative Right such as compulsory repatriation lack widespread public support.

Meanwhile, the Conservative Right continues to question the desirability of multiculturalism. Their longstanding concerns here appeared to be justified by the statements of Trevor Phillips, formerly Chairman of the Equality and Human Rights Commission, that multiculturalism wasn't working. The fact that it was left to Phillips, on the centre left of British politics, to say this showed for some the loss of confidence in the Conservative Party. John Hayes MP said that:

> Leading Conservatives have known for years that multiculturalism was a bankrupt idea, but dared not say so. Any instinctive Conservative knows that a diverse nation coheres when things that unite us are more important than things that divide us.[64]

For Simon Heffer, 'the Tory upholds, in his idea of the nation, a mon-
ocultural society that accepts other cultures at the margins, rather than
the notion of the multicultural society, which would dilute and end the
traditional conception of the British nation.'[65] For Paul Weston, Enoch
Powell had been right all along. Indeed, if anything, he had underestimated the scale of what was to happen: 'I don't think Enoch Powell,
even in his darkest moments, could have envisaged the extent to which
the native English would become second-class citizens in their own
land.'[66]

NOTES

1. For histories of British immigration policy, see Z. Layton-Henry, *The
   Politics of Immigration* (Oxford: Blackwell, 1992); P. Gilroy, *There Ain't
   No Black in the Union Jack* (London: Routledge, 2002).
2. D. Baker, *Ideology of Obsession: A.K. Chesterton and British Fascism*
   (London: Tauris, 2017).
3. R. Skidelsky, *Oswald Mosley* (London: Macmillan, 1981).
4. See A. Gamble, *The Conservative Nation* (London: Routledge & Kegan
   Paul, 1974).
5. C. Osborne, 'The Colour Problem in Britain: Right', *The Spectator*, 4
   December 1964, pp. 7–8.
6. Gamble, *The Conservative Nation*, p. 181.
7. Lord Elton, *The Unarmed Invasion: Survey of Afro-Asian Immigration*
   (London: Collins, 1965).
8. Lord Elton, House of Lords, 3 November 1966, https://api.parliament.
   uk/historic-hansard/lords/1966/nov/03/immigration-problems,
   accessed 6 May 2019.
9. Ibid.
10. Quoted in Gilroy, *There Ain't No Black in the Union Jack*, p. 102.
11. Lord Elton, House of Lords, 3 November 1966.
12. P. Griffiths, *A Question of Colour? The Smethwick Election of 1964*
    (London: Leslie Frewin, 1966).
13. A. Reekes, 'The West Midland and Powell's Birmingham Speech',
    Political Quarterly, 89/3 (September 2018), pp. 400–408.
14. Enoch Powell papers, Churchill College, Cambridge, 1/1/11.
15. P. Foot, *The Rise of Enoch Powell* (Harmondsworth: Penguin, 1969).
16. S. Heffer, *Like the Roman* (London: Weidenfeld & Nicolson, 1998),
    p. 556.

17. N. Jones, 'Enoch Powell: A Personal Insight', *Political Quarterly*, 89/3 (September 2018), pp. 358–361.
18. Ibid.
19. J. Wood (ed.) *Freedom and Reality* (Kingswood: Elliot Right Way Books, 1969), p. 282.
20. J. Atkins, '"Strangers in Their Own Country": Epideictic Rhetoric and Communal Definition in Enoch Powell's "Rivers of Blood" Speech', *Political Quarterly*, 89/3 (September 2018), pp. 362–369.
21. Wood, *Freedom and Reality*, p. 283.
22. Ibid., p. 289.
23. Ibid., p. 300.
24. Ibid.
25. Ibid.
26. J. Wood (ed.) *Powell and the 1970 Election* (London: Elliott Right Way Books, 1970), p. 102.
27. R. Ritchie (ed.) *A Nation or No Nation? Six Years in British Politics* (London: Elliot, 1979).
28. C. Moore, *Margaret Thatcher: The Authorised Biography, Volume 1: Not for Turning* (London: Allen Lane, 2013), p. 195.
29. Powell papers, 1/1/19.
30. Quoted in G. K. Young, *Who Goes Home? Immigration and Repatriation* (London: Monday Club, 1969), p. 4.
31. T. E. Utley, *Enoch Powell: The Man and His Thinking* (London: HarperCollins, 1968).
32. Interview with John Biffen, London, 26 April 2007.
33. H. Taylor, '"Rivers of Blood" and Britain's Far Right', *Political Quarterly*, 89/3 (September 2018), pp. 385–391.
34. Interview with Sir Adrian Fitzgerald, 10 April 2017.
35. Monday Club papers in private possession of Sir Adrian Fitzgerald.
36. *Monday World*, 1/2 (Spring/Summer 1968).
37. Young, *Who Goes Home?*
38. Ibid., pp. 10–11.
39. Ibid.
40. Ibid., p. 22.
41. Ibid., p. 23.
42. Ibid., p. 38.
43. M. Pitchford, *The Conservative Party and the Extreme Right, 1945–75* (Manchester: Manchester University Press, 2013).
44. A. Clark, *Diaries: Into Politics* (London: Weidenfeld & Nicolson, 2000), p. 337.
45. J. Casey, 'One Nation: The Politics of Race', *The Salisbury Review*, 1 (Autumn 1982), p. 26.

46. Ibid., p. 27.
47. P. Worsthorne, *The Socialist Myth* (London: Cassell, 1971), p. 211.
48. P. Worsthorne, *By the Right* (Dublin: Brophy, 1987), p. 78.
49. R. Honeyford, 'Education and Race', *The Salisbury Review*, 2/2 (Winter 1984).
50. R. Honeyford, 'The Race Relations Act 2000', *The Salisbury Review*, 19/4 (2001).
51. P. Weston, 'Degrees of Racism', *The Salisbury Review*, 37/3 (2019).
52. Interview with Gordon Burns, *World in Action*, 27 January 1978, https://www.margaretthatcher.org/document/103485, accessed 6 May 2019.
53. Moore, *Margaret Thatcher*, p. 392.
54. T. E. Utley, *One Nation: 100 Years On* (London: Conservative Political Centre, 1981), p. 12.
55. Worsthorne, *By the Right*, pp. 74–77.
56. E. Powell, 'The UK and Immigration', *The Salisbury Review*, 7/2 (December 1988), p. 42.
57. E. J. Mishan, 'What Future for a Multi-racial Britain: Part Two', *The Salisbury Review*, 7/1 (September 1988).
58. D. Dale, 'The New Ideology of Race', *The Salisbury Review*, 4/1 (October 1985), p. 22.
59. Migration watch, 'The History of Immigration in the UK', 3 September 2018, https://www.migrationwatchuk.org/key-topics/history-of-immigration, accessed 6 May 2019.
60. Full report, available at https://www.youtube.com/watch?v=CTr8IVW-BuPE, accessed 6 May 2019.
61. N. Winterton, *Right Now*, July–September 1999, p. 10.
62. Lord Ashcroft's polling data, http://lordashcroftpolls.com/2016/06/how-the-united-kingdom-voted-and-why/, accessed 6 May 2019.
63. A. Asthana, 'Boris Johnson: Cameron Can't Cut Immigration and Stay in EU', *Guardian*, 9 May 2016, https://www.theguardian.com/politics/2016/may/09/boris-johnson-cameron-cant-cut-immigration-and-stay-in-eu, accessed 6 May 2019.
64. J. Hayes, 'Being Conservative', in *Being Conservative: A Cornerstone of Policies to Revive Tory Britain* (London: Cornerstone Group, 2005), p. 9.
65. S. Heffer, 'Traditional Toryism', in K. Hickson (ed.) *The Political Thought of the Conservative Party Since 1945* (Basingstoke: Palgrave, 2005), p. 201.
66. P. Weston, 'The Whip Hand', *The Salisbury Review*, 36/4 (Summer 2018), p. 22.

CHAPTER 4

Europe

Today European (dis)integration is the issue which most inflames the passions of the Conservative Right. It was not always thus. Indeed, in the early period of our study the attitude of the Conservative Right was best understood as ambivalent for some and strongly supportive for others. The aim of this chapter is therefore to explore how and why the attitude of the Conservative Right moved in an increasingly Eurosceptic direction. It will begin by examining the initial attitude of the Conservative Right to early advocacy of closer European integration after the horrors of the Second World War through to membership. It will then explore the increasingly sceptical approach of the Conservative Right and the reasons for this including further European integration and Margaret Thatcher's Bruges speech (1988) which in turn led to the open divisions over the Maastricht Treaty and during the years of opposition after 1997. Finally, the chapter will examine current Conservative Right attitudes towards Brexit. Although the decision to leave the European Union (EU) could be heralded a success for the Conservative Right there are deep suspicions regarding the terms of departure.

THE NATURE OF CONSERVATIVE RIGHT EUROSCEPTICISM

Euroscepticism as a concept has been deeply problematic for academics. The term began in the UK as a journalistic concept. However, its continued use led academics to seek to define it with greater clarity. One of the first writers on Euroscepticism in the UK, Jim Bulpitt, argued correctly

© The Author(s) 2020
K. Hickson, *Britain's Conservative Right since 1945*,
https://doi.org/10.1007/978-3-030-27697-3_4

that it is a term complicated by being value laden and also riddled with associated contested concepts.[1] For Bulpitt, Eurosceptics were those who resisted and criticised each subsequent step towards integration. However, he also felt that ultimately they would go along with it on the basis that there was 'no alternative'. In contrast, anti-Europeans wish to renegotiate the terms of membership and, should they prove unsatisfactory, withdraw. This view was echoed by Andrew Fear in *The Salisbury Review* when arguing that the Conservative Party needed to be more resolute in its opposition to the EU:

> Euroscepticism is worse than merely futile: it is highly damaging to the cause of preserving national sovereignty... The only difference between a federalist and a Euro-sceptic is that the former offers British sovereignty an honest summary execution and the latter a deceitful slow death of a thousand cuts.[2]

Another useful distinction is that between 'hard' and 'soft' Euroscepticism made by Paul Taggart.[3] Those who subscribe to the former believe in withdrawing or at least fundamentally altering the nature of Britain's membership, whereas the latter is concerned with criticising certain policies, aspects of treaties, the institutions of the EEC/EU or resisting further integrationist steps. The classifications are fluid. One may start off as a soft Eurosceptic and then become 'harder' over time as the nature of the EEC/EU changes. Others may move in the opposite direction as Britain becomes more closely integrated, believing that withdrawal is no longer viable. Both of these types of Eurosceptic can be found on the Conservative Right. A third distinction within the Euroscepticism literature is between inclusive and exclusive.[4] The former category subscribes to the view that European integration should be avoided or opposed because it damages the social fabric and imposes economic liberal policies on member states. Such a view is more characteristic of the Left. In contrast, exclusive Euroscepticism tends to focus on integration as a threat to the nation state through the loss of sovereignty, the negative effects of immigration, budgetary contributions and other factors. This certainly accounts for the Euroscepticism of the Conservative Right.

Euroscepticism is not limited to the Conservatives.[5] Indeed, one of the key reasons why 'Europe' has been such a divisive issue in British politics has been that there is not a pro-European and an anti-European party.[6] Both major parties contain pro's and anti's. At any one moment one of those strands will be predominant. Up until the mid-1980s Euroscepticism was stronger in the Labour Party, and from the late 1980s it was the Conservatives who have become more hostile and Labour became an essentially pro-European party with a few dissenting voices. This partly reflects the strategic self interest of competing political parties and also the changing nature of the European project itself. The growth in Conservative Euroscepticism reflects the fact that it had become a free-market party under Thatcher's leadership and the EEC/EU was seen as a barrier to the promotion of the market, especially as it developed a social policy competency. However, their reasons for doing so are very different. A common argument on the right was that the EEC/EU blocked the creation of the free market, for left Eurosceptics the EEC/EU was a 'capitalist' club. Hence, Euroscepticism is best seen as a thin-centred ideology defined only by what it is against and not what it is for.

A central concept within the European debate is that of sovereignty. For both Labour and Conservative hard Eurosceptics membership of this transnational organisation takes away Britain's sovereignty. Sovereignty is an absolute, something either possessed or dispossessed. The return of sovereignty to Westminster is therefore essential to the attainment of domestic ideological objectives. Critics of this view of sovereignty argue instead that it is divisible, something which can be shared and increased in sum by being part of a larger political and economic block. Both have ran through the post-1945 history of the Conservative Right. It was certainly this latter view of sovereignty which motivated those who sought British membership of the EEC. While the contemporary view of the Conservative Right is very much to see sovereignty in its first sense, this has not always been the case with figures on the Conservative Right being leading advocates of membership as we will now discuss.

EUROPEAN UNITY

The catastrophic consequences of the Second World War combined with the belief that a third conflict was best avoided through the interdependence of the nations of Europe led to calls for formal integration. The initial stages would be in specific, but strategically important, sectors of the economy and this would then necessitate closer integration leading, ultimately, to full political and economic unity. This call for European unity appeared to have the support of Winston Churchill in his appeal for a 'kind of united states of Europe' in a speech in Zurich in 1946. However, what he meant by this and the extent to which he wished Britain to be involved are unclear. Of the three spheres of influence Churchill claimed Britain had after 1945—Europe, America and the Commonwealth—the former was the least significant. For many senior politicians there was ambivalence on the question of European integration. When integrationist steps were taken Britain preferred to be on the side of the looser terms of the European Free Trade Area (EFTA) rather than the more strict terms of membership of the EEC.

At this stage attitudes of politicians in the UK can best be described as falling into one of three categories. For most, as stated, there was ambivalence. Europe was simply not the major issue. Some were openly hostile. Finally, there were those who were advocates of Britain's closer integration in Europe. The issue split both major parties, but Labour was the most sceptical and, although the Conservatives did contain some vocal opponents of membership, was more favourable than Labour. Certainly, this was true of the leaderships of the two major parties in the early 1960s as Britain made its first application for membership, with Harold Macmillan keen to join and Hugh Gaitskell strongly against. Unfortunately for British politics these attitudes did not fit neatly into the party system with all three attitudes present within the two major parties.

The first major test came when the attitude of the British government changed towards the end of the 1950s. Part of the reason for this was the belief that Britain was no longer of sufficient power to be able to pursue an independent course. In the era of the Cold War, Britain needed to be firmly aligned with America. But growing concern over relative economic decline also encouraged the Government to believe that it additionally needed to ally with an economic block, which would be the EEC. Many within the Conservative Party were, to varying degrees, supportive. Partly this was out of loyalty to the party leader, especially when Hugh Gaitskell, as Leader of the Opposition, came out strongly against membership on the grounds that it would end a 'thousand years of British history'. However, France was wary of Britain's application believing that it was a way for the USA to extend its influence and the application was vetoed by de Gaulle. The issues exposed the divisions within the major parties.

The Conservative Right was, even at this early stage, divided. The most prominent MP to speak out against membership was Derek Walker-Smith, who had been an MP since 1945, a Vice Chair of the 1922 Committee and a minister under Macmillan. In what was to become a consistent refrain from opponents of the EEC/EU he argued that the consequences of joining the EEC would be the, 'loss or impairment of our prized national institutions, the sovereignty of Parliament and the common law'.[7] Peter Walker, who was later to serve as a Cabinet Minister under Thatcher despite his association with the Tory Wets, also opposed membership on similar grounds.[8] A further high-profile opponent of membership was Victor Montagu who served as President of the Anti-Common Market League. Montagu (under his title Lord Hinchingbrooke) held a distinctive position within Conservatism. In the war years he had written *Full Speed Ahead: Essays in Tory Reform*[9] which advocated social reform, but had allied this with a strongly imperialist position. He became a prominent member of the Monday Club, arguing in 1970 that Britain should not join the EEC because it was against the interests of the nation and the Commonwealth.[10] Instead, he supported a form of Commonwealth preference in agriculture. The Anti-Common Market League was founded in 1961 to oppose membership, led by John Paul and Michael Shay. The League stood two candidates in the 1964 General Election, though neither performed well.

Another strand of the Conservative Right was at this stage, and subsequently, much more sympathetic to European integration. This predominantly consisted of the old imperialist wing of the party, most prominently Julian Amery and John Biggs-Davison. Both had been supporters of the International Pan-European Union, founded in 1923 under the direction of Count Richard von Coudenhove-Kalergi. In the post-war period they associated with the European Movement. Their belief was that, firstly—as discussed in Chapter 2—America acted against the interests of the UK and its Empire, which they wished to see destroyed. However, other European countries also had empires they wished to defend. Separately they could not compete against the two superpowers but more closely integrated they could do so. There would be no loss of sovereignty by entering the EEC. Indeed, closer integration with Western Europe would increase Britain's international power. Biggs-Davison wrote to Julian Amery in 1955 expressing his regret that the Conservatives had failed to back the Western European Union—which they had supported but others opposed.[11] In 1960, Julian Amery met Coudenhove-Kalergi and was reassured that sovereignty was not at stake.[12] Macmillan encouraged Amery to engage in diplomatic manoeuvres with the French.[13] They therefore rejected the arguments put forward by the likes of Gaitskell that there was a fundamental incompatibility between the Commonwealth and EEC membership believing that the best way to preserve the empire and commonwealth was through European unity.

Biggs-Davison argued that Britain should be fully committed to both the EEC and the Commonwealth:

> London should become the centre of a world system of sovereign nations based on the Commonwealth, the Sterling Area and those European institutions which are flexible enough to allow our full cooperation.[14]

He believed that Britain should have become a member of the Schuman Plan, which was a precursor to the EEC, though fellow MP Harry Legge-Bourke disagreed.[15] He maintained that there was no trade-off between the Commonwealth and the EEC: 'you may be a good European and also a good Commonwealth man.'[16] As late as 1987, Biggs-Davison argued that Britain should have been much more fully committed to European integration from the outset.[17]

If the splits between the imperialistic right and the nationalistic right was not yet apparent then it soon was to become so and 'Europe' was to be a key battleground.

THE THREAT TO SOVEREIGNTY

The veto on Britain's membership and the change of Government in 1964 did not halt the pressures for closer European integration and the Wilson Government made a second application. This again was to be vetoed but the oppositionist voices were heard more clearly. This was partly for ideological and partly for strategic reasons. The Tories had lost the 1964 General Election and Edward Heath had replaced Alec Douglas-Home as Leader. He was struggling to find a new agenda for the Conservatives and to make serious strikes against Harold Wilson. Meanwhile, Powell—who had stood in the 1965 leadership contest only to come a long way last—was seeking to build up his profile within the Party against his old foe Heath. In a number of speeches he set out his alternative vision. This included a u-turn on the European issue. Powell had supported the first application for membership, which he later explained by saying that, 'I didn't raise dissent because at that stage it was presented as a free-trade exercise.'[18] He had also supported membership when the subsequent Labour Administration applied.

However, by the end of the decade he was strongly against membership on grounds of parliamentary sovereignty. His younger followers, including John Biffen and Richard Body, supported him in this opinion. Writing in 1969, Biffen argued that the coolness of public opinion towards European integration contrasted starkly with the enthusiasm of the political elite.[19] Although Nicholas Ridley was to become an ardent opponent of closer integration in the 1980s, in 1970 he argued—against Biffen—that the UK needed to fully commit to European integration.[20] Again, the tensions on the Conservative Right between the imperialists such as Amery and Biggs-Davison contrasted starkly with the now fully emerged nationalist/populist wing.

The battle lines were more clearly drawn by the time of the 1970 General Election. Heath said in his manifesto that he would explore the possibility of membership, but no more. In power he came out strongly in support of membership, which in the absence of de Gaulle was successful. Several Conservative figures opposed membership. They felt that sovereignty was at stake and that a deception was being practiced on the British people. Neil Marten stated that:

> The basic question is whether Britain should remain an independent country or become a province in a United States of "Europe". No criticism is levelled at those who genuinely advocate the latter course; at least it is an honest recognition of the total implications of belonging to the Common Market. But every form of criticism should be made of those who avoid the issue, who wilfully conceal it with honeyed words or who simply don't bother to study the reality.[21]

Enoch Powell also opposed membership on these ground.[22] Heath had said that the full implications of membership should be known by the people, but in what was to become a recurring theme in Powell's speeches on this issue, he felt that the full facts were not being presented by those who argued that sovereignty was not at stake. In the 1970 General Election campaign he said: 'what the "full implications" are, becomes clearer on the side of the Economic Community with almost every week that passes'.[23] Britain would lose sovereignty on issues including the economy and defence. The EEC was clearly moving in a federalist direction with plans already in place for a single currency and direct elections.

A younger generation of Conservative politicians on the free-market right of the Party were also opposed to membership; partly on sovereignty grounds but also because they felt that their desire to pursue free-market policies would be hampered by membership. The main organisation for this position was the Selsdon Group which had been established to oppose what they regarded as Heath's u-turns on economic policy away from the agreement which they believed had been reached at the Selsdon Park Hotel, London in 1969.[24]

The principal organisation on the Conservative Right at this time was still the Monday Club, which was divided over the issue. Already suffering from the splits over immigration (see Chapter 3) the European issue also created tensions for them. The followers of Powell were largely against membership believing that sovereignty would effectively be handed over to the European Commission. However, there was still the presence of the older, more imperialistic wing in the form of Biggs-Davison who was to become Chairman in 1974.

The issue was of sufficient seriousness for Powell that in 1974 he effectively encouraged people to vote Labour on the basis that they had pledged a referendum.[25] The act was considered a betrayal, even by some of his closest supporters. He re-emerged as an Ulster Unionist later in the year and took a prominent part in the referendum the following year along with several other senior figures on the Conservative right (as well as several Labour and other politicians). Powell believed that Heath had taken Britain into the EEC against the wishes of the people who were not consulted. The defeat—by a majority of two to one—was a bitter disappointment for Powell, who claimed that the scale of what he and others were saying—that this marked the end of the nation state—was simply too vast for the public to comprehend. However, he would continue to oppose subsequent steps towards closer European unity and eventually the people would come to see the truth.

He supported the Labour Government's refusal to participate in the European Monetary System but strongly criticised the decision to have direct elections to the European Parliament as this further undermined the sovereignty of the Westminster Parliament. This was a further deception since the people had been told when Britain joined in 1973 that no further loss of sovereignty would take place.

> The British people are about to have practiced upon them a trick even cruder and more shameless than that by which they were cheated out of their inheritance of parliamentary self-government in the first place when we acceded to the European Economic Community.[26]

Just because the referendum had been lost was no reason not to oppose further integration. John Biffen warned of the dangers for his party in seeking to ally too closely with the EEC: 'the Conservative Party must not become identified in the public mind with foreign bureaucratic rule, out of a foolish fear of appearing insufficiently "European"'.[27] On the establishment of direct elections, Biffen stated that, 'I have received more letters from constituents advocating direct elections for the Severn Trent Water Authority than I have for the Strasbourg Assembly.'[28]

Once again, this position contrasted with that of Amery, Biggs-Davison and others. Amery wrote to Biggs-Davison stating his support for direct elections: 'I am in favour of a directly elected assembly simply because I think it might raise the level of debate above the parish pump.'[29] In 1980 Biggs-Davison invited Amery to become Patron of the Pan-Europe Club, whose aim was 'to promote the role of Britain as a European nation and to work for the unity of all the nations of Europe founded on the Christian tradition and ultimately for their political union'.[30] Hugh Fraser, also on the imperialist wing of the party—who had stood unsuccessfully for the leadership in 1975—argued for Britain's continued membership of the EEC. 'My greatest fear is of this growing present derogation of parliamentary sovereignty', he argued.[31] But this was not a derogation of sovereignty to the EEC, but rather by promising a referendum.[32] 'There is only one party which is absolutely solid in favour of coming out of Europe, and that party wishes to do what? It wishes to destroy democracy. It is the Communist Party in Britain.'[33]

THE MOUNTING TIDE OF EUROSCEPTICISM

No minister had resigned from Heath's Cabinet, indeed prominent right-wingers such as Margaret Thatcher were to go on to campaign enthusiastically during the referendum for continued membership. She did have moments of open hostility towards the EEC and overall her governments became more hostile but there were also significant moments of integration which the likes of Powell criticised her for strongly.

Writing in 1983, David Storey and Teddy Taylor argued that after a decade it was necessary to take stock of Britain's membership of the EEC.[34] The experience had been overwhelmingly negative. There had been a large financial transfer to the EEC, food costs had increased under the Common Agricultural Policy, Britain's trade with the rest of the world had declined, and the veto powers—which Heath had said Britain would retain—had been significantly reduced. The options facing Britain included maintaining the status quo, gradual reform, renegotiation or ending membership. They argued that the first two would not work. The logic of integration meant that standing still was not an option and previous attempts to achieve even modest reform in the national interest had not worked. The only options were, therefore, renegotiation, or outright withdrawal. This was an early contribution to what was to become the standard position of the anti-Europeans.

Thatcher's first significant difference with the EEC was over the budget where she demanded 'our money' back at Fontainebleau in June 1984, eventually obtaining a rebate. Nevertheless Britain remained a major contributor to the EEC budget. Two years later Thatcher persuaded Parliament to pass the Single European Act (SEA) which set out the path towards the single market. She was attracted to the notion of an extended economic market, but the Treaty also involved reducing the scope of the veto in favour of qualified majority voting, which the Right regarded as a further erosion of sovereignty, with Thatcher herself seeking to limit its use.[35] John Biffen was by this time the Leader of the House of Commons, and later said he regretted the passing of the Act.[36] There were just 17 Conservative rebels on the bill. Charles Moore says that as Thatcher's opposition to federalism was already known she was able to convert doubters. 'In that sense, if in no other, Mrs Thatcher was the most effective promoter of European integration Britain has ever known,' he argued.[37] Thatcher continued to defend the decision subsequently, even in the 1990s when she was opposing the Maastricht Treaty. She said that she was right to have signed the SEA but had underestimated the will behind the political rhetoric of ever closer union. However, Moore records that in private she was going further and saying that she should never have signed it, 'because it had pushed on towards the European Union which she feared'.[38]

Once again, criticism from the right was led by Powell, who believed that the single market was a major loss of parliamentary sovereignty. He argued that, 'the doctrine of harmonisation is incompatible, and was always intended to be incompatible, with sovereign British institutions.'[39] He argued consistently against Britain becoming a member of the single market, which would mean loss of control over key economic activities and especially borders, and would lead to the creation of a single currency and ultimately political union. He argued that, 'every alteration proposed in the new treaty is an alteration which diminishes the powers of this House...which means a further erosion of the opportunity for the British people to influence the policy and the laws under which they live'.[40] At this stage, this was a minority opinion, even on the Conservative Right. The No Turning Back Group of mostly younger Conservative MP's, which was established to defend the Thatcherite reform agenda against the likes of John Biffen, who had called for consolidation, rejected Powell's arguments. 'Some, who otherwise share our views, appear pessimistic about our prospects for full sovereignty under the Single European Act. We do not share such despondency.'[41] In contrast, Lord Denning argued that the Single European Act had clearly eroded national sovereignty in a legal, or absolute, sense: 'gone is the concept of national sovereignty – to be replaced by European Unity'.[42]

By the end of the 1980s Thatcher had become vocally hostile to European integration. She believed that the EEC had taken on increased policy competences aimed at creating a federal Europe. Her speech in Bruges was to be the moment when she set out her opposition to the direction the EEC had decided to take:

> My first guiding principle is this: willing and active cooperation between independent sovereign states is the best way to build a successful European Community. To try to suppress nationhood and concentrate power at the centre of a European conglomerate would be highly damaging and would jeopardise the objectives we seek to achieve. Europe will be stronger precisely because it has France as France, Spain as Spain, Britain as Britain, each with its own customs, traditions and identity. It would be folly to try to fit them into some sort of identikit European personality.[43]

She also opposed the development of a social dimension under the EEC Commission Presidency of Jacques Delors. The development of this policy competence, which also led to the Labour Party adopting a more pro-EEC stance, was anathema to Thatcher who believed that socialists would achieve through the EEC what she had been seeking to destroy at home: 'we have not successfully rolled back the frontiers of the state in Britain, only to see them re-imposed at a European level with a European super-state exercising a new dominance from Brussels.'[44]

The impact of the Bruges speech was significant. The Conservative Right largely followed her in criticising the EEC. The right-wing press also supported her, with the notorious *Sun* headline, 'Up Yours Delors'. However, there were those who opposed this harder form of

Euroscepticism which was now on the rise in the Conservative Party. This was not just limited to the One Nation Conservatives but also those on the Right who had always favoured Britain's integration. There were also those who believed that the battle to take Britain out of the EEC— the ultimate logic of those who took a more hard-line position—was fruitless because Britain was already deeply integrated. Arthur Aughey argued in *The Salisbury Review* in 1989 that, 'after 15 years of membership of the EC the argument about whether the UK should stay in or come out is now dead.'[45]

The removal of Thatcher in November 1990 was partly over her new-found hostility towards the EEC with her former Chancellor, Geoffrey Howe, leading the criticism. For him closer integration was not a threat to either sovereignty, which could be pooled, or to the free market, which could be rolled out to a wider economic area.[46] The tensions, which had always been present within the New Right, between free-market economics and nationalism were therefore exposed. Despite the arguments of Howe and others it was the nationalistic right which was in the ascendant.

When Thatcher's successor, John Major, stated that he wished Britain to be at the 'heart of Europe'[47] the nationalist fervour created by the Bruges speech was inevitably going to resist. Thatcher, until she became ill, was to lead this revolt, saying that she intended to be a 'back seat driver'. Her key aide Norman Tebbit was also to figure prominently in whipping up opposition to Major from his new seat in the House of Lords.

Major believed that it was in Britain's interests to sign the Maastricht Treaty, albeit with two opt-outs, one from the Social Chapter and one from the single currency. If he had believed that this would placate the rebels he was to be mistaken. Although he had performed an unprecedented feat in the democratic era in winning a fourth successive general election in 1992, it was with a reduced majority. The rebellion therefore had more impact than had there been a larger majority. Several MPs voted consistently against the whip and even had the whip withdrawn for a period. Eventually, the Maastricht Treaty was ratified. However, the rebellions did not stop there with further protests over the size of Britain's budget contribution. Finally, Major said that it was time to 'put up or shut up' and encouraged Eurosceptics to challenge him for the leadership. In indiscrete remarks believing he wasn't being recorded Major had already referred to the 'bastards' within his Cabinet. One of them, Welsh Secretary John Redwood, was to resign. Though he was roundly defeated—Major secured 218 to Redwood's 89—it did nothing to restore Major's credibility and eventually he went down to a thumping defeat at the hands of Tony Blair's resurgent Labour Party in 1997, by 418 seats to 165. Hence, the second Conservative Leader in a row had been brought down at least in part by the European issue.

European integration clearly divided the Right from the Left of the Tory party at this stage. The moderates, which included Major, Michael Heseltine and Ken Clarke were pro-European. The Right became increasingly more trenchant in their views in Opposition from 1997. Here Bulpitt's distinction between anti-Europeans and Eurosceptics comes to the fore again. The Right had opposed the Maastricht Treaty because they saw it as a further erosion of sovereignty. They also opposed what they saw as the socialist direction of the EU. But they did not advocate renegotiation or referendum unlike the Referendum Party at the time of the 1997 General Election under the leadership of James Goldsmith, or the newly emerging United Kingdom Independence Party that had been established under the leadership of Alan Sked in 1993. For Roger Scruton, the Maastricht Treaty showed that a choice would have to be made: 'we are told that our sovereignty is in no way threatened by the Maastricht Treaty; yet the Treaty at every point implies that our Parliament can be overridden where its decisions conflict with those of the Commission.'[48] Britain's interests and history were fundamentally different from those of the continental countries. A choice would have to be made between independence and European integration.

The opposition to the EU continued after the 1997 defeat where the possibility of Britain's membership of the single currency was the main concern. For the Conservative Right this was a direct challenge to the nation state, requiring a patriotic response. *Right Now* magazine argued that all true patriots needed to oppose membership of the single currency[49] and Peter Goodchild argued in *The Salisbury Review* that the main argument against membership should be, 'fear of domination by, or falling under the control of, people who do not belong to this place and to this culture'.[50] However, the decision of the then Labour Government to rule out membership of the single currency did not quell the fears of the Conservative Right who continued to argue for a more fundamental rebalancing of the relationship between the UK and the EU. Prominent advocates for this view at the time included Norman Lamont, who had presided over the economy in September 1992 when Britain was forced out of the Exchange Rate Mechanism.[51] He later told of how he had sang in the bath that evening. Far from being 'Black Wednesday' as it was initially dubbed, Eurosceptics called it 'Golden Wednesday' as the country was freed from the shackles of the fixed exchange rate system and the economy grew. John Redwood remained a strong critic of the EU and the leadership first of William Hague and then more so Iain Duncan Smith was seen as a victory for the Eurosceptics as the pro-European Kenneth Clarke was defeated in both leadership contests. This partly reflected the changing composition of the parliamentary party. A further concern for the Conservative Right at this time was the proposal for a 'European Army'. Lord Chalfont, amongst others, argued that this was only likely to antagonise the western alliance. NATO should be maintained and there was no need for an EU armed forces capability.[52]

However, after a third successive election defeat in 2005, where the Conservatives had stood on a platform including Euroscepticism, there was a feeling that the Party needed to modernise. David Davis stood for the leadership and would have maintained a more Eurosceptic position. However, David Cameron was to win the contest and professed to be a 'liberal Conservative'. Although far from the pro-Europeanism of earlier leaders such as Macmillan and Heath—and even more hostile than Thatcher for much of her premiership—it did halt the further rise of Euroscepticism and the Coalition agreement with a pro-European party also appeared to marginalise the Eurosceptics. The establishment of the Cornerstone Group was in order for those MPs on the Conservative Right to resist Cameron's modernisation. In terms of European integration this meant maintaining a Eurosceptic voice. According to Bill Cash: 'modernisation is bunk. In the hands of the Party's left wing, One Nation politics is No Nation politics.'[53] Further European integration needed to be opposed, including the Treaties of Amsterdam, Nice and Lisbon.

The growth of Euroscepticism was deemed one of the reasons for the Conservative Party being dubbed the 'nasty party' and the party seemed to be obsessing over the issue. Polls frequently showed that 'Europe' was near the bottom of voters' priorities, but for the anti-Europeans the issue was fundamental. For Roger Helmer, 'those of us engaged in politics know (or ought to know) that Brussels influences virtually every policy area'.[54] It was therefore inadequate for senior Conservatives to 'keep mouthing the same platitudes'. Lord Rannoch called for a Treasury White Paper which would show the costs and benefits of membership.[55] Any benefits which Britain derived from being a member of the EU would still be available to the country through a bi-lateral trade deal.

Another fundamental reason for withdrawing is that, 'the EU is not, and cannot be, democratic' for 'there is no European *demos*, no underlying European public opinion, on which representative government can be based.'[56] This was to be a relatively early statement of the anti-Europeans case which became central to the Brexit debate.

BREXIT

However, the pause in the Party's drift to a more hardline Eurosceptic position was to prove temporary. Largely as a result of growing UKIP success Cameron pledged to hold an in-out referendum on continued membership if the Conservatives were re-elected in 2015. The polls appeared to predict a Conservative defeat but the surprise return of a small Conservative majority—the first since 1992—led to the holding of the referendum the following year. Cameron, eschewing the neutralist position adopted by Wilson in 1975, campaigned strongly for remaining in the EU as did his Chancellor.

Several senior Conservative backbench MPs campaigned openly to Leave the EU, most notably veteran Eurosceptics such as Bill Cash and John Redwood but also a new generation including, notably, Jacob Rees-Mogg. Cash had argued in 2005 that 'assuming that other member states will not fundamentally renegotiate the existing European treaties, withdrawal will become necessary'.[57] However, he also argued that a straight in-out referendum would be an oversimplification, preferring a vote between leaving the EU and renegotiating the terms of membership 'into a trading association of nation states with political cooperation'.[58] Cameron entered into renegotiations in 2015 but his critics felt that he had extracted nothing from the EU. Many of the Cornerstone Group of right-wing Conservative MPs campaigned for Leave. They were joined by the members of the European Research Group, which had been founded by Michael Spicer in 1993 to oppose the Maastricht Treaty and was now led by Rees-Mogg. But their activities were boosted considerably by the decision of frontbenchers Boris Johnson and Michael Gove to support Leave. When the results were announced 17,410,742 (51.89%) voted Leave and 16,141, 241 voted Remain (48.11%). Of the constituent parts of the UK, Scotland had voted strongly to Remain as had Northern Ireland by a smaller margin. Wales, surprisingly, had voted to Leave as had England by a bigger margin. Of the English regions only Greater London had voted to Remain. Cameron resigned immediately.

The results also revealed significant social cleavages. Older people generally voted Leave and younger voters Remain. Generally, the better educated voted Remain and the least well educated voted Leave. This led to certain arguments being deployed by Remain campaigners, who felt that the Leave campaign had lied and that the less well educated had fallen for such lies. Pressure for a second referendum began almost immediately and some Europhiles in Parliament also argued that Britain should simply remain in the European Union and effectively ignore the referendum result. However, for the Conservative Right this amounted to the establishment seeking to overturn the will of the people. For Theodore Dalrymple, calls for a second referendum by people 'so certain of the virtue of their own opinion'[59] amounted to an attempt to overturn the democratic process.

> They were so far Europeanised (in the Union's sense of the term) that they saw referenda as the means to endorse a predetermined "correct" answer, to be repeated until the population got the answer right. A referendum was a kind of exam; if you failed, you took it again until you passed, but once you had passed, you had passed. There was no need to take it again: indeed, there was a need not to take it again.[60]

While, for Philip Davies: 'these people (remainers) are very patronising. They honestly think the only reason anyone could have voted to leave is because they are either thick, racist or duped.'[61] The majority for leaving the EU boosted the morale of the Conservative Right who had almost all campaigned for it. However, successive events such as the inability to find a suitable pro-Leave successor to Cameron, the loss of the Conservative majority in the 2017 General Election and the direction of the negotiations led to a revival of the innate sense of Tory pessimism. While the eventual passing of the Withdrawal Bill in June 2018 was a significant achievement for the pro-Leave forces there has been consistent concern over the terms on which Britain would leave the EU. Theresa May's proposals, agreed at the Chequers meeting of Cabinet on 6th July 2018, led to the resignation of her Brexit Secretary, David Davis and later Boris Johnson.

Matters deteriorated later in 2018 as the Conservative Eurosceptics believed that May was making even more concessions in negotiating with the EU, most notably on the financial settlement, transition arrangements and measures on the Irish border. In late 2018, the ERG organised a no confidence vote in May's leadership, which she survived. However, the inability to secure the passing of her deal through Parliament led to gridlock, the granting of extensions to Article 50 and the commencement of talks with the Opposition. The Conservative Right feared a Brexit betrayal. In response the Right split between those who supported—without enthusiasm—May's deal as the only form of Brexit available and those who held out for a different form of Brexit, one which they said would honour the referendum decision, namely leaving on World Trade Organisation (WTO) terms if necessary. Although a WTO Brexit is now regarded by some as the only way to restore national sovereignty, early figures such as Julian Amery and John Biggs-Davison regarded its predecessor, GATT as the loss of national sovereignty. The willingness of the contemporary Parliamentary Right to see a WTO Brexit shows the now unanimous support for free trade, in contrast to the national protectionist tradition. The Conservative Right also adopted a strongly populist rhetoric in the summer and autumn of 2019, believing that the establishment were conspiring so as to overturn the expressed will of the people to leave the EU. This included the Speaker of the House of Commons allowing backbenchers to take control of the Order Paper and thus passing legislation which appeared to rule out a 'no deal' departure; and the Supreme Court in ruling unanimously that Parliament was unlawfully prorogued by Boris Johnson.

Conclusion

The Conservative Right was slow to adopt a Eurosceptic position. Although there were, from the start of the process of European integration, those who opposed membership of the EEC there was also the persistence among at least some of the imperialist wing of the Party a belief that membership of the EEC was not incompatible with the maintenance of Empire. Indeed, it assisted it by creating a counterweight to the USA. However, with the declining salience of Empire, and even for some the Commonwealth, the main objective of policy was to preserve national sovereignty, now under threat from the EEC as the earliest sceptics had forewarned. These tensions between the imperialist wing and the nationalistic wing within the Conservative Right were present in organisations such as the Monday Club, which split over the issue of membership of the EEC.

The furthering of European integration only acted to heighten the concerns of Eurosceptics within the Party, and were given a major boost by Thatcher's speech in Bruges in 1988 and her subsequent actions over Maastricht after she had ceased to be Prime Minister. That this has culminated in a sizeable proportion of the Conservative Party, and especially its right-wing supporting full withdrawal of the EU should not come as a surprise. The ultimate logic of Euroscepticism is to withdraw from the EU given the fundamental incompatibility of the aims of the EU and the anti-Europeans. However, initial euphoria has given way to frustration with the Brexit process. Moreover, as we will discuss in subsequent chapters, Brexit may also put at risk some of the other objectives of the Conservative Right such as the preservation of the Union. The explanation for this can be found within Conservative philosophy, the unintended—if not unforeseen—consequences of radical change.

NOTES

1. J. Bulpitt, 'Conservative Leaders and the Euro Ratchet: Five Doses of Scepticism', *The Political Quarterly*, 63/3 (1992), pp. 258–275; J. Bulpitt, 'The European Question', in D. Marquand and A. Seldon (eds.) *The Ideas That Shaped Postwar Britain* (London: Fontana, 1996).
2. A. Fear, 'Euroscepticism Is Not Enough', *The Salisbury Review*, 14/3 (Spring 1996), pp. 23, 25.
3. P. Taggart, 'A Touchstone of Dissent: Euroscepticism in Contemporary Western European Party Systems', *European Journal of Political Research*, 33/3 (1988), pp. 363–388.
4. A. Baluch, 'The Dynamics of Euroscepticism in Germany', in B. Leruth, N. Startin, and S. Usherwood (eds.) *The Routledge Handbook of Euroscepticism* (London: Routledge, 2018).
5. For historical accounts of Euroscepticism in the UK see, H. Young, *This Blessed Plot* (London: Macmillan, 1999); A. George, *An Awkward Partner* (Oxford: Oxford University Press, 1998); and A. Forster, *Euroscepticism in Contemporary British Politics* (London: Routledge, 2002).
6. Nor is it a Left-Right issue within the major parties. For an account of the Labour Right's Euroscepticism see K. Hickson and J. Miles, 'Social Democratic Euroscepticism: Labour's Neglected Tradition', *British Journal of Politics and International Relations*, 20/4 (2018), pp. 864–879.
7. Quoted in A. Gamble, *The Conservative Nation* (London: Routledge & Kegan Paul, 1974).
8. D. Walker-Scott and P. Walker, *A Call to the Commonwealth* (London: Worcester, 1962).
9. Lord Hinchingbrooke, *Full Speed Ahead: Essays in Tory Reform* (London: Simpkin Marshall, 1944).
10. V. Montagu, *The Conservative Dilemma* (London: Monday Club, 1970).
11. Julian Amery papers, Churchill College, Cambridge, AMEJ/2/1/18.
12. Ibid., AMEJ/2/1/36.

13. R. Bassett, *Last Imperialist* (Settrington: Stone Trough, 2015), p. 185.
14. John Biggs-Davison papers, Parliamentary Archives, letter to M. L. Graham dated 13 December 1957, BD/1/117.
15. John Biggs-Davison papers, Parliamentary Archives Letter from H. Legge-Bourke dated 4 May 1953, BD/1/117.
16. J. Biggs-Davison, *Europe: Faith Not Despair* (London: Monday Club, 1967), p. 1.
17. J. Biggs-Davison, 'The Special Relationship', *The Salisbury Review*, 6/2 (December 1987), p. 64.
18. S. Heffer, *Like the Roman* (London: Weidenfeld & Nicolson, 1998), p. 304.
19. J. Biffen, 'Tory Nationalism', *Solon*, 1/1 (October 1969), pp. 19–24.
20. N. Ridley, 'Europeanism Not Nationalism', *Solon*, 1/2 (January 1970).
21. N. Marten, *The Common Market: No Middle Way* (London: Common Market Safeguard Campaign, 1974), p. 2.
22. J. Wood (ed.) *Still to Decide* (Kingswood: Elliot Right Way Books, 1972).
23. J. Wood (ed.) *Powell and the 1970 Election* (Kingswood: Elliot Right Way Books, 1970), p. 115.
24. Interview with Tim Janman, London, 27 March 2017.
25. E. Powell, '"Vote Labour" Election Speech', in R. Collings (ed.) *Reflections: Selected Writings and Speeches of Enoch Powell* (London: Bellew, 1992).
26. Speech, available at https://www.youtube.com/watch?v=Ob6Wv_FPp7w, accessed on 7 May 2019.
27. J. Biffen, *Political Office or Political Power?* (London: Centre for Policy Studies, 1977), p. 5.
28. Ibid., p. 21.
29. John Biggs-Davison papers, Parliamentary Archives Letter from J. Amery, 13 July 1977, BD/1/750.
30. Julian Amery papers, Churchill College, Cambridge, letter from J. Biggs-Davison, 25 September 1980, AMEJ/2/1/103.
31. H. Fraser, *A Rebel for the Right Reasons* (Stafford: Stafford and Stone Conservative Association, 1975), p. 64.
32. Ibid.
33. Ibid.
34. D. Storey and T. Taylor, *The Conservative Party and the Common Market* (London: Monday Club, 1983).
35. C. Moore, *Margaret Thatcher, The Authorised Biography; Vol. 2: Everything She Wants* (London: Allen Lane, 2015), pp. 395, 406.
36. Interview with John Biffen, London, 26 April 2007.
37. C. Moore, *Margaret Thatcher, The Authorised Biography; Vol. 2: Everything She Wants*, p. 406.
38. Ibid., p. 408.

39. E. Powell, 'By Our Consent', *The Salisbury Review*, 6/3 (March 1988), p. 22.
40. Quoted in Heffer, *Like the Roman*, p. 902. See also, R. Ritchie (ed.) *Enoch Powell on 1992* (London: Anaya, 1989).
41. No Turning Back Group, *Choice and Responsibility: The Enabling State* (London: Conservative Political Centre, 1990), p. 10.
42. Lord Denning, 'The Single European Act', *The Salisbury Review*, 5/3 (April 1987), p. 13.
43. M. Thatcher, Speech to the College of Europe, 20 September 1988, https://www.margaretthatcher.org/document/107332, accessed 7 May 2019.
44. Ibid.
45. A. Aughey, 'Mrs Thatcher and the European Community', *The Salisbury Review*, 7/4 (June 1989), p. 24.
46. G. Howe, 'Sovereignty and Interdependence: Britain's Place in the World', *International Affairs*, 66/4 (October 1990), pp. 675–695.
47. J. Major, Speech to Conservative Central Council, 23 March 1991, http://www.johnmajorarchive.org.uk/1990-1997/mr-majors-speech-to-conservative-central-council-23-march-1991/, accessed 7 May 2019.
48. R. Scruton, *The Conservative Idea of Community* (London: Conservative 2000 Foundation, 1996), p. 28.
49. *Right Now*, July–September 1998, p. 2.
50. P. Goodchild, 'Keeping Britain Out of the Euro', *The Salisbury Review*, 21/1 (Autumn 2002), p. 36.
51. N. Lamont, *Sovereign Britain* (London: Duckworth, 1995).
52. A. Chalfont, 'The European Army', *The Salisbury Review*, 201/1 (Autumn 2001).
53. B. Cash, 'Rediscovering Conservatism for the British Nation', in Cornerstone Group, *Being Conservative: A Cornerstone of Policies to Revive Tory Britain* (London: Cornerstone Group, 2005), p. 31.
54. R. Helmer, 'Europe: A Conservative Rethink', in Cornerstone Group, *Being Conservative: A Cornerstone of Policies to Revive Tory Britain* (London: Cornerstone Group, 2005), p. 26.
55. Ibid., p. 27.
56. Ibid., p. 28.
57. Cash, 'Rediscovering Conservatism for the British Nation', p. 32.
58. B. Cash, 'A Better Britain in a Better Europe: Time for a Dose of "Eurorealism"', in D. Davis, B. Binley, and J. Baron (eds.) *The Future of Conservatism: Values Revisited* (London: ConservativeHome, 2011), p. 311.
59. T. Dalrymple, 'Brexomania', *The Salisbury Review*, 37/3 (Spring 2019), p. 17.
60. Ibid.
61. Interview with Philip Davies MP, London, 19 January 2017.

CHAPTER 5

Constitution

Constitutionalism features prominently in this book. The central objective for the Conservative Right was how to defend the British system of government from internal and external threat. On the one hand the Conservative Right wished to defend the constitutional principle of parliamentary sovereignty but also seek to stop the abuse of that principle—as they saw it—by their political opponents. The defence of parliamentary sovereignty against the EEC/EU was explored in the previous chapter. Defence of the Union of Great Britain and Northern Ireland will be examined in the following chapter. The aim of this chapter is to discuss the preservation of the Westminster Parliament while also seeking ways to limit the growth of the state's economic and social functions. The unifying thread is the defence of parliamentary sovereignty.

For constitutional conservatives, following Edmund Burke, the constitution is of major importance. It is the system of rules, practices and norms which allow government to operate. According to Philip Norton, the constitution is 'real' in the sense that it embodies the values of British society: 'it is the embodiment of values that is crucial'.[1] The British constitution represents the accumulated wisdom of centuries of political evolution.

> A combination of institutional structures, conventions and understandings established over time produced what, to Conservatives, has been a perfectly workable system of government for the United Kingdom. It was

© The Author(s) 2020
K. Hickson, *Britain's Conservative Right since 1945*,
https://doi.org/10.1007/978-3-030-27697-3_5

not planned as such – a strength in the eyes of Conservatives – but it has emerged and continues to adapt.[2]

It should therefore be defended against its opponents, especially those whom Conservatives believe wish to destroy it. Defenders of the constitution regard reformers as 'not so much irrelevant as dangerous'.[3] Historically this has been rival political parties who wished to exploit the flexibility inherent within an uncodified constitution to further their ideological agendas. The task of the conservative constitutionalist therefore is to seek to only accept changes where necessary to maintain tradition, as Simon Heffer put it: 'all attempts at modernisation must at some stage reach an accommodation with the living monuments that history has left us'.[4]

However, as Norton has also shown, there are—and have always been—tensions within the Conservative Party between those who believe that reform is necessary in order to avert more radical change and those who wish to defend the status quo.[5] That is to say the tension between 'hedgers' and 'ditchers' first used to describe the rival positions within the Conservative Party over the 'people's budget' of 1909 and the ensuing constitutional crisis.

For the first thirty years of the period under discussion in this book the constitutional arrangements were largely accepted by both major political parties. The Westminster model of democracy remained largely unscathed with commentators seeking to describe the political system rather than calling for its reform. However, there were still concerns in this period as the doctrine of the 'mandate' was used to justify radical reform by successive Labour governments. Constitutional conservatives were therefore concerned to find ways of curtailing what Labour in power could do, with tensions once again erupting in Conservative ranks between those who wished to oppose all reform and those who believed that reform—sometimes major reform—was necessary, especially in the 1970s.

The radical economic and social reforms introduced by the Thatcher and Major Governments heightened demand for constitutional change to limit the powers of an over mighty Executive. This time, demands for reform came from the Centre and Left of the political spectrum. Charter 88 was established on the tercentenary of the Glorious Revolution of 1688 with support from the Labour and Liberal/Liberal Democrat parties. Pressure for constitutional reform increased substantially within the Labour Party. The Labour Government elected in 1997 was marked by its radical constitutional reforms, something which distinguished it from both the Conservatives and 'Old Labour'. The context within which Conservatives found themselves after 1997 was, therefore, radically different to that which had fostered their historic approach to the constitution. Divisions opened up within the Conservative Party towards the constitution, with three positions identifiable. Firstly, those who believed that the task of Conservatives was to operate within whatever the status quo happened to be. Next there were those of a more reactionary disposition who wished to restore the pre-1997 constitution. Finally, there were those who believed that only a radical new constitutional approach was satisfactory. Again, these positions will need to be unpicked with figures on the Conservative Right adopting a mix of these approaches.

THE TORY CONSTITUTION

For Tories the British constitution is one characterised by stability, continuity and authority. Tory historians sought to find an alternative narrative to the dominant Whig view which spoke of the inevitable and triumphant progression to democracy. In contrast to this focus on representative government, Tories stressed the preservation of authoritative government. What distinguished the British constitutional model was less its democratic and participatory nature but rather the emphasis on strong and efficient government. For Ronald King, writing in *Monday World*, the magazine of the Monday Club: 'it would be better for Britain if we accept that we are governed by a permanent oligarchy, and have done with the democratic myth that has evolved since the Reform Bill of 1832.'[6] This underlying continuity had survived the transition from feudalism to capitalism and from an absolute monarchy, tempered only by the Monarch's need to consult powerful nobles in the court, to the Crown in Parliament.

Each institution had a specific role within the balanced constitution. Change was therefore likely to have an unsettling effect. The bias should always be in favour of continuity. As Kenneth Pickthorn put it: 'there will be many who do not doubt that always in politics Change must make her case before receiving a welcome; I believe that in England this has always been the general view.'[7] Each generation is merely the custodian of the constitution. Democratic demands for radical constitutional change are arrogant since the current generation is ignoring the will of the dead and the unborn.

At the heart of the system was the notion of the Crown in Parliament. The executive, legislative and judicial branches were interlinked. The powers once exercised by the Monarch had gradually transferred to the office of Prime Minister in the Eighteenth Century, a post not officially recognised until much later. By the mid-Nineteenth Century the Prime Minister was the leader of the largest political party and sat as a Member of Parliament. Until the end of the Nineteenth Century it was not considered odd for the Prime Minister to be a member of the House of Lords and it was not finally established that the Commons exercised supremacy over the Lords until the start of the last century and even then only through the intervention of the Monarch. Although the Monarchy by this point was largely ceremonial, it did—and still does—contain reserve constitutional powers; even if those powers had not been exercised since 1707. For Roger Scruton, the monarchy represents the continuity and stability of the constitution: 'not being elected by popular vote, the monarch cannot be understood merely as representing the interests of the present generation.'[8] As David Levy put it:

> The monarchy is the articulation of national unity not only because it stands above the factions of the moment but because, in the most concrete possible way, it incarnates the spirit that links us to those dead and those yet to be born.[9]

The electoral system—with its tendency to create large parliamentary majorities for the winning party far in excess of its actual vote share—was justified on the basis that it produced strong government. The political party which could command a parliamentary majority would form the government. Parliament made laws for the whole of its territory and could not be overruled by either judges or a power above the nation state. Individual participation was limited to casting a vote every four to five years. The system of government was administered by civil servants who operated under the principles of permanence, anonymity and neutrality. Civil servants and politicians operated in a state of mutual dependence. The government of the day needed the civil service to implement its decisions, but equally the civil service recognised that it required the steer of political masters accountable to Parliament. The system operated through balance and interdependence. Reform would upset this delicate balance between the different parts of the constitution and was therefore to be avoided.

Critics of this constitutional model said it lacked legitimacy. If one was setting out a constitution from scratch, they argued, then it would be very different from this practice. A democratic polity would require greater participation and an electoral system which more proportionately reflected the wishes of the people. It would also mean that individuals had their rights protected in law. The respective roles and functions of the different institutions should be outlined in a written constitution, with judges able to strike down 'unconstitutional' laws. The unelected elements would be removed; and checks and balances introduced so as to limit the power of the executive. This liberal model of the constitution has inspired reformers in the UK and founders of new constitutions such as that of the USA.

However, constitutional conservatives argued that there was no need for such a new constitutional settlement. The Westminster Model of democracy worked. It had survived major social and economic dislocation in the Nineteenth Century; had absorbed the gradually expanded electorate; and had helped the UK to navigate successfully two world wars. There was very little appetite for constitutional reform after 1945. Even the election of the first majority Labour Government in 1945 did not upset this faith in the Westminster model. The presence of a Labour-dominated Commons and an inbuilt Tory majority in the Lords could have created tension but it was avoided by the establishing of a convention that the Lords would not vote against any commitment which had been contained in the manifesto of the winning party. Reform was only justified to correct a recognised defect and even then should be as limited as possible in scope. For example, Leo Amery argued that the growth of party and the increase in legislation had placed additional burdens on the House of Commons and suggested limited reforms in order to address this problem.[10]

When challenged, constitutional conservatives could be relied on to defend the old order. Constitutional conservatism had been strongly expressed throughout the postwar period by Enoch Powell. This can be seen in at least three examples. In 1953, Powell opposed the Royal Titles Bill. This piece of legislation was intended to settle the titles which the new Queen would hold ahead of her coronation. Powell believed that it was wrong in three respects. Firstly, the Crown was indivisible whereas the legislation would make her Queen of numerous countries separately. Secondly, the term 'British' would be removed from the realms and territories and from the Commonwealth. Finally, he objected to the new title Head of the Commonwealth. To other MPs he said that, 'we have a meaning in this place only in so far as in our time and generation we represent great principles, great elements in the national life, great strands in our society and national being.'[11] This arch constitutional conservatism was based on his growing belief that the Commonwealth was a fiction (see Chapter 2).

Secondly, in 1958 the Conservative Government decided to establish Life Peers to modernise the House of Lords. It was felt that a wholly hereditary chamber was antiquated and would eventually lead to further reform or even abolition. By creating life peers, the composition of the upper chamber would be radically altered. The Labour Party, recognising that it would be likely to reduce the prospects of abolition, opposed the measure. Powell also opposed it, but from strongly constitutional conservative grounds. The House of Lords had existed in its current form since the Middle Ages. It had therefore proved its right to exist through the fact that it had existed for so long. Longevity was sufficient justification. To engage in arguments as to what form political institutions should take was to concede ground to the liberal critics of the constitution. So strongly did Powell feel about this, that he co-authored a detailed history of the Upper House.[12] Later, when he was to finally lose his parliamentary seat in 1987 he refused to take a life peerage. Rhodes Boyson also showed a dislike of life peers: 'they are neither fish nor fowl'.[13] Writing in 1978 he called for all existing life peers to be made hereditary ones instead. The creation of life peers had 'certainly not created an influx of brilliant, independent and courageous thinkers'.[14] Lord Sudeley, setting out his ideal chamber, argued: 'to be excluded from such an upper house would be the present element of life peers – the species the Spaniards would call hidalgos de la gutiera, the nobility of the gutter, because they did not inherit their titles.'[15] Reflecting on the reform in 1991, Lord Sudeley believed that, 'there can be no doubt the Life Peerages Act has further weakened the House of Lords in its role of stable counterpoise to the more fluid lower House.'[16] The hereditary element in the Lords represented the landed interests and provided a source of independent opinion, free as it was from patronage.

His stance on the Lords was to be seen again when the subsequent Labour Government sought to reform it. This again produced an alliance between the Labour Left, particularly Michael Foot, who wished to see complete abolition of the Lords and constitutional conservatives like Powell who wished to defend the unreformed upper chamber. Coming in the immediate aftermath of the 'Rivers of Blood' controversy this was a strained cross-party alliance but it was ultimately successful—primarily because both Foot and Powell used their parliamentary skills to thwart the measure—and the Government withdrew the proposals.

STRESSES AND STRAINS

Mid-Twentieth Century confidence combined with the self-interest of the two major political parties and was reinforced by their corresponding ideologies. For Labour the Westminster model meant that it could form majority governments, unrestricted by the need to form coalitions—which were much more likely under proportional representation—with non-socialist parties. Even the long period of opposition after 1951 did not shatter this faith. The pendulum would eventually swing and Labour could be returned to office with a socialist, or at least social democratic agenda. The only tension between Right and Left was over the extent to which compromise was necessary in order to regain power. Once in office, Labour could claim a mandate and implement social and economic reforms in the interests of 'the people'. The neutral state bureaucracy would then implement its manifesto commitments. It was not only unnecessary to implement constitutional reform, but also a waste of legislative time. What reform that took place was essentially administrative and justified on the basis that it allowed for the more efficient implementation of the manifesto. However, Labour's embrace of the Westminster model created a dilemma for the Conservatives. The great advantage of the Westminster model—namely its flexibility—also proved its great weakness since it allowed Labour to introduce radical reforms. There had always been concerns on this front but by the 1970s it had reached new heights. The concern of the constitutional conservatives was how best to curtail the over-mighty Executive.

From 1945 onwards, the Conservative Right was concerned with the growth in size, powers and functions of the state in both economic management and social policy. Particular concern was expressed about the rise of the doctrines of the manifesto and the mandate. Political parties would put their policy pledges to the electorate and the successful party—bolstered by the large majority which the First Past the Post system usually produced—would then claim to have a mandate to implement its policies unencumbered by the political forces ranged against it. For Michael Oakeshott the fundamental difference between the

two views of the constitution was thus: 'that of socialism is the philosophy of the mandate; that of Conservatism is the philosophy of natural law.'[17] The doctrine of the mandate—which had 'no great antiquity
in British parliamentary history'—was one of will.[18] The government of
the day could claim full authority for what it chose to do based on the
fact that it had been elected on a manifesto. The doctrine of natural law
instead placed restrictions on what the government of the day could do
as it was little more than a custodian for a limited period of time. For
T. E. Utley, the doctrine of the mandate was a worrying political development which overrode the traditional belief in the need for a balanced
constitution.[19] Once elected the governing party could whip its MPs on
the justification that it had a mandate. Leo Amery wrote that, 'the idea
that a majority, just because it is a majority, is entitled to pass without
full discussion what legislation it pleases...is wholly alien to the spirit
of our Constitution'.[20] Writing 30 years later, Rhodes Boyson picked
up the same theme: 'absolute democracy – the tyranny of a majority
empowered to rule unchecked for five years – could be more dangerous
than absolute monarchy or absolute oligarchy, since it can claim more
legitimacy.'[21]

Tory concern over the increasing functions of the state continued to
rise. Keith Joseph argued that Britain had experienced a socialist ratchet
with each successive period of Labour government moving Britain in
an ever more socialist direction.[22] Intervening periods of Conservative
administration had done nothing to halt this process. Following the
1970 election defeat, the Left took control of Labour's policy committees and the 1974 manifestoes were more radical than any since 1945 as
a result. Labour was then elected, but on a relatively low vote share—
obtaining 37.2% in February and 39.2% in October—and for much
of its time in power lacking a parliamentary majority. To claim a mandate was therefore most implausible, yet Conservatives believed that
the Government was embarking on a radical socialist agenda. This led
some to argue for radical constitutional change in order to constrain the
Labour Administration.

Most notable among them was Quintin Hogg (Lord Hailsham) who
used his 1976 Dimbleby Lecture to argue that Britain had an 'elec-
tive dictatorship'.[23] In between elections, the government of the day
had almost complete control. The whip system and growing numbers
of governing party MPs on the 'payroll' vote, together with a subser-
vient House of Lords meant that the government could implement its

manifesto commitments at will. The time had come to restrict the ability of government to do as it wished. He proposed an elected upper chamber to replace the Lords, greater devolution and more extensive use of referenda.

Numerous points here are relevant to our discussion. Hailsham had not been associated previously with the Conservative Right. Indeed, he had been a prominent backbench advocate of the New Conservatism after 1945, as argued in his book *The Case for Conservatism*.[24] However, he had become increasingly concerned with the rise of 'socialism' and had endorsed the calls for a more overtly free-market agenda when penning the Foreword to a set of essays edited by Lord Blake and John Patten, *The Conservative Opportunity*.[25] He remained a loyal member of Thatcher's governments, seemingly unconcerned about her strong governing style and centralisation of power. Indeed, by the 1990s he was arguing that the constitution was in good health as socialism had been defeated.[26] A charitable interpretation of this is that there was an underlying consistency in his beliefs. He believed in the need for political balance. However, imbalance had been created first by the individualism of pre-war society and then by the socialists within the Labour Party of the 1970s. The imbalance was corrected by the Thatcher governments. Others would argue that she dramatically centralised power, undermining Hailsham's credibility as an objective observer of the constitution as he remained silent.

But his warnings on socialism did, naturally, appeal to the Conservative Right. Various arguments for more radical constitutional change were advanced which advocates believed would curtail the powers of the Executive and thereby limit the prospects of socialism in the future. For example, Eric Barendt—writing in a book which argued for a more right-wing form of Conservatism, but with a distinctly liberal approach—argued that, 'Conservatives would surely prefer to remove this danger by well-ordered constitutional reform – reform designed to limit the powers of government and puncture its intolerable arrogance.'[27] Lord Blake believed that Conservatives needed to look again at electoral reform, despite the fact that it had been emphatically rejected at the 1975 party conference.[28] Keith Joseph believed that a Bill of Rights was required to set constitutional limits on taxation.[29] Rhodes Boyson bemoaned the absence of the constitutional constraints which others possessed: 'the lack of checks and balances in our present political situation now strikes me as extremely dangerous. I envy the checks and balances of the American constitution.'[30] Boyson went on to say that the nature of elections was also adding to the economic strains which the country was then facing. He argued in 1978 that:

> There is a growing risk that political elections will be debased to nothing more than an auction in which large sections of the electorate are promised economic advantages either at the expense of others, or by running down national assets, or even through the mulcting of foreign creditors.[31]

This statement appears to be drawn from two arguments which had recently been advocated. Samuel Brittan had argued that democracy had economic consequences since parties would seek to outbid each other in the competition for voters, irrespective of whether they could afford to do.[32] Samuel Finer had also advanced an argument which sought to link Britain's economic malaise with the democratic process.[33] The First Past the Post system led to regular changes in government with the incoming party overturning what its predecessor had done. This adversarial system was hugely unsettling. Boyson advocated other reforms including a Bill of Rights and regular referenda, though his wish to see all peers made hereditary also aligned with more reactionary views on the constitution.[34]

Equally, however, there were those who recognised that such calls for radical reform were inherently unconservative. For Roger Scruton, the constitution was the reflection of the complex and highly specific historical circumstances in which it developed. To seek a new constitutional settlement was therefore ignoring the particular traditions, customs and conventions which it reflects. A constitution evolved, it could not be 'made'.[35] Others argued that the best way to respond to the threat of socialism was to offer a more radical alternative. Conservative commentators argued that for too long the Party had been too moderate. Lord Coleraine argued that there had been a consensus in British politics since the end of the Second World War which had been essentially socialist in character. This included all Conservative leaders since 1945 and had been most shaped by R. A. Butler.[36] Joseph followed suit in arguing that British politics had become 'stranded on the middle ground'.[37] For John Biffen the best way of dealing with one's political opponents was to offer a clearer alternative on social and economic policies rather than reforming the constitution.[38] Writing in 1976 he said that, 'for over a generation British public life has not been disturbed by major domestic constitutional conflicts.'[39] Now all is different. At heart this crisis was a loss of authority. However, constitutional reform was not the answer. Instead, a future Conservative government needed to address three issues above all others: the restoration of sovereignty at Westminster against calls for devolution and the powers of Brussels, restore control over the trades unions and restrict immigration.[40] Ultimately it was this view which prevailed with Thatcher being elected in 1979 committed to upholding the established constitution, but defeating socialism in all its forms.

THE MENACE OF NEW LABOUR

Calls for constitutional reform were effectively taken off the political agenda with the election of the first Thatcher Government. However, if formal constitutional reform was no longer likely, there was still significant change brought about as a result of the more authoritarian and personalised style of government. Critics argued that Thatcher was acting in a way which was fundamentally unconstitutional.[41] However, to her supporters such actions were compatible with the British constitution which had always been justified on the basis that it allowed strong government.

Nonetheless, Thatcher's ability to form governments on less than 50% of the popular vote—and considerably less in Scotland; her alleged politicisation of the civil service; and her attack on local government generated increased demands for reform, leading to the creation of Charter 88. The Labour Party became more influenced by the calls for constitutional reform. By the time Labour was eventually re-elected in 1997 it had committed to a range of reforms. Indeed, given that it had moderated its social and economic position considerably in the run up to the 1997 election, constitutional reform was its most radical and distinctive area. However, the notion that Labour had an alternative constitutional model in mind—as opposed to addressing a series of ad hoc constitutional issues is doubtful. Indeed, the extent to which the agenda was shared by the new Prime Minister is also debateable. However, in British terms the measures were radical and altered the constitution in fundamental respects.

For the Conservative Right, New Labour posed new dangers. Indeed, in some ways they felt it was more dangerous than Old Labour. For although Old Labour was more overtly socialist in its economic and social policies it was constitutionally and culturally conservative. While the economic and social measures could be controlled and at least temporarily halted by the periodic election of Conservative governments, cultural and constitutional change was more damaging due to its lasting effects. For some, New Labour despised everything that was traditionally British, as embodied in cultural and constitutional practices.[42] In its desire to destroy traditional Britain it looked to the supposedly superior continental model. For Philip Norton, New Labour was 'wreaking havoc with the nation's constitution, borne not out of malice but political imperatives and ignorance'.[43] Cultural change will be explored in a later chapter. The remainder of this chapter will examine the response of constitutional conservatives to the challenges posed by New Labour. Within the space available, not all of the reforms can be examined. New Labour's devolution measures will be discussed in the following chapter. Here we will focus on Lords reform since this was the other issue on which the Conservative Right was most vocal.

Labour pledged in its 1997 manifesto that the House of Lords would be reformed so as to remove the hereditary peers, with the potential for further reform left open. Hereditary peerages were seen as anachronistic and an offence to modern democratic politics. It was pushing at an open door. While constitutional reform was generally seen as an unimportant issue on voters' priorities there were few public defenders of the hereditary principle. The opposition of the Conservative Right to the measure was therefore one of principle rather than electoral advantage. One of the advantages of the hereditary system was the demonstration of independence which the peers had shown. Despite a Conservative majority they had rebelled almost 300 times between 1979 and 1997. Simon Heffer thought this proved its 'independence as an institution, its vigour in the constitution, and its value as a revising chamber' and should not therefore have been subject to radical reform.[44] It had worked perfectly well since 1911 when it had accepted its secondary status to the Commons. The Salisbury-Addison convention, agreed in 1945, which accepted not to overturn legislation contained in the governing party's manifesto, was 'as close to perfection in constitutional matters as one was likely to get'.[45] For Lord Cranborne (later the 7th Marquess of Saisbury), 'Mr Blair (planned) to remove the only truly independent element left in Parliament, the hereditary peerage'.[46] Roger Scruton believed that Tony Blair wished to, 'remake the Lords as a kind of TV chat show, in which dignities are discarded and opinions assessed for their "political correctness" rather than their truth.'[47]

However, in government it was recognised by New Labour that this measure had the potential to become bogged down in a dispute between the two chambers of Parliament and thus reduce legislative time for other measures. Equally, senior peers recognised that they could only resist a manifesto pledge of the winning party—especially one on the scale of Labour in 1997—for a short period of time or face a constitutional crisis. This was certainly the belief of the Conservative Leader in the House of Lords at this time, Lord Cranborne, who reached agreement with the Labour Government that the Tory peers would accept the removal of all but 92 hereditary peers. The move allowed the Bill to pass fairly quickly, but not without controversy.

The Conservative Right held firm on both the initial proposal and the Cranborne concession. For them, Labour's proposal marked an attack on the foundations of the constitution. Particularly vocal in this regard was Simon Heffer who argued that the hereditary principle was defensible but the fact that the Conservative leadership was failing to do so highlighted how far they had moved away from the traditions of constitutional conservatism. There was nothing new in the fact that the Conservative Party was failing in this regard since, 'the worst and most effective enemy of the House of Lords since the War has unquestionably been the Conservative Party'.[48] This was so because the party had generally had a historically uninformed approach to the constitution and also because Leaders since the 1960s had failed to refresh the hereditary peers by creating new ones.[49] The proposed reforms would lead to stalemate since a revised upper House would seek to exert its authority. It would also increase the power of the whips and of Prime Ministerial patronage.[50] Instead, there were reforms which would work with the grain of the constitution including removing the non-attending peers and creating one or two extra ministerial posts in the Lords.[51]

Another vocal critic at this time and subsequently on this matter was Lord Sudeley, a hereditary peer who had long associations with the Conservative Right. Sudeley had persistently argued the merits of the hereditary principle, writing a pamphlet in the 1970s in support of heredity in politics.[52] The proposal for 92 peers—a 'dirty trick'—could have been avoided had the political direction of the Conservative peers been stronger at the time.[53] In 2004 when Blair tried to remove the remaining hereditaries, the then Conservative Leader in the Lords, Lord Strathclyde threatened to block all of the Government's more important legislation and Blair backed down. Sudeley argues that this would have been the right approach in 1997 but Cranborne had refused to make such a move.[54] He argues that the only alternatives to a hereditary House of Lords—appointment and election—don't work.[55] The lack of consensus over the way forward with Lords reform, which has resulted in no 'stage two' as New Labour had intended, means that it is now time to reinstate the hereditaries.[56]

The defence of the hereditary principle by Heffer, Sudeley and others echoed the case for the aristocratic principle made over a long period by Peregrine Worsthorne. For Worsthorne a ruling class was an inevitable feature of any political system.[57] The only real option was who governs. The traditional ruling class in Britain was imbued with a keen sense of national history having been a part of it for so long and maintained a firm attachment to an ethos of public service. 'A Parliament with an hereditary element is likely, quite simply, to be a better Parliament, truer to its nature and to its traditions,' he argued.[58] Since 1945 that traditional class had been undermined by socialism which preached the doctrine of equality and therefore removed the sense of distance that was needed between elite and mass, not just economic but also cultural. Thatcher had been elected to defeat socialism but she did so by unleashing a new ruling class, which was much more selfish and lacked the sense of public duty associated with the old class. New Labour completed the task of destroying respect for the nation's past rulers. The job of removing the hereditary peers was relatively straightforward since no one was left to defend them: 'their fate is worst of all, since not only is the current generation ignorant of their history but also of the very principles on which their authority rested.'[59]

However, while Worsthorne regretted the loss of the old order, Sudeley sought its restoration. Hence, once again, we see the tension between a pessimistic conservatism and a more reactionary approach. Sudeley continues to argue that the hereditary peers should be readmitted to the House of Lords. His book, *Peers Through the Mists of Time* argues that the current composition of the House of Lords is unjustifiable.[60] The alternatives both lacked legitimacy—an appointed upper House created vast powers of Prime Ministerial patronage; an elected Chamber would create gridlock. The only way to re-establish the legitimacy of the Lords is through the restoration of all hereditary peers, which respects tradition and allows an important estate of the realm to be represented in Parliament.[61] However, this view is not widely shared. Indeed, when Sudeley has sought re-election to the Lords upon a vacancy for a hereditary peer becoming available he has been unsuccessful, showing the lack of appetite for such a policy even in the Lords.

A further reform which involved the House of Lords was the Constitutional Reform Act (2005) which removed the judicial responsibilities of the Law Lords in the House of Lords and of the Lord Chancellor, and created the Supreme Court. For Geoffrey Cox this amounted to the further encroachment of liberal constitutionalism, whereby the judges had an increased role in the constitution. This had already been significantly enhanced with the Human Rights Act (1998) having started with accession to the EEC in 1973. Liberal constitutionalism was an erosion of parliamentary sovereignty and ought to be avoided as far as was possible.[62] The decision of the Supreme Court in September 2019 to rule that the prorogation of Parliament was unlawful was criticised by some on the Leave side of the Brexit debate as a major extension of the role of the judiciary in the constitution.

THE UNSTOPPABLE RISE OF CONSTITUTIONAL LIBERALISM?

New Labour's constitutional reform agenda was to come to a halt. While phase one of House of Lords reform was to be conducted quickly, phase two never materialised. In a series of indicative votes in the House of Commons, MPs could not agree on what the balance should be between election and appointment in the upper chamber and the impetus for further reform was lost. The House of Commons was largely unscathed in terms of reform. New Labour's constitutional reform agenda had resulted from a general pressure for change which had accumulated in the Thatcher years and the support of particular senior party figures for change in specific areas. It did not come from the wish to create a new model constitution. Blair himself—having talked of wishing to see a new constitutional settlement before the 1997 election—quickly lost interest in it after winning his landslide, as Paddy Ashdown commented in his diaries.[63] There was continuing interest in moving towards a more pluralistic model of the constitution in some quarters but this resulted in very little action post 1997. By 2001, constitutional reform had ran out of steam. Indeed, the dominance of New Labour in the House of Commons led to the resurfacing of the arguments of executive dominance from the 1970s. For instance, in 2005 Bill Cash proposed a number of constitutional changes which were designed to reduce the control of the Executive. These included increasing the powers of the Speaker, of Select Committees, election of 80% of the House of Lords and an Act establishing parliamentary supremacy.[64]

The inability of David Cameron to secure a parliamentary majority in 2010 reopened the prospect of further constitutional reform, and specifically electoral reform. The Liberal Democrats held the balance of power. For a combination of ideological reasons—with the Liberal Democrats moving rightwards under Nick Clegg—and of parliamentary arithmetic, the Coalition Government between Conservative and Liberal Democrats was formed. A condition of the deal was a commitment to hold a referendum on changing the electoral system, although a more full-blooded form of proportional representation was ruled out in favour of the Alternative Vote (AV). Figures on the Conservative Right were critical of this concession. They believed it risked the prospect of major constitutional change. However, Cameron and the overwhelming majority of the Conservatives campaigned solidly for the retention of First Past the Post and the AV proposal was easily defeated by 68 to 32%.

According to its supporters, the virtue of First Past the Post lay in its simplicity—people understood what happened to their vote—the link between the constituency and the representative was maintained and, ordinarily, the election resulted in a strong government with a clear parliamentary majority. Proportional representation was based on the myth that democracy meant rule by the people. However, direct democracy was an impossibility. Instead, a government needed to be elected which could make decisions on their behalf, what, drawing on Joseph Schumpeter, can be called 'democratic elitism'.[65] The most appropriate system was first-past-the-post since it allowed for clear results between two opposing sides. Karl Popper made a similar argument in calling the election 'judgement day' on the performance of the government.[66] It didn't matter who was governing as long as there was an ability to either kick them out or reaffirm their right to govern at periodic moments. Given that the British constitution was justified on grounds of authoritative, rather than representative, government the current electoral system worked well. But it was also argued that proportional representation would increase the power of the political class by leading to post-election trade offs in order to form governments—something alien to the British system of government.[67]

Broadly speaking, the Conservative Right has been firmly on the side of constitutional conservatism. It has sought to defend the constitution against change on the basis that it was the repository of established wisdom, allowed for strong and effective government, and provided a balance between the different social interests. However, reform in other areas of policy has led to indirect and unintended changes to the constitution. On occasions where they believed that the current danger to be too great—as with the 'threat' of socialism in the 1970s—they have advocated radical change in order to curtail the power of their political opponents. Although the Thatcher Governments ruled out formal constitutional change, the seismic economic and social measures that were introduced and abrasive nature of the Prime Minister herself fuelled demands for more radical reform. Just as in other areas explored in this book, the legacy of the Thatcher Governments was ultimately damaging to the traditional beliefs of the Conservative Right. New Labour's incomplete constitutional reform agenda created a dilemma for defenders of the old order. Either they had to consolidate or embrace further reforms to rectify the damage which they believed had been heaped on the constitution. Arguably, these tensions are still unresolved. This is most visible in terms of the challenge to constitutional conservatives caused by devolution and this is what will be explored in the following chapter.

NOTES

1. P. Norton, *The Constitution: The Conservative Way Forward* (London: Conservative Political Centre, 1992), p. 7.
2. P. Norton, 'The Constitution', in K. Hickson (ed.) *The Political Thought of the Conservative Party Since 1945* (Basingstoke: Palgrave, 2005), p. 96.
3. Norton, *The Constitution: The Conservative Way Forward*, p. 6.
4. S. Heffer, 'Traditional Toryism', in K. Hickson (ed.) *The Political Thought of the Conservative Party Since 1945* (Basingstoke: Palgrave, 2005), p. 198.
5. Norton, 'The Constitution'.
6. R. King, 'The Anarchical Order of Power', *Monday World*, 2/6 (Summer 1970), p. 15.
7. K. Pickthorn, *Principles or Prejudices* (London: Signpost Booklets, 1943).
8. R. Scruton, *The Meaning of Conservatism* (Basingstoke: Palgrave, 2001, 3rd edition), p. 48.
9. D. Levy, 'The Real and the Royal', *The Salisbury Review*, 3 (Spring 1983), p. 20.
10. L. S. Amery, *Thoughts on the Constitution* (Oxford: Oxford University Press, 1947).
11. S. Heffer, *Like the Roman* (London: Weidenfeld & Nicolson, 1998), p. 185.

12. E. Powell and K. Wallis, *The House of Lords in the Middle Ages* (London: Weidenfeld & Nicolson, 1968).
13. R. Boyson, *Centre Forward: A Radical Conservative Programme* (London: Temple Smith, 1978), p. 165.
14. Ibid.
15. Lord Sudeley, 'The Role of Heredity in Politics', *Monday World* (Winter 1971), p. 72.
16. Lord Sudeley, *The Preservation of the House of Lords* (London: Monday Club, 1991), p. 10.
17. M. Oakeshott, 'Contemporary British Politics', *The Cambridge Journal*, 1/8 (May 1948), p. 474.
18. Ibid.
19. T. E. Utley, 'The Mandate', *Cambridge Journal*, 3/10 (July 1950).
20. Amery, *Thoughts on the Constitution*, p. 46.
21. Boyson, *Centre Forward*, p. 160.
22. K. Joseph, *Stranded on the Middle Ground* (London: Centre for Policy Studies, 1976).
23. Lord Hailsham, *Dilemma of Democracy* (London: HarperCollins, 1978).
24. Q. Hogg, *The Case for Conservatism* (London: Penguin, 1947).
25. Lord Hailsham, 'Foreword', in Lord Blake and J. Patten (eds.) *The Conservative Opportunity* (London: Macmillan, 1976).
26. Lord Hailsham, *On the Constitution* (London: HarperCollins, 1992).
27. E. Barendt, 'Constitutional Reforms', in Blake and Patten (eds.) *The Conservative Opportunity*, p. 30.
28. Lord Blake, 'A Changed Climate', in Blake and Patten (eds.) *The Conservative Opportunity*, p. 8.
29. K. Joseph, *Freedom Under the Law* (London: Conservative Political Centre, 1975).
30. Boyson, *Centre Forward*, p. 159.
31. Ibid., p. 161.
32. S. Brittan, *The Economic Consequences of Democracy* (London: Holmes and Meier, 1979).
33. S. Finer (ed.) *Adversary Politics and Electoral Reform* (London: Wigram, 1975).
34. Boyson, *Centre Forward*, p. 165.
35. Scruton, *The Meaning of Conservatism*.
36. Lord Coleraine, *For Conservatives Only* (London: Tom Stacey, 1970).
37. Joseph, *Stranded on the Middle Ground*.
38. J. Biffen, *A Nation in Doubt* (London: Conservative Political Centre, 1996).
39. Ibid., p. 5.
40. Ibid., p. 18.

41. C. Graham and T. Prosser (eds.) *Waiving the Rules: The Constitution Under Thatcher* (Buckingham: Open University Press, 1988).
42. G. Wheatcroft, *The Strange Death of Tory England* (Harmondsworth: Penguin, 2005).
43. Norton, 'The Constitution', p. 106.
44. Heffer, 'Traditional Toryism', p. 199.
45. Ibid., p. 200.
46. Lord Cranborne, *The Chain of Authority* (London: Politeia, 1997), p. 14.
47. Scruton, *The Meaning of Conservatism*, p. 52.
48. S. Heffer, *The End of the Peer Show?* (London: Centre for Policy Studies, 1996), p. 26.
49. Ibid., pp. 34–36.
50. Ibid., pp. 30–31.
51. Ibid., pp. 39–43.
52. Sudeley, 'The Role of Heredity in Politics'.
53. Lord Sudeley, *Peers Through the Mists of Time* (London: Diehard, 2018), p. 151.
54. Ibid., pp. 151–152.
55. Ibid., pp. 154–155.
56. Ibid.
57. P. Worsthorne, *The Socialist Myth* (London: Cassell, 1971).
58. P. Worsthorne, *By the Right* (Dublin: Brophy, 1987), p. 47.
59. P. Worsthorne, *In Defence of Aristocracy* (London: HarperCollins, 2004), p. 59.
60. Sudeley, *Peers Through the Mists of Time*.
61. Ibid.
62. G. Cox, 'The Living Constitution: A Conservative Response to Liberal Constitutionalism', in D. Davis, B. Binley, and J. Baron (eds.) *The Future of Conservatism: Values Revisited* (London: ConservativeHome, 2011).
63. P. Ashdown, *Diaries, Volume 1: 1988–1997* (London: Allen Lane, 2000).
64. B. Cash, 'Rediscovering Conservatism for the British Nation', in Cornerstone Group, *Being Conservative: A Cornerstone of Policies to Revive Tory Britain* (London: Cornerstone, 2005).
65. J. Schumpeter, *Capitalism, Socialism and Democracy* (New York: Harper, 1942).
66. K. Popper, 'The Open Society and Its Enemies Revisited', *The Economist*, 23 April 1988.
67. Ibid.

CHAPTER 6

Union

The most fundamental objective of the state is to defend the nation from internal and external threat. According to the Conservative Right, the greatest internal threats to the territorial integrity of the nation state are those political and, in the case of Northern Ireland, paramilitary organisations which seek to break up the Union between England, Scotland, Wales and Northern Ireland. This raises questions both constitutional and of national identity. While Tories have sought to defend the territorial integrity of the UK and the sovereignty of the Westminster Parliament, nationalist parties have sought to break it up and to divide power between the constituent parts of the UK. While Tories have spoken in terms of a Union understood primarily in English terms, their opponents have sought to establish separate Irish, Welsh and Scottish identities in which England is perceived as a colonial power from which they seek their liberation. This chapter will begin with an exploration of the ways in which the Conservative Right has responded to the rise of nationalism and devolution in Scotland and Wales, including the rise of an English nationalism within the Conservative Right. It will then go on to examine the politics of Northern Ireland, where Tories have associated firmly with Unionism.

© The Author(s) 2020
K. Hickson, *Britain's Conservative Right since 1945*,
https://doi.org/10.1007/978-3-030-27697-3_6

Scotland and Wales

Up until the 1959 General Election the Conservatives were the largest single Party in Scotland. The Scottish Unionist Party (only renamed in 1965) was the dominant force throughout the interwar years, despite the phenomenon of radical politics in Clydeside. This Tory dominance of Scotland had been due to a number of reasons. The Conservative Party's appeal to nation and empire had secured it support in all parts of Great Britain. There was a shared sense of sacrifice from two world wars and the Conservatives' acceptance of nationalised industries and the welfare state after 1945 strengthened the UK-wide sense of allegiance. Finally, those who questioned the Union had little electoral appeal. The Scottish National Party had been established in 1934, however it wasn't until the 1960s that its support began to noticeably grow. It had fielded just five candidates in 1959. The postwar boom helped retain Conservative electoral support in Scotland until the end of the decade.

The Conservative position in Scotland was also bolstered by the importance of continuing sectarian politics in Glasgow. Whereas many other industrial cities in the UK had long since become Labour strongholds, Glasgow—like Liverpool—continued to have strong Conservative representation. In Glasgow and Liverpool the main social cleavage was religious rather than class-based. Protestant and Catholic tensions remained strong, evidenced through cultural and sporting divides. Organisations such as Rangers football club and the Boys' Brigade led to support for the Conservative Party. Catholics tended to vote Labour and Protestants Conservative. The Catholic community remained wary of the SNP believing it to be dominated by Presbyterians. Active Orange Lodges remained recruiting grounds for Conservative politicians.

However, this picture started to change in the early 1960s.[1] Wider social changes led to decline in religious observation. Moreover, economic decline—relatively if not absolutely—created greater pressure for political change. The economic benefits of remaining in the Union began to be challenged. Moreover, the power of the United Kingdom internationally markedly declined with the process of decolonisation. The political consequence of these changes was the rise of Scottish nationalism. SNP support increased and their strength was recognised in the Hamilton by-election victory of Winnie Ewing in 1967.

Fearing the electoral challenge of the SNP to its now dominant position in Scotland, Labour began to contemplate the possibility of devolution. This first took the form of greater administrative devolution, but pressure mounted for legislative devolution too. Indeed, this was not isolated to the Labour Party. Moderate Conservatives also embraced Scottish devolution, fearing that the alternative would be independence. As stressed in the previous chapter, Conservatives embraced constitutional reform as a way to reduce the scope for Labour governments to introduce 'socialism'. Devolution was also seen as the way to defeat nationalism. Edward Heath had declared support for devolution in his Declaration of Perth in 1968. Senior Conservatives had openly supported the idea.

Scottish nationalism had continued to rise. The extraction of North Sea oil had led to the notion that it was 'Scottish oil'. The SNP won 11 seats in the autumn election. Had Edward Heath won the February 1974 election he may well have embarked on the path to legislative devolution. The proposal of devolution had made its way into the 1974 manifestoes. However, it was left to the Labour Party to deal with. Although there were keen supporters of devolution, notably John Smith, there were also those who believed that electoral pragmatism dictated devolution. Labour had been the dominant party since the 1959 election. Their parliamentary majorities at Westminster depended on MPs from Scotland. The rise of support for the SNP threatened all of this. Equally, though, there were strong opponents inside the Labour Party to devolution. This included those on the Left who believed that devolution was pandering to nationalism, as well as constitutionalists who opposed devolution on principle. Most notable among this latter group was Tam Dalyell, who posed what became known as the West Lothian Question—why should, under devolution, Scottish and Welsh MPs be able to vote on matters which only affected England at the Westminster Parliament.

While support for devolution within the Conservative Party came from moderates who had supported Heath's inclusion of it in his manifestoes, many on the Conservative Right were staunchly opposed. Although the constitutional question was associated with Dalyell, it in fact was originally raised in response to William Gladstone's proposals for Home Rule in Ireland. The issue had split the Liberal Party with Unionists such as Joseph Chamberlain opposing devolution. Conservative opponents of devolution questioned its application to Scotland and Wales on the same grounds. The Act of Union of 1707 was a mutual agreement between Scotland and England, based on a shared perception of self interest. While that perception continued to exist there was a case for the continuation of the Union. If one party decided that the arrangement no longer benefited them they were free to leave. The Act of Union was not the result of military conquest and did not mean the suppression of one side by the other. So much for independence. But devolution was another step altogether and one which could only take place by disadvantaging one party at the expense of another. It was therefore an unacceptable measure which should be opposed.

Anti-devolution Conservative MPs argued instead that measures should be taken which would strengthen the Union. Enoch Powell emerged as a staunch advocate of the unitary state principle. It was Powell's view that sovereignty was an absolute and was held by the Westminster Parliament: 'the House of Commons brooks no competition and no concurrent authority in any part of the realm'.[2] Just as membership of the EEC posed an external threat to the sovereignty of the Westminster Parliament so too did devolution. Sovereignty could not be 'pooled' between Westminster and Edinburgh or Westminster and Cardiff, just as it could not between Westminster and Brussels. If the Scots wanted independence then that was acceptable, but devolution was unacceptable. It was what Jim Bulpitt was to describe as the 'sod off' school of devolution.[3] Powell's preference was for a committee concentrating on Scottish affairs under the authority of the House of Commons, but this failed to gain support.

For Scottish Conservative MP, Teddy Taylor, the Tory appeal in Scotland should be on the 'bread and butter' issues affecting his working-class constituents including a strong approach to law and order.[4] His appeal became known as 'tenement politics' due to his capacity to win in unlikely working-class areas of Glasgow. Taylor felt that his appointment to the Shadow Cabinet from late 1976 was to balance the pro-devolution Shadow Scottish Secretary, Alick Buchanan-Smith who he was to succeed after one month.[5] However, Charles Moore reports that Taylor was seen as an eccentric and that Thatcher had reluctantly agreed to appoint him in the absence of anyone else. Better a Scot opposing devolution than an English politician telling the Scots what they could do.[6] The party was divided on the issue. Pro-devolution MPs saw it mainly as the way to defeat the SNP. Opponents believed variously that it would undermine the unity of the United Kingdom, create an unnecessary extra tier of government or a 'permanent socialist administration'.[7] Taylor said that when the referendum came his approach against the moderates—was 'bashing devolution head on'.[8] He felt that the success in defeating the devolution proposal was a major boost for the Party, not only as the nationalists refused to support Labour in the no confidence vote but also because the Conservatives saw off the SNP challenge in the election that followed.[9] However, Taylor lost his seat.

John Biffen was a firm critic of devolution.[10] For him the rise of Scottish nationalism had little to do with the discovery of North Sea oil. It in fact predated it. The main cause, instead, was the decline of empire: 'London was no longer the hub of the Empire it was, rather, the headquarters of a distant and growing bureaucracy'.[11] However, oil had acted as a catalyst for nationalism. Looking at the possible solutions in the mid-1970s, Biffen rejected the case for federation. There was simply no demand for it. A referendum would not resolve the issue since what was on offer from Labour was a half-way-house which would do nothing to stop the further rise of nationalism in Scotland. Biffen was a Unionist and believed that a more positive case for the Union could be advanced. However, if this failed he believed that the only option was independence.

In Wales, things had been different for the Tories for much longer.[12] They had never been the dominant party since the establishment of party politics in the 1860s. Firstly being second to the Liberals and then from 1918 to Labour. The number of Welsh Conservative MPs between 1945 and 1979 had been in single figures. However, there was a small rise in the number of Conservative MPs in Wales in 1979 and again in 1983 when they had 11 and 14 respectively as Labour lost support.

The failure of the Labour Government to implement devolution in 1979—Wales rejecting it outright and Scotland by an insufficient margin to meet the threshold imposed as a concession to anti-devolution MPs— led to the nationalist parties withdrawing their support from Labour and the successful no confidence motion tabled by the Opposition in 1979.

Margaret Thatcher was instinctively a Unionist.[13] However, she inherited a party which had only just committed to devolution the previous year. Recognising her lack of support at the top of the Party she trod carefully initially on this issue, as much else. She made a speech in Perth in May 1975 in favour of devolution. The Party document, *The Right Approach* (1976) also contained a commitment to devolution. However, as it was the moderates who were mostly supporting devolution she came to oppose it. But, after 1979 there was no serious prospect of legislative devolution to either Scotland or Wales. Charles Moore says that 'although she was an instinctive Unionist, it did not engage her passionate interest'.[14] For her the issue was one of pragmatism rather than principle. Hence, Thatcher's position can be distinguished from Powell, Taylor and Biffen on the Right of the Party who opposed devolution as a matter of firm constitutional principle.

However, the social and economic policies pursued by the Thatcher Governments placed strain on the Union. Over the course of the 1980s, Conservative support in Scotland, Wales and Northern England declined. Just as pressure for constitutional change increased (see previous chapter) so too for devolution. By the 1990s, Labour was firmly committed to legislative devolution in Scotland and Wales, seeing it as unfinished business from the 1970s. Neil Kinnock had changed from his earlier opposition to legislative devolution in Wales and John Smith remained a firm advocate of devolution. By the time of Blair's accession to the leadership in 1994, the policy was set in stone—even if Blair appeared to cast doubt on the strength of his own personal commitment by likening devolved legislatures to parish councils.

The Conservative Party remained strongly anti-devolutionist on the same grounds as previously. For John Major—in many ways disappointing the Conservative Right but very much articulating their constitutional conservatism—devolution would lead inexorably to the breakup of the United Kingdom. This was not only because of the resentment that would be fostered in England due to the legislative disadvantage articulated in the West Lothian Question, but also that it would fuel the rise of nationalism rather than stop it. The decisive victory for New Labour in 1997 provided a strong electoral mandate for devolution. This time, unlike the 1970s, the referendums would be held first so as to strengthen the mandate and push Parliament into granting legislative devolution. There was a clear majority for a Scottish Parliament (74.2–25.7%) and a smaller one for a Welsh Assembly (50.3–49.7%) and both institutions were created by statute in 1999.

Commenting on the consequences of the 1997 General Election towards the end of his life, Enoch Powell argued that it was a vote to break up the United Kingdom.[15] Roger Scruton argued that the devolved bodies introduced by Tony Blair had 'incalculable consequences'.[16] In contrast, Labour claimed that devolution was the best way to preserve the Union. The failure to allow a greater voice for Scotland and Wales had created tensions, especially when the Conservative Governments of Thatcher and Major had relied on English MPs to impose measures on them. Now that devolution was enacted it would remove the impetus given to nationalism in Scotland and Wales. At first, this seemed justified with Labour dominating the two devolved legislatures. However, the proportional electoral systems used in Scottish elections, combined with political failings by the Labour Party, resulted in a nationalist revival until securing a majority in a system designed to stop one party control. From the vantage point of more recent times it would seem that devolution had failed to halt the forces of separation. From this perspective Powell had been proven correct his supporters argued.

Yet again, in the context of radical constitutional change, the Conservatives faced a strategic political dilemma. William Cash moved an amendment in 1997/1998 calling for a UK-wide referendum on the Scottish devolution legislation supported by over half of Conservative MPs as devolution was an issue for the whole of the UK.[17] However, for some, post-devolution the only option was reaction. The devolution of legislative powers was alien to the British constitution and created inherent unfairnesses with the West Lothian Question. The only principled course of action was to repeal the new legislatures. In theory this was a viable course of action since the principle of parliamentary sovereignty meant that no Parliament at Westminster could bind its successors. In practice, there had always been severe constraints to this principle. Once certain measures were introduced they could not be repealed, the reason why conservative constitutionalists had so strongly opposed its creation in the first place. However, Lord Pearson of Rannoch proposed such a measure.[18]

Others argued that the Parliament and Assembly were now realities and that the Conservatives had to work within them. Indeed, there had to be a genuine conversion to Scottish and Welsh devolution for electoral revival. The new electoral system allowed for this to happen, it would provide a springboard for Tory revival in Scotland. This combination of the new constitutional reality and electoral pragmatism would eventually win through, despite the reservations of the Tory Right. Ruth Davidson was to prove particularly adept at achieving this revival, but only by embracing things which the Right would not like.[19] The new Scottish Conservatism would retain its commitment to the Union, albeit a post-devolution Unionism, but would be significantly different from English Conservatism in key respects including being less hostile to the EU and more socially liberal. The centre of gravity in Scottish politics was to the left of England and Scottish Conservatism would reflect this.

Moreover, it has allowed the Conservatives to gain a particular niche in Scottish politics from which it could rival the Scottish National Party. Labour remains uncertain as to its direction—outflanked by the SNP, which is more pro-European and more left-wing on social and economic issues, but also by the Conservatives. The 'New Conservatism' in Scotland is markedly different in form from what the Right would have wished, but it seems there is little scope for a Conservative Right revival in Scotland.

THE ENGLISH QUESTION

Devolution to Scotland and Wales threw into sharper relief the question of England's place within the Union. According to Norman Tebbit, 'the creation of a Welsh Assembly and a Scottish Parliament...critically unbalanced the former constitutional settlement to the disadvantage of England'.[20] The Conservative Right became more interested in the politics of England from 1997 onwards in stark contrast to their earlier Unionism.[21]

While the Union was stable the terms England and Britain were frequently interchangeable. In his classic text, John Robert Seeley had written of the expansion of England when referring to the British Empire.[22] The Union was predominantly English in terms of land and population. There was no need to distinguish a separate English identity. Hence, Englishness lagged behind Welsh and Scottish identities. The reforging of those latter distinctive cultural identities led to demands for devolution. The 'English Question' has therefore been how to address the constitutional disadvantage which devolution had placed England in.[23]

Again, Conservatives were forced to confront the dilemma within their thought over how to respond to a change they did not wish to see. If Enoch Powell had been right in 1997 that the election of the Labour Government was a vote to abolish the Union, then how should Conservatives who were loyal to the Union react?

For many the best option was to ignore the West Lothian Question and hope that it would go away. After all, this was Labour's approach and there was little sense of English grievance at the time of devolution or subsequently despite the protestations of those who felt that the English had been aggrieved. If the Scots and Welsh wanted devolution who were the English to complain? The English would accept it. However, the issue would not entirely go away. Against the conservative disposition, some believed that anomalies needed resolving. Separate parties were formed to campaign for the English interest and a campaign for an English Parliament was established. New Labour allowed a referendum for a North East regional assembly in 2004 but this was rejected emphatically with 78% voting against. Those who had argued against federation previously felt vindicated by this outcome. There was no appetite for a new tier of regional authority in England. People did not identify particularly strongly with their region. Moreover, Tebbit asserted that if the plan for regional government had been implemented it would have meant that England would have been the most divided it had been for eleven hundred years.[24] Other constitutional devices were sought, especially after controversial aspects of Labour's legislative programme was passed only with the votes of Scottish and Welsh MPs even though, under devolution, they only affected England.

From the moment of its defeat in 1997 the Conservative Party said that it must express the views of England.[25] After all, it was now an exclusively English party in terms of representation at Westminster. Party Chairman, Michael Ancram said that the Party needed to speak with a more English voice. This was taken up by new Leader, William Hague. But what response? Those who held a more reactionary view, as we have seen, proposed abolishing the Welsh Assembly and Scottish Parliament. The conservative response was to settle on English Votes for English Laws (EVEL), within the existing chamber. There was a clear logic to this proposal from a traditionalist Conservative perspective since the only justification for constitutional reform was to fix a recognised problem with only the most modest reform on offer. Moreover, there was evidence of public support for the measure. It was eventually to come into effect in 2015.

However, others thought that only a radical option was suitable. Philip Davies felt that EVEL was more like an English veto than a vote to do things and was therefore an inadequate response to the West Lothian Question.[26] In January 1998 Teresa Gorman proposed an English Parliament. As the federal Parliament at Westminster would have less to do it would no longer need to sit each day. Therefore, the English Parliament could meet in the same chamber on the other days to discuss exclusively English matters. Arthur Aughey described this as a 'serious but not serious' approach.[27] Serious in feeling a sense of political grievance at the constitutional imbalance but not serious in the sense that it could sit for a couple of days per week without having to move out of the existing Parliament at Westminster.

For Simon Heffer, the only course available was to accept the logic of Powell's summation of the 1997 election outcome and accept that the Union was no more.[28] Heffer felt that the government of New Labour was 'probably the most anti-British and certainly the most anti-English in history'.[29] The English would be permanently disadvantaged by remaining in the Union post-devolution. No other option was appropriate. There was no appetite for regional government in England, as the referendum in 2004 would show. They went against the English desire to be little governed. Moreover, people did not see themselves as belonging to regions, which would end up being dominated by their biggest cities. Their loyalty was to England. The creation of an English Parliament would meet the second objection to regional legislatures but not the first; it would simply create an extra tier of government. Empowering local government may be desirable in itself but would not answer the English Question. Elected mayors in the major cities would do nothing for those in the shires. Therefore, Conservatives should accept that they are a predominantly English Party and embrace the English national interest, which was to leave the Union.

Another figure on the Conservative Right who wished to see the emergence of a separate English political identity was Richard Body.[30] He argued that devolution to Scotland and Wales made separation inevitable. 'The English will have no alternative but to come to terms with what will in due course be a fact of history,' he said.[31] For some this may seem 'quite absurd, at best a romantic dream and at worst plainly suicidal'.[32] However, there was no reason to fear the dissolution of the United Kingdom, he thought. England had much of the land mass and most of the people of the UK. It would still be one of the largest economies in the world and would be able to defend itself. It would be in line with a longer international trend of small countries being created. The world was not moving in the direction of regional blocs but smaller nations. 'Events will force the pace, and the English, we can be sure, will find their way'.[33]

There has also been growing concern on the Conservative Right over the declining cultural significance of England. Cultural conservatives feel that there was a consistent attempt to undermine all things English. 'To be English in the twentieth century was to breathe in a climate of unrelieved pessimism' thought Theodore Dalrymple.[34] While Englishness was seen in essentially negative terms, Scottish and Welsh identity was seen as something in need of promotion; something needing liberation from the oppressive English. Compared to the backward English, being 'European' was seen as enlightened. To be progressive was to be critical of all things English according to the critics of progressivism. Norman Tebbit believed that the blame lay with Tony Blair: 'never before have we had in office a government and, most particularly, a Prime Minister who detests our history, our constitution, our institutions and indeed the very nation we are'.[35] For some the forces of the Left had taken over institutions and had sought to discredit English history and culture. Roger Scruton emphasised the Marxists such as E. P. Thompson and Eric Hobsbawm.[36] Their stated aim was to liberate the working class, but they provided a way for intellectuals to 'feel good about the destruction of working-class life' as traditional communities were destroyed after the Second World War.[37] They had also changed the school curriculum. History, in particular, was seen as a discipline in which the English were disparaged and alternative histories had taken the place of national history. Literature was revised to take account of the demands of feminism and multiculturalism. For Alistair Miller, writing in a recent edition of *The Salisbury Review*, the very notion of an English culture has been 'banished from polite conversation'.[38] The Conservative Right would also agree with David Starkey in his argument that English identity had been so debased that 'we stand inarticulate and naked among nations - as you will find out if you ask an Englishman to define his Englishness'. From such a low base the recreation of English identity would be very difficult indeed. Conservatives such as Michael Gove, as Education Secretary between 2010 and 2014, have sought to re-emphasise the teaching of English history on the school curriculum. However, when he did this it led to controversy amongst historians.[39]

On the whole, then, Conservatives have been slow to cultivate particularly English constitutional and cultural forms. One reason for this is the point made by Scruton in terms of the forbidding of England.[40] Unlike Scotland and Wales, England is seen by some—especially the intellectuals—in overwhelmingly negative terms. England is seen as backward, prejudiced and reactionary. Something to be ridiculed and of which to be ashamed. Devolution, Scruton said, was 'not so much a gesture in favour of the Welsh and the Scots as a gesture against *England*'.[41] Progressives see in the idea of England everything they wish to destroy. This is why they have been strongly in favour of European integration.

In contrast to perceptions of English things, 'Europe' offers the hope of modernity, more cultured and enlightened. To be sure, other countries have experienced national decline, but, for Scruton, what is significant about England is that the decay has been achieved by the English themselves:

> It is the fact that England has been forbidden - and forbidden by the English... Every practice in which the spirit of England can still be discerned seems fated now to arouse contempt, not in the world at large, but in the English.[42]

NORTHERN IRELAND

Between the establishment of the Ulster Parliament in 1920–1921 through to the mid-1960s the affairs of Northern Ireland were of limited interest to Conservative politicians. There were historic ties between the Conservative Party and the Unionists in Northern Ireland. The Conservatives were also a Unionist party. They had demonstrated their Unionism in the Home Rule crisis of 1886 and had gone on to absorb the Liberal Unionists. The Unionist politicians who were returned to the Westminster Parliament would frequently vote with the Conservatives. There was an instinctive sympathy and a shared interest in preserving the then status quo. Unionists in Northern Ireland had wanted, as the *Ballymoney Free Press* had put it in 1912, to be 'let alone'.[43] Northern Ireland was effectively a semi-autonomous province. As long as there was relative stability, then the affairs of Northern Ireland were no business of Westminster. Westminster politicians had no interest in intervening in sectarian politics.

However, this changed in the 1960s. Growing hostility was directed to the Unionist dominated Northern Ireland legislature against what aggrieved Catholics felt was political corruption and social injustice. Protests took place throughout the 1960s, culminating in British troops being sent to Northern Ireland to keep the peace in 1969 and the imposition of direct rule in 1972. However, the troops quickly came to be seen as a manifestation of colonial rule. British politicians from this point on sought to compromise with the protestors. This was a grave mistake according to T. E. Utley, who became fascinated by Ulster politics and stood for the Ulster Unionist Party in the February, 1974 General Election.[44] Although the Catholics had originally had legitimate grievances, Utley felt that the human rights protests were really Republican inspired. Indeed, they had allowed the Republicans to revive their fortunes after a marked decline. This was to be the first mistake of Westminster politicians who did not understand the reality of Ulster politics. Northern Ireland was always seen as a problem in need of a solution by Westminster politicians.

Following the imposition of direct rule, a constitutional solution was sought for Northern Ireland. This began with the Sunningdale Agreement in December 1973. The Agreement had the support of the moderate element of the Unionists, with Prime Minister Brian Faulkner who became the Chief Executive of the new power-sharing executive. However, other Unionists were opposed. In the new year, the Ulster Unionists voted against the deal and Faulkner resigned, to be replaced by the more hard-line Harry West. In the General Election the following month there was the formation of an anti-agreement United Ulster Unionist Council (UUUC). Following strikes in May of that year the Agreement collapsed. Unionists felt that this was the start of an approach which was badly flawed and offensive. Firstly, it was a 'solution' which was being sought above their heads, something to be imposed upon them. Secondly, it meant that the South would be given a greater say over the affairs of the North.

For Enoch Powell, who became a Unionist MP in the autumn 1974 election, Northern Ireland needed to be seen as a full and integral part of the United Kingdom.[45] However, politicians from all quarters did not wish to see this. For British politicians, who openly or secretly wanted Ireland reunited, it served their interests to see Northern Ireland as separate from the rest of the UK. 'The object is to persuade the people of Great Britain that the inhabitants of Ulster are quarrelling among themselves and unable to refrain from sectarian and internecine violence' in order to push the British into a position where they say it would be better to leave them to it.[46] Moreover, the British army was said to be an impartial peacekeeping force as if it were in a separate country, when in fact it should be there to defeat an enemy of the state. It was really a state of war. The British state should accept 'as historically and politically valid the continuing massive plebiscite of the Ulster electorate for membership of the United Kingdom'.[47] However, Powell's belief that Ulster should be fully integrated into the rest of the UK also distinguished him from many of the Unionists in Northern Ireland who desired a return to a separate, Unionist-dominated Parliament. He persuaded James

Molyneaux (Leader of the UUP, 1979–1995) to support integration, but Molyneuaux admitted he had been criticised by his own party for not wanting home rule.[48]

For contributors to a Monday Club pamphlet, *Ireland: Our Cuba?*, the issue was one of communist threat.[49] Jonathan Guinness said that the threat was not one of Catholicism or nationalism but of communism. The civil rights protests had been stirred up by communists. To counter this, the Catholics should be absorbed more into the establishment: 'I should like to see the Catholic minority have a permanent place in the ruling Unionist Party.'[50] For John Biggs-Davison a consistent aim was to foster a Catholic Unionism.[51] A decade later, he felt that, 'the Northern Irish Catholic loyal to the Crown and faithful to the Union receive(d) little encouragement'.[52] Others, notably Powell, argued that the foreign intervention in Northern Ireland came from America.

Margaret Thatcher initiated talks with the Irish Government in 1980. However, IRA violence and the hunger strikes meant this had not developed far. On 15th November 1985, Margaret Thatcher signed the Anglo-Irish Agreement. It established the Anglo-Irish Intergovernmental Conference which gave the Irish Republic a greater say over the affairs of the North. The Agreement easily passed through the House of Commons, with just 47 MPs voting against. However, it was met with outrage from Unionists and Unionist-supporting Conservatives. Both the Ulster Unionist Party and the Democratic Unionist Party were against the Agreement and there was a series of protests, rallies and strikes.[53] Unionist MPs resigned their seats at Westminster in protest. Enoch Powell accused Thatcher of betraying the people of Ulster: 'does the Right Hon. Lady understand—if she does not yet understand she soon will—that the penalty for treachery is to fall into public contempt?'[54] John Biggs-Davison and Julian Amery sought to whip up opposition in the Conservative Party.[55]

Ian Gow resigned from the Government in opposition to the Agreement. 'Unionists have been treated badly by the Government' he said.[56] The Agreement played into the hands of the paramilitaries, who would not rest until Ireland was reunited. The Anglo-Irish Agreement resulted in the formation of Friends of the Union to foster closer links between the Conservative Right and the Unionists. Biggs-Davison believed that the Ulster Parliament had created a wedge between Northern Ireland and Great Britain and therefore, 'an integration that put the Union beyond doubt would serve notice on all manner of terrorists that their game was up'.[57] Integration was a consistent theme of the Friends of the Union lectures. So too was the British government's misunderstanding of the situation. For Conor Cruise O'Brien, Thatcher's claim that the Agreement would strengthen the Union was not shared by anyone in Northern Ireland: 'the Agreement has alienated the majority, without reconciling the minority'.[58] She instinctively felt sympathy for a Unionist cause. However, she was also a pragmatist seeking a solution. For Charles Moore, 'there is an almost tragic pathos in the determination of most people in Northern Ireland to stay loyal to the institutions whose present leaders treat them with contempt'.[59] Lord Cranborne (now the 7th Marquess of Salisbury) had been an MP at the time and was one of a relatively small number of Conservatives to vote against the Agreement: 'a decision which I have never regretted'.[60] The episode highlights the difference in approach between Thatcher and her critics to the Right.

The talks which culminated in the Belfast Agreement in 1998 were more successful since they included a wider range of objectives than the previous agreements and involved a wider range of political actors in Northern Ireland. These included Martin McGuinness, Jerry Adams and Ian Paisley. It was therefore only opposed by hard-line Republicans on one side and the more hard-line Unionists on the other. The Conservative Right largely accepted the Agreement, though traditional Unionist voices could still be heard. Patrick Roche argued in *The Salisbury Review* that, 'republican terror lurks at the heart of this process'. 'The "peace process" is directed towards meeting the demands of Irish republicanism backed by so-called constitutional nationalists and by the Clinton administration'.[61] Roche was active in anti-Agreement Unionist politics. Traditional Unionist Voice was also established to articulate this position.

In conclusion, the Conservative Right has sought to defend the Union of Great Britain and Northern Ireland. This meant that it sought to defend the sovereignty of the Westminster Parliament, which it felt was incompatible with devolution. However, post-devolution the Conservative Right has taken on a greater English tendency. Brexit may prove to throw the Union into doubt once again. Scottish nationalists see the Brexit issue as a further point of contention between England and Scotland. The Northern Ireland border issue has the potential to place a further strain on the Union. The Conservative Right may well find itself—by choice or not—becoming even more an English movement.

NOTES

1. C. Sutherland, *The Decline of the Scottish Conservative Party* (Leicester: Book Guild, 2016).
2. S. Heffer, *Like the Roman* (London: Weidenfeld & Nicolson, 1998).
3. Cited in A. Aughey, *The Politics of Englishness* (Manchester: Manchester University Press, 2007), p. 189.
4. E. Taylor, *Teddy Boy Blue* (Glasgow: Kennedy & Boyd, 2008).
5. Ibid., pp. 171–173.
6. C. Moore, *Margaret Thatcher: The Authorised Biography, Volume One: Not for Turning* (London: Allen Lane, 2013), p. 376.
7. Taylor, *Teddy Boy Blue*, p. 173.
8. Ibid., p. 177.
9. Ibid., pp. 178–179.
10. J. Biffen, *A Nation in Doubt* (London: Conservative Political Centre, 1976); J. Biffen, *Political Office or Political Power?* (London: Centre for Policy Studies, 1977).
11. Biffen, *Political Office or Political Power?* p. 42.
12. A. Convery, *The Territorial Conservative Party: Devolution and Party Change in Scotland and Wales* (Manchester: Manchester University Press, 2016).
13. Moore, *Margaret Thatcher*, p. 375.
14. Ibid.
15. Heffer, *Like the Roman*, p. 950.
16. R. Scruton, *The Meaning of Conservatism* (Basingstoke: Palgrave, 2001), pp. 60–61.
17. Interview with Sir William Cash, London, 13 October 2016.
18. P. Norton, 'The Constitution', in K. Hickson (ed.) *The Political Thought of the Conservative Party Since 1945* (Basingstoke: Palgrave, 2005), p. 107.
19. A. Liddle, *Ruth Davidson and the Resurgence of the Scottish Tories* (London: Biteback, 2018).
20. N. Tebbit, *By Their Fruits Ye Shall Know Them* (London: Friends of the Union, 2002), p. 8.
21. A. Aughey, *The Politics of Englishness*.
22. J. Seeley, *The Expansion of England* (London, Macmillan, 1899, first published 1880).
23. R. Hazell (ed.) *The English Question* (Manchester: Manchester University Press, 2006).
24. Tebbit, *By Their Fruits Ye Shall Know Them*, p. 9.
25. Aughey, *The Politics of Englishness*, pp. 192–193.
26. Interview with Philip Davies MP, London, 19 January 2017.

27. Ibid., p. 195.
28. S. Heffer, *Nor Shall My Sword: The Reinvention of England* (London: Weidenfeld & Nicolson, 1999).
29. Quoted in Aughey, *The Politics of Englishness*, p. 128.
30. R. Body, *England for the English* (London: New European Publications, 2001).
31. Ibid., p. 155.
32. Ibid.
33. Ibid., p. 159.
34. T. Dalrymple, *Our Culture: What's Left of It* (Chicago: Ivan R. Dee, 2005), pp. 106–107.
35. Tebbit, *By Their Fruits Ye Shall Know Them*, p. 15.
36. R. Scruton, *England: An Elegy* (London: Continuum, 2006).
37. Ibid., p. 145.
38. A. Miller, 'Transit Camp Britain', *The Salisbury Review*, 37/2 (Winter 2018), p. 19.
39. K. Sellgren, 'Historians Split Over Gove's Curriculum Plans', *BBC News*, 27 February 2013, https://www.bbc.co.uk/news/education-21600298, accessed 16 May 2019.
40. Scruton, *England: An Elegy*, pp. 244–257.
41. Ibid., p. 252.
42. Ibid., p. 247.
43. Quoted in A. Aughey, 'Traditional Toryism', in Hickson (ed.) *The Political Thought of the Conservative Party Since 1945*, p. 7.
44. T. E. Utley, *Lessons of Ulster* (London: Dent, 1975).
45. E. Powell, 'Northern Ireland', in R. Collings (ed.) *Reflections: Selected Writings and Speeches of Enoch Powell* (London: Bellew, 1992), pp. 223–227.
46. E. Powell, speech to the South Buckinghamshire Conservative Women's Annual Luncheon, 19 March 1971, in ibid., p. 220.
47. E. Powell, 'Northern Ireland', p. 227.
48. J. Molyneaux, Sixth Ian Gow Memorial Lecture, 19 November 1996 (London: Friends of the Union, 1996), p. 9.
49. J. Harwood, J. Guinness and J. Biggs-Davison, *Ireland: Our Cuba?* (London: Monday Club, 1972).
50. J. Guinness in ibid., p. 8.
51. J. Biggs-Davison in ibid., p. 11.
52. J. Biggs-Davison, *Ulster Catholics and the Union* (London: Friends of the Union, 1987).
53. A. Aughey, *Under Siege: Ulster Unionism and the Anglo-Irish Agreement* (Belfast: Blackstaff, 1989).

54. E. Powell, 'House of Commons', 14 November 1985, available at https://www.margaretthatcher.org/document/106172, accessed 16 May 2019.
55. Letter from John Biggs-Davison to Julian Amery, 13 June 1986, Julian Amery papers, Churchill College, Cambridge, AMEJ/2/1/138.
56. I. Gow, *Ulster After the Agreement* (London: Friends of the Union, 1986), p. 4.
57. Biggs-Davison, *Ulster Catholics and the Union*, p. 8.
58. C. Cruise O'Brien, 'Address to the Friends of the Union' (London: Friends of the Union, 1988), p. 4.
59. C. Moore, 'First Ian Gow Memorial Lecture' (London: Friends of the Union, 1991), p. 5.
60. Lord Cranborne, *The Renewal of Unionism* (London: Friends of the Union, 1997), p. 4
61. P. Roche, 'Unionism', *The Salisbury Review*, 17/2 (Winter 1998), p. 4.

CHAPTER 7

Economy

Since the 1980s under Margaret Thatcher's direction, if not earlier under the lead of Enoch Powell, the Conservative Right has been associated with advocacy of the free market. The influence of economic liberalism within the Conservative Party has become predominant. However, this has not always been the case, not even among the right-wing elements of the Conservative Party. Indeed, it will be argued in this chapter that the pursuit of free-market economics has been deleterious to the other goals of the Conservative Right.

This chapter begins by exploring the political economy of the neo-liberals in theory and in practice before going on to examine those who became increasingly concerned with the rise of the free-market agenda. Finally, it will explore the arguments of those who opposed free-market economics and proposed alternatives to it. Two main alternatives, both put forward in the 1970s and both representative of older traditions, will be examined alongside the reasons why they failed to have any impact on the agenda of the Conservative Party. These two traditions were distributism and protectionism. Although they failed to have any impact it will be argued that both would have been more consistent with the wider objectives of the traditionalists than free markets. Hence, the chapter highlights the central tension between the 'Old Right' and the 'New Right' of the Party.

© The Author(s) 2020
K. Hickson, *Britain's Conservative Right since 1945*,
https://doi.org/10.1007/978-3-030-27697-3_7

ECONOMIC LIBERALISM IN THEORY

Traditionally, the Conservative Right had been sceptical of free-market economics. That is not to say, as some have, that there was never a free-market (or small state) tradition within the Conservative Party until Mrs Thatcher brought in 'classical liberalism' from a long forgotten Victorian era. There had always been advocates of a small state within the Conservative Party, those who believed in the inefficiencies of state provision and the dependency culture which it engendered. This tradition was represented in the Victorian era by the likes of Herbert Spencer and Samuel Smiles. It was maintained by Lord Salisbury (3rd Marquess) at the end of the nineteenth century against the 'One Nation' approach of Disraeli and the 'Tory Reform' of Randolph Churchill. In the immediate aftermath of the Second World War there were also advocates of free-market economics, influenced by theorists such as Friedrich Hayek and Michael Oakeshott who both opposed—in their different ways— the 'rationalism' of the era. Prominent amongst them were the MPs Sir Waldron Smithers and Richard Law (later Lord Coleraine).

However, the tone of their utterances was more one of scepticism against the claims made for a larger state by advocates of the 'New Conservatism' than the positive virtues of the market. For T. E. Utley, the new economic model contained a central problem 'of how to combine full employment with low prices and a production great enough to make the welfare state safe'.[1] However, the belief that this would lead to a revival of economic liberalism was misplaced since:

> The present, or some future, socialist government may fail, but the socialist economic system which it has created will remain, and the public will demand not a government of liberal revolutionaries to restore the economic system of the nineteenth century, but a competent technocracy to apply the ultra revolutionary and coercive measures necessary to rescue a socialist economy from disaster.[2]

In contrast, the general tone of the economic liberals was a much more optimistic and radical one. Utley was later to complain of the absence of a genuinely conservative tone in public life in the early 1980s. In the midst of the debate between the so-called wets and dries, 'what is absent is anything which corresponds even remotely to the description of a traditional English Conservative as that phrase would have been understood right up until 1939'.[3] Ideology had replaced the inherent scepticism of traditional conservatism.

The principal theorist of economic liberalism in the UK was, of course, Hayek.[4] For Hayek there were only two economic models available. One was planning and the other free markets. Only the latter could protect individual freedom. In contrast, any moves towards planning, no matter how benign to begin with, would create the conditions which led to totalitarianism.[5] This was because the state would need to possess sufficient power to be able to implement its plan. The imposition of a plan would lead to unintended consequences which would then require more government intervention. Anyone not complying with the plan would also need to be forced in to doing so. The extension of the plan would lead to the erosion of individual liberty, a liberty only protected through the market which calculated for individual subjective preferences. As Sir Frederick Sykes put it: 'to the doctrinaire politician and the crank the plan is mainly a stalking-horse to enable him to impose his fads on his reluctant fellows and to gratify his incurable itch for ordering other people about'.[6]

Hayek's belief in the virtue of competition extended to national currency.[7] Here he admonished Milton Friedman's advocacy of monetarism for its belief in the role of the government in setting interest rates to control inflation. For Hayek, even this allowed too great a role for government. Instead, the currency should be 'denationalised' so as to allow for competing currencies. Consumers and producers would then settle on the one which secured the greatest level of confidence.

Friedman's monetarist thesis otherwise shared many of the same objectives as Hayek.[8] The government should not seek to maintain full employment. Whereas Keynes had advocated government borrowing in order to stimulate aggregate demand at a time of recession, with the debts being paid back once economic growth was resumed, Friedman believed that this policy would only result in ever higher doses of inflation due to the attempts by government to push unemployment below its 'natural' market level.

In a narrow sense, monetarism could be held to be politically neutral between left and right as the deficit could be reduced through either tax increases or expenditure cuts. The choice between them would be an empirical one exploring the likely impact of tax rises versus spending cuts. However, in an ideological form monetarism was clearly supportive of government spending cuts and in this aim was buttressed by three further economic liberal theories.

The first was the 'crowding out' thesis which distinguished between a wealth-creating private sector and a wealth-consuming public sector.[9] The government did not produce wealth, instead it acted in a parasitical fashion living off the wealth creation of the private sector. A growth in the size of the public sector would therefore 'crowd out' the resources which would otherwise have been available for the dynamic market sector. The thesis, espoused most clearly in the UK by Bacon and Eltis, maintained that this phenomenon was the cause of Britain's economic malaise in the 1970s and that resources therefore needed to be diverted from the public to the private sectors.

The second argument was that of supply-side theorists in America, Britain and elsewhere.[10] This concerned the impact of taxation rates on the economy. As taxes increased the tax yield would initially rise to an optimum point at which it would then become a disincentive beyond which further increases in taxation would lead to a fall in the government's revenues. While almost nobody would disagree with this thesis in principle the assertion was that current tax rates in the 1970s had already had this effect. It was therefore necessary to reduce tax rates in order to increase economic activity.

There was one further argument presented by the economic liberals which critiqued the social democratic state. This was the public choice thesis which argued that government bureaucracies had expanded out of self interest.[11] Far from being the benign custodian of the 'general good' public administrators had their own interests at heart, seeking to expand their personnel, power and resources. It was this which had explained their inexorable rise over the course of the twentieth century.

Taken together these arguments provided a rebuttal of all aspects of the social democratic state. Monetarism rejected the Keynesian theory of demand management and goal of full employment, crowding out theory rejected claims to increase public expenditure, supply-side theory undermined faith in higher levels of taxation and public choice theorists questioned the socially beneficial role of public sector bureaucracies.

However, these arguments would not have taken root without powerful and influential supporters. The thesis that the Keynesian welfare state was deeply flawed fed into middle-class concerns that they were over taxed.[12] Various pressure groups sprung up which claimed to represent the interests of the 'squeezed' middle class. Most notably, The Freedom

Association led by Ross and Norris McWhirter and the Middle Class Alliance.

In addition, numerous think tanks helped to disseminate the ideas of the economic liberals by arranging speaking tours and publishing their ideas in accessible and relatively inexpensive pamphlets.[13] Prominent amongst these were the Institute of Economic Affairs (IEA), the Centre for Policy Studies (CPS), the Adam Smith Institute (ASI) and Aims of Industry. The IEA had been established in the mid-1950s when it appeared that no major political party (including the Liberals) supported their position. The group explicitly drew on the ideas of Hayek. In the 1950s it received little attention under the direction of Arthur Seldon and Ralph Harris, but by the later 1960s they were starting to attract the attention of prominent Conservatives such as Enoch Powell and Geoffrey Howe. In the context of the economic downturn of the 1970s they received more traction, especially after the election of Thatcher as Leader of the Opposition in 1975. However, the IEA maintained its independence and so Thatcher and her key ally, Keith Joseph established the CPS as a free-market think tank within the Party to oppose what they characterised as the overly 'wet' nature of the Conservative Research Department which contained figures still broadly sympathetic to the old Heathite wing of the Party. The ASI also sought to promote free-market thinking, increasingly in the domain of social policy. Moreover, there was significant media support for the emerging economic liberal theory.

All of these arguments appeared increasingly relevant in the Britain of the 1970s. The period was also known as one of 'stagflation' which appeared to undermine the Keynesian economic view that there was a trade-off between inflation and unemployment. Now both inflation and unemployment rose together. Confidence in the British economy was further reduced when the then Labour Government went 'cap in hand' to the International Monetary Fund in 1976.[14] Finally, Labour's pledge to be able to manage the trade unions came to an end in the Winter of Discontent in 1978–1979. For many it appeared that the postwar days of economic boom had long passed and that a new phase of policy was needed, one which the economic liberals appeared to have advocated. As Lord Blake put it in the middle of the decade: 'there are signs of one of those rare and profound changes in the intellectual climate which occur only once or twice in a hundred years... There is a wind of change in Britain...and it comes from the right, not the left'.[15]

In short, we can see that the economic liberals succeeded because of two things in particular. Firstly, there was considerable institutional support for economic liberalism ranging from business interests, think tanks and prominent journalists. Economic liberalism also appealed to those in the private-sector middle class. However, to see it as an essentially class-based phenomena would be wrong. In the strained economic context of the 1970s, and in particular the growing sense that Britain was becoming ungovernable, the arguments of the economic liberals also appealed to a growing number of the working classes as well.

ECONOMIC LIBERALISM IN PRACTICE

Economic liberal policies have always had a presence within the Conservative Party going back to the late nineteenth century. It would therefore be incorrect to see the Thatcher governments as initiating economic liberalism within the Party, but it was always a marginal doctrine until the advent of Thatcherism. In the late nineteenth century the ideas of Herbert Spencer, with his emphasis on self-help and the survival of the fittest, was influential on some within the Conservative Party.[16] This was given a boost by the premiership of Lord Salisbury who was highly sceptical of positive state action—apart from isolated cases where he accepted there was a clear and overwhelming case for intervention.[17] His approach was based more upon scepticism of what good the state could achieve rather than a positive belief in what the market could achieve. Defectors from the declining Liberal Party in the early years of the twentieth century provided stronger advocates of the virtues of the 'free' market. However, interwar Conservative governments moved closer to the protectionism advocated by Joseph Chamberlain, to which we return below.

By 1945, therefore, free-market ideas had a foothold within the Conservative Party, but it was far from the dominant mode of thought. Indeed, the apparent success of the free-market wing in opposing the Beveridge Report acted as a catalyst for the more collectively-minded Conservatives. Winston Churchill's notorious intervention in the 1945 election campaign that Labour's domestic policies would require a British variant of the Gestapo in order to implement them showed the apparent influence of Hayek, whose *The Road to Serfdom* had been first published the preceding year. However, the damage that utterance caused to the Conservatives and the scale of the election defeat encouraged a further move in the direction of the collectivists, who drew inspiration from Harold Macmillan's *The Middle Way*.[18] The publication of the *Industrial Charter*—coupled with further charters—marked the triumph of a more interventionist form of Conservatism.[19] The veteran free-market Conservative, Sir Waldron Smithers, complained of the 'socialist bug' then infecting the Party.[20] However, his voice was in the minority, if the Conservatives did not wholeheartedly embrace the collectivist consensus they did at least recognise that such a move was needed if the Party's electoral fortunes were to be revived.

The dominance of the more collectivist form of Conservatism by the 1950s was highlighted by two developments. The incoming Chancellor of the Exchequer in 1951, R. A. Butler initially supported a speedy transition to free floating exchange rates.[21] Revisionist historians of the period have argued that this is evidence of the lack of consensus in economic policy at this time. That far from being the eponymous 'Mr Butskell' as *The Economist* had suggested, the economic policy of Butler was very different from that of his immediate predecessor, Labour's Hugh Gaitskell.[22] However, the more significant point is the speed with which this policy—designated Operation ROBOT, was abandoned in favour of continuing use of exchange controls. Similarly, when Peter Thorneycroft was Chancellor he demanded public expenditure cuts believing that inflation, and not unemployment, was the main problem then facing the economy. However, Macmillan—by this time Prime Minister—refused to sanction the full extent of the cuts in spending and the entire Treasury team resigned in 1958. The episode demonstrated, apart from Macmillan's political skills in dismissing the 'little local difficulty', the dominance of Keynesian policy since a measure which would increase unemployment was ruled out.

It was against this dominance of Keynesian policy for nearly two decades that Enoch Powell began to articulate a policy of economic liberalism following the Conservative defeat in 1964. In a series of speeches—soon to be overshadowed by his outburst on immigration in 1968—he advanced arguments for privatisation (or, as he preferred to call it, denationalisation—meaning a return of nationalised industries to their 'natural' state), monetarism, tax and public expenditure cuts, laws to restrict the trade unions and deregulation. Edward Heath also appeared to move towards economic liberalism when he convened a special meeting of his Shadow Cabinet at the Selsdon Park Hotel in London in early 1970. For later founders of the Seldson Group, Heath had embraced free-market economics only to betray his manifesto commitments at the first sign of economic difficulty.[23] The Right never forgave Heath for this and the idea of the u-turn took hold, hence Thatcher's comment in 1980—greeted enthusiastically by the party conference delegates—that she was not for turning. Lord Blake criticised the Heath Government rather differently.[24] In Opposition between 1965 and 1970 Heath had developed a lot of detailed policy proposals but had failed to change the climate of ideas: 'the Conservatives did not go into the election of 1970 devoid of policies, but they did go into it without... freshly articulated doctrinal support'.[25]

It was with the election of Thatcher in 1979 that the economic liberal philosophy became the dominant approach to economic policy. Thatcher was a believing monetarist alongside her first Chancellor, Geoffrey Howe, and the new approach was highlighted in the Medium Term Financial Strategy (MTFS) which committed the Government to a set of money supply targets.[26] In order to meet these targets public expenditure would need to be reduced, especially as the Government was also committed to reducing tax levels. The policy of monetary supply constraint appeared one which was easy to implement. Monetarists believed that inflation was purely a monetary phenomenon; control the money supply and inflation would inevitably fall. Moreover, there was a political opportunity which monetarism appeared to offer. If inflation was seen as being caused by excessive wage rises then governments needed to intervene in the labour market to restrict wages in order to bring down inflation, something which postwar governments of both political persuasions had tried to do. However, if inflation was instead seen as a purely monetary phenomenon then only governments could correct it and therefore there was no need to negotiate with the unions. However, monetarism proved a far from easy theory for governments to implement since there were numerous measurements of the money supply with different targets responding differently to each other and often with lengthy time tags between the implementation of policy and the change to the money supply target that was desired. By 1981 unemployment had risen towards three million and the Thatcher Government was facing a political crisis which she only survived due to the prevarication of her opponents within the Party, the even greater crisis facing Labour and the outbreak of war in the Falkland Islands the following year. Monetarism—in a conventional sense—was abandoned and replaced by a decision to shadow the Deutschmark under the Chancellorship of Nigel Lawson and eventually to the decision to join the European Exchange Rate Mechanism (ERM) in 1990.

Writing in 1979 on the eve of Thatcher's election victory, Peregrine Worsthorne expressed his suspicion that the new Conservative Government would not result in significant changes: 'it seems to me unrealistic, not to say absurd, to hope for a capitalist counter-revolution'.[27] He had already expressed his belief that Thatcher was far too influenced by classical liberalism, as evidenced by her emphasis on freedom: 'what Britain is suffering from is "riotous disorder" and to argue, as Mrs Thatcher does, that "setting the people free" will cure it is as senseless as trying to smooth raging waters with a stick of dynamite or to quieten hubbub with a brass band'.[28] Hayek, Worsthorne argued, was not an appropriate guide for the realities of class politics.[29] His predictions may have initially had some substance. Despite the tougher rhetoric of the new premier, her Government—with moderate, Jim Prior, as Employment Secretary—was initially slow in introducing measures to significantly reduce the power of the unions. However, plans had already been put into place prior to the General Election on how to deal with the unions—and especially the miners who had often been in the vanguard of industrial unrest, including that which had brought down the Heath Government in 1974. Under Prior's successor, the resolutely right-wing Norman Tebbit, the Government's approach towards the unions became tougher. The seemingly inevitable conflict between the miners and the Government took place over the long strike of 1984–1985 during which time the powers of the police and secret state were increased. The defeat of the National Union of Mineworkers led to the implementation of the closure programme of numerous mines and the implementation of measures designed to restrict the capacity of trade unions to strike, to take secondary action and to fund the Labour Party.

A further core objective of the Thatcher Governments was the privatisation programme. The Labour Government had resorted to asset sales in 1976 in order to meet the demands of the International Monetary Fund. However, the Thatcher Governments pursued privatisation with ideological passion. Again, this started more slowly with low hanging fruit being the first to be sold off. The first Thatcher Government legislated quickly for the sale of council houses to sitting tenants, something which it was able to do because the previous Labour Government had been contemplating. However, the swing to the left by Labour after the 1979 defeat led to it being ideologically opposed to council house sales. Thatcher also ignored the warnings of those who believed that the sale of houses without a corresponding house building programme would create a social housing shortage. Thatcher, with her own ideological aversion to state provision—national and local—refused to allow this to happen. The second and third Thatcher administrations were most distinguished by its sale of major state-owned industries including gas, electricity, water and telecommunications. In order to ensure that these sales were successful the shares were often sold at a lower rate and accompanied with mass marketing campaigns. The measures were designed to create a 'popular capitalism' as a principal architect for privatisation, John Redwood, put it.[30]

Further measures were designed to reconstitute the state so as to fit the model of economic liberalism. The welfare state had largely avoided direct reform for the first two of Thatcher's Governments as she concentrated on inflation, trade unions and privatisation. But in the third term she initiated measures to replicate the operation of a competitive market in health and education. The initial preference had been for cash vouchers given to patients and parents, which could then be used by them to choose between competing providers of health and education. However, this policy was deemed too politically and administratively difficult and so internal markets were introduced in the National Health Service, facilitated by published league tables. The civil service was also reformed—inspired by public choice theorists—with cuts to civil service personnel, the creation of arms-length government agencies with clear performance management targets, and numerous private sector audits of civil service departments. Local government was also subjected to greater exposure to market forces either by direct transfer of local government services to private providers, restrictions on councils' ability to borrow and the implementation of the Community which would supposedly make local authorities more accountable to the electors by making more of the electorate pay local taxation. Although the policy—dubbed the Poll Tax—seemed attractive in principle it quickly became highly controversial and led to the eventual removal of Thatcher from office in 1990.

Certainly, the pursuit of economic liberalism during the 1980s led to significant social tensions. This was not only true of the miners' strike and poll tax riots but more generally through the combined effect of tax changes which significantly widened the gap between richest and poorest as discussed in the following chapter on welfare reform. For her admirers such social upheaval was necessary in order to bring about fundamental improvement in the operation of the economy. Indeed, Thatcher's forced removal from office in 1990 led her supporters to argue that her agenda must continue. Her successor was deemed to be closest to her ideologically although he quickly dismayed her supporters by saying that he wished to be at the heart of Europe and softening some of her reforms, including replacing the Poll Tax almost immediately. The free-market wing of the Conservative Party became openly hostile to Major. This is despite the fact that in many ways Major not only continued with Thatcherite reform but also pushed it even further. For instance, the more controversial privatisations occurred not under Thatcher but under Major, especially rail privatisation in the mid-1990s. The marketisation of the welfare state also reached its furthest extent under Major, with the full implementation of the internal market policy. Despite the fact that the trade union issue had been largely dealt with under Thatcher, there was further legislation in this area under Major.

By 1997, therefore, Britain had had 18 years of economic liberal reform, a reform programme which became increasingly strident in its nature as time went on. The election of the Labour Government in 1997 did little to change this in many ways. Despite sustained redistribution and record levels of public expenditure on health and education following the Comprehensive Spending Review in 1998, the marketisation of public services was sustained, alongside further privatisation measures. To the dismay of those on the left of the Party, there was no attempt to repeal any of the trade union legislation. The new approach to welfare was also maintained (see next chapter). However, the prevailing view within the Conservative Party was that the Labour Government needed to be criticised from the vantage point of economic liberalism, which many in the Party—certainly those on the right—regarded as an unfinished agenda. Just as Euroscepticism within the Conservative Party hardened in Opposition, so too did economic liberalism. Debate over the future direction of the Party was somewhat muted at first as the Party came to terms with the scale of its defeat in 1997. However, when debate did occur the economic direction of the Party was never seriously questioned. This can be seen in the debate between the so-called 'Mods' and 'Rockers' around 2000. Both sides shared an economic liberal outlook but disagreed on social issues (as explored in Chapter 9). For modernisers the greater freedom in economic life should be accompanied with greater freedom in personal morality. The emergence of localism within the Party also took place within the paradigm of economic liberalism. The Thatcher Governments had sought to liberate people in the economic sphere but had not done so in the political sphere. Economic liberalism decentralised economic decision making to individual consumers but political power was still overly centralised. Therefore decentralisation of non-economic decisions should now go side by side with the free market. The opponents of modernisation wanted to maintain the Thatcher mix of strong state in social issues and free markets in the economic sphere. Both sides could agree with Simon Heffer that, 'there is no finer mechanism to encourage the enterprise in which Tories believe than free markets and low taxes'.[31] Traditional Tories had historically had little to say about economics because they 'left those sorts of things principally to the workings of the market and private enterprise'.[32]

The third consecutive electoral defeat in 2005 did finally challenge Conservatives to think much more seriously about their ideological pitch. David Cameron was elected Leader over the more experienced David Davis on the basis that he was better placed to modernise the Party. Thatcher had notoriously stated in the 1980s that there was 'no such thing as society'.[33] Cameron asserted that there was indeed such a thing as society, but that this did not equate with the larger state which New Labour was implementing. More centralised state activity reduced the scope for localised community action. The Big Society would be more compassionate than Thatcherism had apparently been but the state would still need to be reduced in order to encourage not so much the private sector as the voluntary sector. However, if this was designed to be a break with economic liberalism it was quickly overtaken by events. Almost as soon as Cameron had announced his Big Society vision the economy collapsed and the Conservatives quickly reverted to their comfort zone of economic liberalism. Blame was placed on the profligacy of the Labour Government for spending too much money when the economy was growing, meaning that there was no money left to spend in the bad times. What was initially a crisis created by lax regulation in the banking sector—a sector deregulated when Thatcher became Prime Minister in 1979—was portrayed as a crisis in public expenditure. The Coalition Government formed in 2010 embarked on public expenditure restraint. However, for some 'austerity' was a slogan used by the political left against the Conservatives. What cuts there were, were necessary given the state of public finances in 2010. Indeed, for some, 'the truth is that there just hasn't been any austerity in Britain'.[34]

Theresa May served as Home Secretary throughout the Coalition Government, indeed she could be regarded as a loyal follower of the austerity agenda through substantial cuts to policing budgets throughout her tenure at the Home Office. However, on assuming the Premiership in 2016 she signalled a reduction in the pace of austerity. This could be seen as a departure from economic liberalism and was accompanied by a One Nation rhetoric. However, May's premiership was consistently vulnerable. Her failure to win a majority in the 2017 General Election and to secure a majority for her Brexit proposals undermined any attempt to move beyond rhetoric into actual domestic policy achievements and she was eventually forced to quit. Numerous interviews conducted for this book with Conservative MPs have shown the extent to which economic liberalism still dominates thinking in the Conservative Party.

CRITICISMS AND ALTERNATIVES ON THE RIGHT

Such dominance of economic liberal ideas was the result of Thatcherism. Prior to that, as we have seen, economic liberalism was far from paradigmatic. However, the relationship between economic liberalism and the Conservative Right is not as simple as this may suggest. There were numerous critics of economic liberalism from the Right of the Conservative Party from those who believed that, far from being consistent with their wider objectives, it was actually antithetical to them. Maurice Cowling's pithy comment on Hayek's major work, *The Constitution of Liberty*, was that it 'left me cold'.[35] There was little to no account of economics in the set of essays which Cowling edited in 1978.[36]

Michael Oakeshott argued that Hayek had come close to his preferred model of nomocracy—a system where the state acts as the enforcer of a system of rules which allow individuals to pursue their own ends—but had ultimately failed.[37] The modern state takes the form of a teleocracy, seeking to impose its own predetermined ends on society. Social democracy, socialism and social liberalism all took the form of teleocratic politics. It was an 'enterprise association' rather than a 'civil association' which they desired. It meant the imposition of a government plan to reform society so as to achieve a certain goal—social justice, a planned economy, equality etc. As postwar Conservatives had embraced the welfare and economic policy objectives of their opponents, even if they had moderated them somewhat, they had accepted a teleocratic form of politics. This was ultimately dangerous since it would lead to the suppression of individual freedom in pursuit of a collective goal. Hayek had appeared to endorse this when he distinguished two modes of politics—a free economy, in which individuals pursued their own notion of the good, and planning, in which a central and shared purpose was implemented by the state. The latter would inevitably lead to a loss of freedom. However, Oakeshott believed that Hayek had ultimately failed in his attempt to forge a nomocratic alternative to the dominance of teleocracy. The state would be required to legislate so as to create, and then defend, a free-market model. This may be against the wishes of the majority of the citizens, something which Hayek recognised as he sought to develop a range of constitutional devices to protect the free market from democratic pressures. Such measures were justified since the market would be a guarantor of greater economic efficiency and productivity. The long-term rate of growth would be higher under a market model than under planning. Hence, there was an ends-based justification for the market economy, something which Oakeshott argued moved Hayek's mode of thought from nomocracy to teleocracy.

A related argument was made by Angus Maude in his book, *The Common Problem* (1969).[38] Maude had been a close associate of Powell, establishing with him the One Nation Group and writing their 1959 pamphlet, *Change Is Our Ally* which was widely interpreted as a call for a less collectivist economic approach.[39] Maude, therefore, may well have been expected to have endorsed Powell's advocacy of free markets. However, he did not do so, believing Powell guilty of 'militant economic liberalism'.[40] Instead, he regarded the central challenge of politics at that time to end the dominance of technocracy and to rediscover a more fundamental, principled form of politics. Political debate had for too long been about the best way to manage the system. Instead, he argued that politics should be about rediscovering the conditions which would allow individual citizens to pursue their own definition of the good within the rule of law. The problem with the collectivist model was that it made individuals means to some wider purpose rather than ends in and of themselves. However, Maude also believed that the free-market model did the same. Individuals would be means to the attainment of some wider end goal, namely the profit maximisation of the large corporations who were engaged in selling consumers things they did not need. Maude—surprisingly for someone on the Right—endorsed the arguments of environmentalists and those, notably J. K. Galbraith,[41] on the power of advertisers to determine consumer demand: 'it is impossible to ignore Galbraith's message, and almost impossible to deny rationally its essential truth'.[42] Rather than consumers being sovereign, they would become tools for large capitalist enterprises, often operating under conditions of limited competition despite the claims of economic liberals that the economy was essentially competitive. While Maude's argument can be interpreted as novel and a significant challenge to economic liberalism, it did nothing to stop its rise in the Conservative Party and ultimately failed to provide a coherent alternative position. Maude campaigned for the election of Thatcher as Conservative Party Leader in 1975 but did not survive in Government for long after 1979.[43]

For others, it was the pace of change and specific aspects of Thatcherism which proved problematic. Thatcher had decided to appoint Peter Thorneycroft as Party Chairman. In doing so she looked back to his resignation in January 1958 and, for some, he had come to be regarded as the first monetarist Chancellor, at least in the post-1945 era. He had also been recommended by Thatcher's loyal Deputy, Willie Whitelaw. However, if he had been expected to support the economic liberal agenda he was to disappoint. In 1981, just prior to the summer recess, Geoffrey Howe had proudly announced that the recession was now over. With mounting unemployment this was a step too far for some including Thorneycroft. In the discussions concerning the 'wets' and the 'dries' at that time, he gave an interview in which he said he detected rising damp in his own political persuasion. The interview was seen as disloyal to Thatcher and he was later removed from his role as Party Chairman.[44]

A similar fate was to befall John Biffen. He was a supporter and close personal friend of Powell who had been an outspoken critic of Keynesian social democracy. If Thorneycroft was not a committed monetarist, Biffen was much closer to being so. Recognising that she was outnumbered in her own Shadow, and then later real, Cabinet, Thatcher determined that the key battles would be in the economic sphere and she appointed ministers to key economic portfolios who she believed she could trust. Biffen was appointed Chief Secretary to the Treasury, responsible for overseeing public spending restraint. However, he was not an advocate of low taxation. Indeed, he was quite relaxed about higher public expenditure so long as it was funded through taxation rather than borrowing: 'high public spending is not in itself inflationary if it is accompanied by high taxation'.[45] When Thatcher embarked on a tax-cutting agenda—especially for the rich so as to create greater entrepreneurial incentive, Biffen was sceptical. He was publicly and privately critical of the direction of policy and seen increasingly as being 'semi-detached' in Bernard Ingham's phrase.[46] He called for a period of consolidation believing that there had been sufficient reform in the early 1980s, objecting to those who wished to see permanent revolution from the Right: 'they are, as it were, Tory Maoists. Their quest for further far-reaching reform is vigorous and uninhibited. I clearly dissent from this viewpoint'.[47] For Michael Portillo, writing in 1992, this was misguided: 'the would-be consolidators were asking us to throw away our greatest single advantage'.[48] By carrying on with economic liberal reform, Thatcher had changed Britain:

> At the end of the 1970s, the Conservatives rewrote the political agenda. We emphasised the independence of the individual, the free operation of the market, and the need for improved incentives. These ideas are scarcely questioned in Britain today.[49]

Roger Scruton was sufficiently concerned about the undue influence of the economic liberals to pen *The Meaning of Conservatism*.[50] For Scruton, there was nothing inherently incompatible between conservatism and free markets. However, the latter was only a method and should not be regarded as an end in itself. He was critical of the ideas of Robert Nozick, who argued that taxation amounted to the confiscation of private income by the state.[51] Instead, levels of taxation should not be determined in accordance with abstract principles. Individuals owed a loyalty to the state and the government therefore had a right to take what it needed in taxation so as to fund the defence of the nation from external and internal threats. Given that her internal party critics had made the defence of public spending a defining issue, Thatcher had identified spending cuts as an essential part of her project. However, the issue was not so much one of higher or lower public expenditure but rather spending on the areas necessary for the state to fulfil its core responsibilities. Scruton was concerned that this meaning of conservatism had been lost on the current Government, and was to continue to have doubts up until the Falklands War when Thatcher's patriotism was finally established.

In justification of its free-market agenda, the Government had seized on the arguments of Martin Wiener that Britain's long-term economic decline was caused by the persistence of an aristocratic culture which looked down on industrialism and commercialism.[52] Keith Joseph had circulated copies of the book to his civil servants.[53] However, for Peregrine Worsthorne this was a blessing since it had managed to civilise the bourgeoisie: 'the transference of power, protracted over a century, resembled a merger rather than a conquest; a marriage (in many cases literally) rather than a rape'.[54] He opposed the attempt to create an enterprise culture. Ian Crowther also opposed the emphasis on such a culture: 'teaching people that the "enterprise culture" is the only or pre-dominant culture is tantamount to teaching them that acquisitiveness and self-seeking are identical with the fulfilled human life'.[55]

Enoch Powell voiced concerns over the education policies of the Thatcher Government which stemmed from this. Thatcher said she wanted to divert education funding into science and technology in order to increase national prosperity. For Powell this would lead to a 'inhuman and barbarous state' since learning was an end in itself, 'to the glory of God'.[56] He had written long before against attempts by politicians to use education as a means to the end goal of higher economic growth.[57] This was a product of Powell's underpinning belief in the role and limits of markets.[58] For Powell, there was a clear distinction between economic and non-economic spheres. In the former the market should be dominant, but in the latter the market should have little to no role. The Thatcher and Major Governments had gone too far in their pursuit of market forces by encroaching into the non-economic sphere. However, Powell's distinction between economic and non-economic sectors is difficult to sustain and highlights a central tension between economic liberalism and traditional Toryism. While the former believe markets are superior in any area bar a few natural monopolies, the latter regards a wider area of activity as the proper function of the state.

A specific tension was over reforms to Sunday trading laws.[59] For traditionalists, Sundays needed to be kept special for reasons both of Christian observation and family life and required separate trading laws. This led to an unusual alliance of traditionalists and the trades unions who believed that Sunday opening would reduce the rights of their members. However, free marketeers believed that existing Sunday trading laws restricted the operation of the market and the right of consumers to shop as they wished. It was one of the few issues which led to the Thatcher Governments being defeated on the floor of the House of Commons.

If there was scepticism expressed on the Conservative Right to the economic liberal direction of policy from 1979 onwards, alternative models were harder to find. There were in fact two main alternatives put forward in the 1970s from different quarters of the Conservative Right, both of which failed to make significant headway. Arguably, both were more consistent with the traditional aims of the Conservative Right. However, both failed to receive the institutional or financial support which economic liberalism garnered, nor the media exposure.

The first was the tradition of national protectionism which had a history within the Conservative Party going back to the turn of the last century with the ideas of Joseph Chamberlain. The Chamberlainite tradition was examined in Chapter Two, with its aim to preserve the empire by creating a stronger economic unity between the UK and her colonies. The argument for tariff reform split the Party and left it in Opposition for a decade after 1906. However, it eventually was adopted—albeit in a watered down form—by the 1930s. Although the British Empire continued to decline after the Second World War there remained support for protectionism through to the 1970s. Membership of the EEC further reduced support for protectionism since it was no longer viable under the Treaty of Rome, at least at the level of the nation-state. However, there was still support for protectionism in this period. Tim Janman felt that some on the Right, particularly those in the Monday Club, were protectionist, but most Conservative students were supporters of free trade.[60] There was a growing generational divide. There was also criticism of the rise of economic liberalism in publications of the period. The Monday Club was far from united in its approach to economic matters. Its periodical, *Monday World* continued to have its advocates for national protectionism. One Monday Club member dismissed influential Thatcherite, Rhodes Boyson as a classical liberal.[61] For the economic liberals, following Powell, the Empire was now a costly historical legacy and the way to revive the strength of the nation was through free-market economics. Others disagreed believing that economic liberalism was no respecter of nation states. Robert Henderson, a contributor to *Right Now* magazine, believed that the Thatcher years had seen the government lose control of the national economy.[62] The editorial of the same publication also lamented that 'the essential problem with free trade is that it has become a doctrine, rather than a tool'.[63] When asked who most closely resembled his own approach to Conservatism in the period since 1945, Lord Sudeley—former Chairman and President of the Monday Club and founder member of Traditional Britain—said Julian Amery and John Biggs-Davison rather than Enoch Powell.[64] Both were critical of the larger state after 1945 in social and economic matters, without being advocates of free markets at home or free trade in the international economy. Writing in 1957, Biggs-Davison warned that 'the subordination of economic policy to GATT and IMF is incompatible with national independence'.[65] Economic liberalism had led to national decline and undermined the country's traditions. It had also allowed American interests to dominate. Brexit and the rise of Donald Trump both created a new opportunity for the revival of national protectionism.[66] Britain should not only leave the economic liberal EU but should also withdraw from the World Trade Organisation so as to recreate the conditions for national autonomy over economic matters.[67]

A second alternative was put forward by Ian Crowther, regular contributor to *Monday World* and later Literary Editor of the *Salisbury Review* for many years. Crowther was especially influenced by the ideas of G. K. Chesterton and the Catholic social tradition.[68] For Chesterton, the English national tradition was not so much one of free markets, but rather a more corporatist one.[69] This tradition was established in a feudal society in which everyone had a defined station within the social hierarchy with corresponding duties and obligations. However, the twin processes of urbanisation and industrialisation had shattered this holistic social model in favour of individualism. As Biggs-Davison put it: 'capitalism, freed from the restraints imposed by the Tudors and the early Stuarts, had made its own laws and broken society into a medley of competing individuals'.[70] The professed aim of the Catholic social tradition from the late nineteenth century was to respond to these conditions by creating partnerships between different social classes. Corporate governance would need to be changed so that there was partnership between workers and bosses within industry.[71] Biggs-Davison gave a speech in 1952 arguing for partnership in industry including profit sharing.[72] He also felt that in Opposition after 1945, the Party had 'taken an element of distributism into its doctrine'.[73] Writing to Edward Heath in 1974, Julian Amery said that, 'co-partnership has been a hobby horse of mine since 1948 and I shall always regret that we have been so slow to adopt it as official party policy'.[74] Amery proposed a 'Chamber of Industry'—a corporate body which would be able to exercise greater control over the trade unions by absorbing them.[75] The ideas of 'Chesterbelloc' (Chesterton and Hillaire Belloc), or distributism, would replace the antagonistic relationships of modern capitalism with something more harmonious. According to authors of a Monday Club pamphlet, not only would this lead to a more cohesive society but also greater economic tranquillity:

There is far too great a gap between management and union or management and workers in a large number of industries and we believe that a sound economy can only be built up if the employees in industry have a greater insight into the affairs of their company.[76]

Crowther argued that the emergence of the welfare state since 1945 had compounded these tensions, rather than resolving them, with issues concerning distributive justice also being a source of social antagonism and further reducing the scope for direct opportunities for community action.[77] The central state had crowded out voluntary and community organisation and eroded personal responsibility as the un-personal welfare state had now taken on those responsibilities. The welfare state should therefore be largely abolished, with companies reorganised as partnerships between employers and trades unions who could then take responsibility for the welfare needs of the workers and their families. 'An escape from the evils of irresponsibility,' he argued, 'may yet be found by making the industry and the union jointly responsible for all those social benefits which at present are supplied by the welfare state'.[78] Such reform would amount to the revival of the medieval guild system.[79] The retrenchment of the welfare state in the 1980s had not, however, revived morality and individual responsibility since, 'little today is left of the old, pre-economic, social and moral order into which capitalism fitted in the Nineteenth Century'.[80] The main difficulty with distributist ideas is that they appeared other worldly, strangely utopian and feudal in an era of increasingly internationalised capitalism. Crowther felt that there was in reality, 'no practical counterpart in policy to free markets, my musings not withstanding'.[81] However, in response to many years of economic liberal hegemony, there are those who have argued for a revised form of distributism as a way of recreating conservatism. The principal exponent of modern distributism in the UK has been Phillip Blond through his notion of 'Red Toryism' in which local communities take greater responsibility for economic and social activities from the central state.[82] Rather than seeing the state as a countervailing power to corporations, it had in fact cooperated with them against the needs of communities. Once again, whether Red Toryism offered a viable alternative model to economic liberalism is very much open to dispute. David Cameron appeared to take up the idea with his talk of the 'Big Society'. But to earlier exponents of distributism this soon evaporated: as Crowther put it, 'the bubble burst quite quickly'.[83] Perhaps the main significance of these

ideas is that they highlight the tensions between Traditional Toryism—
with its scepticism of both government and market—and economic liberalism, which is seen by traditionalists as having an essentially destructive
and dislocating impact on civil society.

NOTES

1. T. E. Utley, *Not Guilty: The Conservative Reply* (London: MacGibbon and
   Kee, 1957), p. 10.
2. Quoted in A. Gamble, *The Conservative Nation* (London: Routledge,
   1974), p. 50.
3. C. Moore and S. Heffer (eds.) *Tory Seer: The Selected Journalism of
   T. E. Utley* (London: Hamilton, 1989), p. 65.
4. F. Hayek, *The Constitution of Liberty* (Chicago: University of Chicago,
   1960).
5. F. Hayek, *The Road to Serfdom* (London: Routledge, 1944).
6. F. Sykes, *Roads to Recovery* (London: Signpost Booklets, 1944), p. 3.
7. F. Hayek, *Denationalisation of Money* (London: Institute of Economic
   Affairs, 1978).
8. M. Friedman and R. Friedman, *Free to Choose* (Harmondsworth: Penguin,
   1970).
9. R. Bacon and W. Eltis, *Britain's Economic Problem: Too Few Producers*
   (London: Macmillan, 1976).
10. B. Bartlett and T. Roth, *The Supply-Side Solution* (London: Macmillan,
    1984).
11. J. Buchanan and G. Tullock, *The Calculus of Consent* (Ann Arbor:
    University of Michigan, 1962).
12. P. Hutber, *The Decline and Fall of the Middle Class and How It Can Fight
    Back* (Harmondsworth: Penguin, 1977).
13. R. Cockett, *Thinking the Unthinkable: Think Tanks and the Economic
    Counter-Revolution, 1931–83* (London: HarperCollins, 1994).
14. K. Hickson, *The IMF Crisis of 1976 and British Politics* (London: I.B.
    Tauris, 2005).
15. Lord Blake, 'A Changed Climate', in Lord Blake and J. Patten (eds.) *The
    Conservative Opportunity* (London: Macmillan, 1976), p. 4.
16. H. Spencer, *The Man Versus the State* (London: Williams and Norgate,
    1884).
17. A. Roberts, *Salisbury: Victorian Titan* (London: Phoenix, 2000).
18. H. Macmillan, *The Middle Way* (London: Macmillan, 1938).
19. R. A. Butler (ed.) *Conservatism, 1945–1950* (London: Conservative
    Political Centre, 1950).

20. Quoted in M. Garnett and K. Hickson, *Conservative Thinkers* (Manchester: Manchester University Press, 2008), p. 28.
21. See M. Jago, *Rab Butler* (London: Biteback, 2015).
22. S. Kelly, *The Myth of Mr Butskell* (Aldershot: Ashgate, 2002).
23. See J. Bruce-Gardyne, *Whatever Happened to the Quiet Revolution?* (London: Knight, 1974).
24. Blake, 'A Changed Climate', pp. 1–4.
25. Ibid., p. 2.
26. See A. Gamble, *The Free Economy and the Strong State: The Politics of Thatcherism* (Basingstoke: Macmillan, 1994), pp. 105–138 for a discussion of the economic policies.
27. P. Worsthorne, *Peregrinations* (London: Weidenfeld & Nicolson, 1980), p. 276.
28. P. Worsthorne, 'Too Much Freedom', in M. Cowling (ed.) *Conservative Essays* (London: Cassell, 1978), p. 149.
29. P. Worsthorne, 'F. A. Hayek: Next Construction for the Giant', in M. Ivens (ed.) *Prophets of Freedom* (London: Aims of Industry, 1975).
30. J. Redwood, *Popular Capitalism* (London: Routledge, 1988).
31. S. Heffer, *What Tories Want* (London: Politeia, 2000), p. 14.
32. S. Heffer, 'Traditional Toryism', in K. Hickson (ed.) *The Political Thought of the Conservative Party Since 1945* (Basingstoke: Palgrave, 2005), p. 198.
33. M. Thatcher, 'Interview', *Woman's Own*, 23 September 1987, https://www.margaretthatcher.org/document/106689, accessed 10 May 2019.
34. T. Worstall, 'There Hasn't Been Any Austerity so How Can the Cabinet Be Split on Reversing It?' *Forbes*, 2 July 2017, https://www.forbes.com/sites/timworstall/2017/07/02/there-hasnt-been-any-austerity-so-how-can-the-cabinet-be-split-on-reversing-it/#34bbd692f5e7, accessed 10 May 2019.
35. M. Cowling, 'The Sources of the New Right: Irony, Geniality and Malice', *Encounter*, November 1989, p. 6.
36. Cowling (ed.) *Conservative Essays*.
37. M. Oakeshott, 'Rationalism in Politics', in M. Oakeshott, *Rationalism in Politics and Other Essays* (Indianapolis: Liberty, 1991).
38. A. Maude, *The Common Problem* (London: Constable, 1969).
39. E. Powell and A. Maude (eds.) *Change Is Our Ally* (London: Conservative Political Centre, 1954).
40. Maude, *The Common Problem*, p. 201.
41. J. K. Galbraith, *The New Industrial State* (London: Hamilton, 1967).
42. Maude, *The Common Problem*, p. 215.
43. See Garnett and Hickson, *Conservative Thinkers*.
44. C. Moore, *Margaret Thatcher: The Authorised Biography, Volume 1: Not for Turning* (London: Allen Lane, 2013), p. 643.

45. J. Biffen, *Political Office or Political Power?* (London: Centre for Policy Studies, 1977), p. 14.
46. C. Moore, *Margaret Thatcher: The Authorised Biography, Volume Two: Everything She Wants* (London: Allen Lane, 2015), p. 524.
47. J. Biffen, *Forward from Conviction* (London: Conservative Political Centre, 1986), p. 9.
48. M. Portillo, *A Vision for the 1990s* (London: Conservative Political Centre, 1992), p. 6.
49. Ibid.
50. R. Scruton, *The Meaning of Conservatism* (Harmondsworth: Penguin, 1980). Correspondence with Roger Scruton.
51. R. Nozick, *Anarchy, State and Utopia* (Oxford: Blackwell, 1974).
52. M. Wiener, *English Culture and the Decline of the Industrial Spirit, 1850–1980* (Cambridge: Cambridge University Press, 1981).
53. 'Empty Shelves', *The Economist*, 27 April 2010.
54. Quoted in Wiener, *English Culture*, p. 8.
55. I. Crowther, 'Thatcherism and the Good Life', *The Salisbury Review*, 8/1 (September 1989), p. 6.
56. S. Heffer, *Like the Roman* (London: Weidenfeld and Nicolson, 1998), p. 887.
57. E. Powell, *A View on Education* (London: Working Men's College, 1964).
58. See Garnett and Hickson, *Conservative Thinkers*, for a discussion.
59. Moore, *Margaret Thatcher*, Volume 2, pp. 509–511.
60. Interview with Tim Janman, London, 27 March 2017.
61. T. Beardson, 'Right Turn?' *Monday World* (Winter 1970–1971), pp. 16–17.
62. R. Henderson, *Right Now* (January–March 2000), p. 10.
63. Editorial, *Right Now* (May 2005), p. 2.
64. Interview with Lord Sudeley, London, 6 February 2017.
65. Policy Statement by John Biggs-Davison sent to Julian Amery, 25 July 1957, Julian Amery papers, Churchill College, Cambridge, AMEJ/2/1/29.
66. Interview with Lord Sudeley.
67. Ibid.
68. I. Crowther, *Chesterton* (London: Claridge, 1993).
69. G. K. Chesterton, *A Short History of England* (London: Chatto & Windus, 1907).
70. J. Biggs-Davison, *Look to the Foundations: A Tory Restatement* (London: Edinburgh Press, 1949), pp. 8–9.
71. I. Crowther, 'The Re-creation of Social Order', *Monday World* (Autumn 1972), pp. 3–6.

72. Letter from John Biggs-Davison to Julian Amery, 31 March 1952, Julian Amery papers AMEJ/2/2/6.
73. Letter from John Biggs-Davison to H. W. J. Edwards, 14 October 1953, John Biggs-Davison papers, Parliamentary Archives, BD/1/116.
74. Letter from Julian Amery to Edward Heath, 30 May 1974, John Biggs-Davison papers, BD/1/750.
75. Ibid.
76. Monday Club Home Group, *You: Your Children, Your Job, Your Home, Your Umbrella* (London: Monday Club, 1962), p. 6.
77. I. Crowther, 'Remaking One Nation', *Monday World* (Spring 1974).
78. Ibid.
79. Crowther, 'The Re-creation of Social Order'.
80. I. Crowther, 'Thatcherism and the Good Life', *The Salisbury Review*, 8/1 (September 1989), p. 5.
81. Interview with Ian Crowther, Telephone, 12 May 2017.
82. P. Blond, *Red Tory* (London: Faber, 2010).
83. Interview with Ian Crowther.

CHAPTER 8

Welfare

The Conservative Right has been on the opposing side of the major social changes in the UK in the period under discussion in this book. The two major forms of social change are the growth of the welfare state (the focus of this chapter) and the liberalising social reforms mostly, but not exclusively, associated with the 1960s and to which the term 'permissive' is usually attached (the next chapter). The nature of the these reforms is widely documented and so only a brief description of them is provided here, with the main focus being on the Conservative Right's opposition to these reforms.

The underpinning philosophy to the Conservative Right's approach to welfare was highlighted by Michael Oakeshott in his conception of the individual manqué.[1] The conception of individualism is what most distinguished modern society from feudal society, where the individual had been subjected to the wider needs of the community, a means rather than the ends. The modern individual was one which assumed a certain character. This character was upright, responsible and accepted the full duties of the citizen. To be free was to be responsible. There was, therefore, no distinction between freedom and order. However, modern society had also created an individual who was stripped of his/her sense of personal responsibility. They were the opposite of the individual. This alternative character was the individual manqué. Shorn of his sense of personal responsibility this character instead became dependent on the state, which took many of the decisions—over welfare and so

© The Author(s) 2020
K. Hickson, *Britain's Conservative Right since 1945*,
https://doi.org/10.1007/978-3-030-27697-3_8

forth—which he should take. With the growth of the welfare state since 1945 this dependence had become even greater.

The Conservative Right has, therefore, been consistently critical of the idea and practice of the welfare state. Arguments against the growth of the welfare state were muted in the immediate aftermath of the Second World War. The Conservative Party came to the belief that in order to get back into power it had to accept the broad parameters of the welfare state. The economic crisis and (perceived or real) failures of the welfare state then led to a revival of the Conservative Right generally and of their case against the welfare state specifically. This chapter has three main aims. The first will examine the postwar case against the welfare state made by the Conservative Right. It will then go on to explore Thatcherism and its attitudes to the welfare state. Finally, it will examine the legacy of Thatcherism.

DEPENDENCY

Inevitably with the outbreak of war in 1939 political focus was on the conduct of the hostilities, placing the economy on a wartime footing and ultimately winning the conflict. However, with the turn in fortunes from 1942 onwards there was increased focus on post-war reconstruction.[2] This was most famously the case with the Beveridge Report of 1942 which called for a fundamental reconstruction of society with government action to lay waste the five giants of want, disease, ignorance, idleness and squalor. Other measures included the second Beveridge Report in 1944 and the Education Act of the same year. These measures exposed differences within the Conservative Party. The Right, and probably many in the Centre of the party too, opposed such measures and organisations such as the Progress Trust were established to make the case against such reforms. The moderates within the Party embraced these reforms. The Tory Reform Committee was established to promote the cause of social reform within the Party, while R. A. Butler was the inspiration behind the Education Act. The failure of the Conservatives in the 1945 General Election to mount an effective campaign, let alone to win, meant the return of the first majority Labour government which then set about implementing these and other reforms. For some most credit for these measures goes to the wartime coalition, for others the postwar Labour government. It is true that some of the measures were bitterly opposed, such as the creation of the National Health Service (NHS), but overall the realisation by senior Conservatives that many of these measures were popular led to them being largely maintained by the incoming Conservative government in 1951. The opposition from the Conservative Right therefore, much like the opposition to decolonisation, was therefore forlorn.

For some the War was being used as a justification for postwar economic and social reconstruction. However, that was not why the War was being fought. It could not, therefore, be a justification for the welfare state. Progressive opinion had led to a distortion of the very reasons why the war was being fought at all. It was being conducted to initially save the nation from foreign invasion and then, with the fascist retreat, to defeat the aggressive power. It was not being fought to recreate society from within. The advocates of the New Jerusalem were thereby distorting what the Second World War was about to suit their own ideological ends. Michael Oakeshott stressed the point when he said that the nature of postwar policy was predicated on 'legends':

> Setting aside the philosophy, the projects and methods of contemporary British politics seem to spring from two main sources: a legend of mass unemployment and a legend of war. I say "a legend" because although mass unemployment and war are the two dominating experiences of our time, our politics spring not so much from the experiences themselves as from something that has been made of them.[3]

While it was true that poverty had increased as a result of the Wall Street Crash the recession had been relatively short lived and isolated to particular sectors of the economy. Overall there had been growth and a steady diminution of poverty. Many people had seen their lot improved.[4]

A more theoretical case against reform was made by Friedrich Hayek.[5] Although firmly in the (classical) liberal political tradition and someone who was to later express the reasons as to why he was 'not a conservative' given conservatism's tendency to compromise with social forces,[6] his arguments were in line with those who opposed the projected growth in the size, powers and functions of the state after 1945. Hayek argued that these plans for reconstruction were based on a false prospectus of 'social justice'.[7] Social justice did not exist because there were, in fact, competing claims of social justice, each necessitating different patterns of distribution. There was no way of settling which of these claims was the correct one since they were, in turn, based on subjective moral reasoning. The result would be an almost infinite demand from different groups for more government resources. While government direction of economy and society was both possible and necessary in times of crisis, such as the Second World War—where there was a shared purpose in defeating a common enemy—there was no such shared purpose in times of peace as individuals would prefer to pursue their own version of the good. Hayek's arguments boosted the intellectual case of the Conservative Right in their opposition to the welfare state. However, Hayek's thesis was predicated on value pluralism. The Conservative Right therefore had to look elsewhere to find 'moral' reasons to oppose the welfare state.

An alternative line of argument came from Richard Law, who was explicit in his moralistic case against welfare reform.[8] For Law (later Lord Coleraine) the proposals for postwar society marked the end of civilisation. Civilisation rested upon people being able to make decisions for themselves and to reap the rewards or face the consequences of their own actions. The welfare state undermined the sense of individual responsibility which was enshrined in the poor law. People would be protected from the consequences of their own actions by the provision of universal welfare as of right. The result would be a dependency culture with people unable to act responsibly as they would not have to face the consequences of their actions. What was happening, he said, was 'the collapse of all absolute moral values, the end of man as a moral being'.[9]

The same theme was voiced by the Marquess of Salisbury.[10] People had a responsibility to work. 'In particular I consider that the spectacle of young men and women living on the dole is deplorable' he said.[11] Salisbury argued that it would be better for the private sector to provide employment, but that the state should find work for those unemployed thus that 'it should...be a condition of the provision of such state work that no applicant should be entitled to refuse any reasonable work assigned to him or her'.[12] Occasionally people may find themselves unemployed. Conservatives should have sympathy for the unemployed but this did not equate to endorsing a more generous welfare system. Instead, the focus should be on individual responsibility.

> Insecurity is unfortunately an essential condition of human life. We cannot, I am afraid, altogether avoid it. Admittedly, indeed, it is a great, if not the greatest, stimulus to effort, and we do not want, it is true, a nation of waiters upon Providence or even upon state assistance.[13]

Moreover, the welfare state could not be a substitute for the family. As Frederick Sykes said: 'the family is the foundation of society; its influence cannot be replaced or superseded by any other force'.[14] The concern was, therefore, that the welfare state would erode family values and individual responsibility. This was an early postwar expression of what would later be seen as Thatcherism.

A further argument that was made by those who opposed the welfare state was that welfare was not a proper function of the state. The state, according to Utley, was concerned with the protection of the nation from external threat and the preservation of civil peace. By extending its functions the state was diverting its attentions from these essential tasks.[15] However, just as he argued that there was no alternative viable political option but to accept the mixed economy so too he believed of the new welfare state.[16]

Opponents of the welfare state, expressed their view that society was better organised along paternalistic lines rather than compulsion. Welfare was better understood as a function of charity where individuals and organisations could decide who was worthy of support and who was not. Historically, the churches had fulfilled this role. Charity could not, however, be provided by the state. Charitable acts required voluntarily giving to those deemed needy. It was a private act based on free choice. However, the state worked through compulsion. People did not have a choice as to whether or not they gave away part of their income in taxation. They were compelled to do so. Hence, the sense of paternalism which had existed before the creation of the welfare state had been lost. As Peregrine Worsthorne said the person enjoying the trappings of wealth under these conditions, 'will not regard these advantages as in any way imposing on him a debt of social responsibility... The existence of the welfare state makes any such feeling of paternalism seem absurdly old-fashioned.'[17] The new society was underpinned by an egalitarianism which did not respect privilege. Hence, the rich person would simply keep quiet about his/her wealth which 'requires neither gratitude nor repayment'. However, the new egalitarian ethos would not ensure social solidarity in the way that the old order could rely on through its call for patriotism:

> Of course he (the recipient of welfare) likes to get his social services as a dog feels grateful for his bone. But there is no poetry in a national health service; nothing to set the heart racing as it does to the sound of fife and drum.[18]

Enoch Powell argued that the welfare state required greater application of means testing.[19] Towards the end of the Labour Government, an element of means testing was introduced into the NHS. For Powell and Iain Macleod this was 'more than minor significance'.[20] It undermined the idea of a free, universal system of welfare in the UK. The Labour Left agreed, provoking Aneurin Bevan's resignation. They wanted to maintain a free and universal service. But Powell (Macleod seems to have had little input into their pamphlet, *Social Services: Needs and Means*) argued that means testing was a desirable thing.[21] The original notion of the welfare state was that it would be based on the contributory principle—National Insurance—with a lower level of poverty relief available for those who had not contributed sufficiently, National Assistance. However, the expansion of the welfare state under Attlee meant that more people were in receipt of National Assistance than had been in receipt of its equivalent in 1900. The welfare state was failing in its aim of reducing poverty, measured by this statistic. However, for Powell the idea of means testing needed to be extended. The Labour Government had introduced means testing tentatively. It would remain on the margins of the welfare state. Instead, they argued, the approach should be not whether a means test should be applied to certain benefits but why certain benefits should not be means tested. The welfare state was in crisis and the application of means testing was 'imperative'. Welfare payments would become derisory unless they were means tested.[22] The call for reform was met with little support since means testing still invoked images in the minds of the electorate of the poor law and the work-house.

Not all on the right-wing of the Conservative Party subscribed to the view that the welfare state created dependency, however. One notable exception was Angus Maude.[23] He accepted that there were cases of benefit fraud, but then again there were at any time in history: 'society has always contained a proportion of people who are idle, irresponsible or unscrupulous'.[24] Just as there were those who cheated the welfare state, so too there had been those who had cheated all pre-existing forms of welfare. They were, however, very much the minority. It would be wrong to tarnish the entire system because of this, and it would be too costly to try to eliminate the undeserving from the system. Moreover, the fact that there were such people is itself a reflection of the fact that the modern economy had produced such levels of alienation. People were no longer ends in themselves, but rather fodder for the productive process. This was bound to lead to resentment. The best way to tackle the issue was through reform of the economy away from large scale production, back to meaningful employment.

That voices of opposition were marginalised after 1945 was not surprising to a party with a desire to be re-elected to office at the first available opportunity. Postwar Conservative governments presided over this enlarged welfare state. Indeed, Macmillan, as Housing Minister in the 1950s Conservative government, had boasted of its achievements in this area, building more houses than the previous Labour administration. It was not to be until the election of Margaret Thatcher that the Conservative critique of the welfare state was to be taken up once again.

RESTORING THE VICTORIAN VIRTUES?

The Thatcherite critique of the welfare state rested on both moral and economic grounds. The economic case was that monolithic public services were inefficient and needed to be opened up to competition. The economic theories underpinning this were discussed in the preceding chapter. Of more relevance to this chapter was the moral critique that the welfare state had undermined individual responsibility and created a dependency culture. This change of attitude was apparent when urban riots broke out in inner-city areas. These areas were known for their levels of poverty and unemployment, and the riots also had a racial dimension owing to the fact that there was a high proportion of ethnic minority residents in areas such as Brixton in London, Moss Side in Manchester and Toxteth in Liverpool. The election of the Thatcher Government led to the adoption of monetarist economics with a consequent rise in unemployment. The official committee of enquiry, under Lord Scarman, reported that the causes of the riots were indeed social and economic, with emphasis being attached to the high correlation between poverty and unemployment. For critics of Thatcherism—including those in her own party—this showed how out of touch her own approach was to these issues.

However, Thatcher and her supporters would have none of this. Thatcher said that, 'we are reaping what was sown in the Sixties. The fashionable theories and permissive claptrap set the scene for a society in which the old virtues of discipline and self-restraint were denigrated'.[25] The new, tougher attitude was prominent in the Conservative Party Conference of 1981 in Norman Tebbit's speech: 'I grew up in the '30s with an unemployed father. He didn't riot, he got on his bike and looked for work and he kept looking until he found it'.[26] Rather than seeking to explain the riotous behaviour in social terms, the focus here was very much on individual responsibility. The theme was further emphasised in Thatcher's memoirs when she visited Toxteth once the riots were over. She quickly dismissed the focus on social and economic causes. It was not possible, she believed, that boredom (caused through unemployment) was a cause as those who had rioted had plenty to do cleaning their homes and tending to their gardens.

> They had plenty of constructive things to do if they wanted. Instead, I asked myself how people could live in such circumstances without trying to clear up the mess and improve their surroundings. What was clearly lacking was a sense of pride and personal responsibility – something which the state can easily remove but almost never give back.[27]

For her supporters it showed that they were right to distrust the 'establishment' which they felt was imbued with liberal ideology. Alan Clark noted in his diary that he was not surprised by the recent unrest.[28] Indeed, he felt that it was directly caused by the failure to clamp down on those who had rioted in 1980 in Bristol: 'all this was totally predictable once it was apparent that the people who rioted in St Pauls, Bristol had been handled with kid-gloves... Indeed, I am surprised that it has taken so long for the practice to spread.'[29] The Scarman report had not helped 'with his constant sniping at the police and dreary toleration of endless monologues about social deprivation etc'.[30] The idea that there was a causal link between the riots and unemployment was, Clark felt, 'totally spurious of course'.[31] Utley argued that the riots had demonstrated that:

> Respect for law in these islands is, to put it mildly, no longer something to be taken for granted... You get riots in the inner cities, and the instant response, perhaps not of the people but of many of their self-appointed spokesmen, is not to deplore it, save perfunctorily and ceremonially, but to ask us to examine and remove its causes.[32]

The emphasis on the different outlooks of the 'people' and the elites was also stressed by Charles Moore, who argued that, 'the public were deeply shocked by the scale of the violence, and were disposed, unlike the metropolitan elites, to blame it on the people who had rioted'.[33]

Writing three years before the riots about which Utley spoke, Peregrine Worsthorne said that Britain was suffering from too much freedom:

If one were to probe into the hearts of many potential and actual Tory supporters - and others besides - one might well discover that what worried them most about contemporary Britain was not so much the lack of freedom as its excessive abundance; not so much the threat of dictatorship as the reality of something unpleasantly close to chaos.[34]

The underlying cause of this was that the welfare state had encouraged people to have too much sympathy for the underdog. 'While it is perfectly proper for a society to think *about* the unfortunate' he said, 'it must never be encouraged to think *like* them.'[35] The recession of the early 1980s was welcome to the extent that it undermined the welfare state. In its place would come private charity. However, he also felt that there was still too much fraud in the system, from which the undeserving poor benefitted:

The truth is that vast sums do still get spent on cases which most people would regard as undeserving; on anti-social bums who by no stretch of the imagination deserve help, many of whom even social workers would regard as utterly irredeemable, so far gone as to be beyond the bounds of even pity.[36]

One of Thatcher's key intellectual supporters, Shirley Letwin, claimed that Thatcherism was a moral project.[37] Letwin believed that at heart, Thatcherism had a conception of the individual: 'the individual preferred by Thatcherism is...upright, self-sufficient, energetic, adventurous, independent-minded, loyal to friends and robust against enemies'.[38] These were the 'vigorous virtues'.[39] There were essentially two kinds of virtues, what Letwin called the 'softer' and the 'vigorous' virtues. The softer virtues included things such as 'kindness, humility, gentleness, sympathy, cheerfulness'.[40] While there was nothing wrong with such virtues they would ultimately be destructive of the social order if they were extended too far. This is what had happened by the 1970s: 'Thatcherism has seen Britain at the end of the twentieth century as a place in which the softer virtues have been too much stressed and the vigorous virtues insufficiently regarded'.[41] The result was an overloaded state and a decline in individual responsibility as people looked to government rather than themselves for help. Thatcher had recognised this and had sought to revive the vigorous virtues, including self-help, thrift and hard work. 'Thatcherism has always been a "vigorous" creed' Letwin explained, 'in the sense not that it wishes to abolish the softer virtues but that it emphasises the vigorous virtues, and if necessary, where conflicts arise, at the expense of the softer virtues'.[42] Her policies may have had an overwhelmingly economic focus but the real goal was a moral one, the restoration of the vigorous virtues. Thatcher preferred instead to talk of the 'Victorian values', ones which she believed had been instilled in her by her father. The phrase had been given to her in an interview with Brian Walden in 1983.[43] For Thatcher, the Victorian era was when Britain became a great country. 'As our people prospered' she opined 'so they used their independence and initiative to prosper others, not compulsion by the state'.[44]

Further support for Thatcher's approach came from underclass theorists. Underclass theory emerged initially in the USA. Theorists such as Lawrence Mead and Charles Murray argued that the welfare state created an underclass, a group of people separated from mainstream society not just by their levels of wealth and income but also by morals since they refused to share the morality of the rest of the society.[45] Both argued that the principal cause of this was the welfare state, which had eroded individual responsibility. For Murray the solution was to make welfare provision much more financially unattractive. People would then, rationally, engage in the labour market where they would stand to gain material benefit. In contrast, Mead argued that there needed to be greater conditionality attached to welfare claims making it less attractive to apply for welfare and to make it more difficult to be approved for receipt of welfare. These, initially American, arguments permeated British politics when Murray was invited to speak in the UK by the Institute of Economic Affairs.[46]

Thatcher had sought to restate her moral outlook in an interview for *Woman's Own* magazine in 1987 when she stated that people need to look to themselves rather than to the 'society':

> They are casting their problems on society and who is society? There is no such thing! There are individual men and women and there are families and no government can do anything except through people and people look to themselves first.[47]

This was a clear statement of the Conservative Right view after the Second World War and in response to the riots. The welfare state undermined the social fabric and sense of individual responsibility. Hayek said that 'the adjective "social" is probably the most confusing and misleading term of our whole political vocabulary'. It had come to mean, and to justify, almost anything.[48]

Many, including some on the moderate wing of her own party, regarded this as highlighting the harshness of Thatcher personally and the political project which bore her name. Indeed, it became so notorious that it has continued to cast a shadow long after her departure. David Cameron sought to demonstrate that he had moved the Party on from her day by labelling his own strategy as 'the Big Society'.[49] He argued that it was different from Thatcherism which had an excessive individualism and also from New Labour which had equated the needs of society with those of the state. However, for some this was a misreading of Thatcher's intentions. Her supporters claimed that what she had in fact meant by this statement was that people should look first and foremost to themselves and that individuals had responsibility to their own family.

It was not just Thatcher's opponents to the left who criticised her 'no such thing as society' comment but also her critics on the right. For some it showed the predominance of neo-liberal advisers close to Thatcher and the ideas permeating from think tanks such as the Institute of Economic Affairs (IEA), which had proposed a range of pro-market reforms which the Thatcher governments had taken up with enthusiasm.[50] This had long been a concern for those of a more traditionalist perspective. The Salisbury Group had been set up in 1976 to oppose what it regarded as the liberal bias of the new Conservatism.[51] Instead, it aimed to promote political, cultural and social conservatism. Roger Scruton argued instead that conservatism, properly understood, did hold to a notion of the collective.[52] However, this was a view of society (or community) which was very different from that of the left. Instead of seeing society as an arena in which 'justice' was pursued to correct perceived unfairnesses based around inequality, society was naturally hierarchical and unequal with everyone holding a particular position in relation to everyone else, with that position bestowing certain liberties but also responsibilities to others. Such a conception of society led one to reject both the egalitarianism of the left and also the individualism of the economic liberals. It may entail more government intervention than the latter and different forms of intervention from the former. For instance, the egalitarians had sought to extend the comprehensive school model to further their wish for greater equality but traditional conservatives should recognise the value of a hierarchical education system in a society of marked, and natural, inequalities. Similarly, the need to provide a safety net of welfare and a strong system of public order may mean more intervention than economic liberals would allow and this should be paid for by those most able to afford it. This was a theory of society which Mrs Thatcher could have adopted but she was too susceptible to the influence of economic liberalism.[53]

The controversy which Thatcher's 'no such thing as society' remark created meant that she would have to set out in greater clarity and detail her social philosophy. The opportunity was provided by an invitation to speak at the General Synod of the Church of Scotland in 1988.[54] The speech was always going to be difficult, not least because of the falling stock of the Conservatives north of the border but also the theological differences which existed between Thatcher and her supporters on the one hand and the liberal theologians in the churches on the other, something which had been highlighted in the *Faith in the City* report of the Catholic and Anglican bishops of Liverpool which argued for extended welfare provision amongst other things. Some on the Right felt that there was a clear left-wing bias in the Church of England.

She argued that Christianity had little to do with social reform and the provision of welfare. The liberal clergy had been expressing opinions on all sorts of issues which were political not religious. Critics on the Right had been pointing this out for some time. Ronald Butt highlighted this: 'to many, this general approach seems unacceptably political'[55] and the political adherence was to 'pre-1979 social and economic assumptions and practices'.[56] Instead it had everything to do with salvation:

> We must not profess the Christian faith and go to Church simply because we want social reforms and benefits or a better standard of behaviour; but because we accept the sanctity of life, the responsibility that comes with freedom and the supreme sacrifice of Christ.[57]

She pointedly said that 'we Parliamentarians can legislate for the rule of law. You, the Church, can teach the life of faith.'[58] The role of the clergy was not to interfere in politics. Those who had called her policies immoral were wrong. There was an alternative theological justification to her agenda. The example of the parable of the Good Samaritan was presented as justification.[59] While those on the left had often held this to be a justification for redistribution to Thatcher it was more the fact that the Samaritan had first created his wealth and then that he was choosing what to do with it.

A key influence on her speech was Brian Griffiths, who had been the Head of the Number Ten Policy Unit since mid-1985.[60] Griffiths also believed that the welfare state had created a dependency culture. By restricting state provision, charitable acts would be encouraged. Thatcherism was not—as her critics had characterised it—survival of the fittest. Instead, it was 'in the nineteenth century tradition which always sought to place wealth creation in an effective legal and institutional framework and emphasise our shared responsibility to help others who could not help themselves.'[61] Markets were desirable since 'wherever (they) are allowed to work, the result is an increase in prosperity and jobs'.[62] A market economy would encourage self-help and compassion for those less fortunate. Griffiths argued that Thatcherism aimed to promote 'a sense of personal duty and self-reliance and...a personal obligation to those in need'.[63] There was nothing selfish about Thatcherism and nothing immoral. The critics in the Church were misguided: 'I have always believed...that advocacy of monetarist economic policies is perfectly compatible with a Christian view of the world' he wrote in the mid 1980s when Thatcherism was at its peak.[64] Moreover, 'it is because the Christian faith has such a high view of the dignity of man, created in the image of God, that it also has such a positive view of work and wealth creation'.[65] Lowering taxes would encourage more charitable giving, a laudable Christian aim. After all, America had a lower tax base and more philanthropy. He subsequently admitted, however, that he had been overoptimistic as lowering taxes had not significantly increased charitable donations.[66]

Critics believed that the expansion of the free market in the 1980s had done nothing to tackle personal irresponsibility. Ian Crowther argued that, 'Mrs Thatcher's admiration for the Victorian Virtues...should awaken conservatives to the realisation that the state is not their only enemy. They have inherited, along with the socialist state, the unsocialised individual.'[67] At first, Crowther was willing to give Thatcher the benefit of the doubt that she did intend to revive individual responsibility. However, as time went on he became more critical: 'while Thatcherism has delivered the material goods, the moral have proved more illusive. The asocial individual is still with us'.[68] Merrie Cave also concluded that Thatcher had tried, but failed, to restore individual responsibility: 'the tragedy of the Thatcher years was the refusal to realise that the welfare state had deprived people of responsibility for themselves'.[69] The attempt to restore the vigorous virtues was always likely to fail since the social fabric which had underpinned this set of values in Victorian times had disappeared. As Crowther put it, 'what we have been seeing under Mrs Thatcher is the re-establishment of the free-market economy in moral circumstances far less propitious than those which prevailed a hundred years or more ago'.[70] Peregrine Worsthorne believed that Thatcher had 'set out to create a country in the image of her father but ended up creating one in the image of her son'.[71] All she had succeeded in doing was to promote individualism and materialism. The new rich who had made quick returns in the City and were keen to flaunt it were 'vulgar, loud-mouthed, drunken yobboes, scarcely better, if at all, than football hooligans.'[72]

The impact on policy was initially limited. Thatcher prioritised economic policy, with the adoption of monetarism, measures to restrict the power of trade unions and privatisation of state owned industries. However, by the third term of her government she was beginning to tackle welfare reform with measures to increase both choice and responsibility in the welfare state. Her removal from office in 1990 meant that the welfare reform agenda had by that stage only had limited impact. The No Turning Back Group said in 1990 that, 'having begun cautiously to reform the internal market structure of the welfare state, we believe that the Conservative Party should take heart and make a great leap forward'.[73] On this logic, much was left for John Major's Government. His notable reform was the introduction of Jobseekers' Allowance in place of unemployment benefit in 1996. The new social security benefit would be conditional upon the claimant being able to show that he or she was actively seeking employment. The following Labour administration continued with this more stricter system of welfare policy. For the Conservative Right, much more was still needed in this area of policy. Writing in 2001, Roger Scruton believed that, 'indiscriminate welfare produces crime, family breakdown, illegitimacy and drug abuse'.[74] He acknowledged that there had been a move towards workfare in place of welfare, which was desirable: 'this return to the ethos of the work-house has much to recommend it'.[75] However, it did not tackle the root cause which was illegitimacy. The expanding welfare state was not the cause of 'our social disease' but rather a symptom.[76]

Iain Duncan Smith sought to capture the concept of social justice from the Left. Whereas Hayek had felt that social justice was a mirage, Duncan Smith believed that it could be used to justify a concern with social responsibility. He established the Centre for Social Justice in 2004. Its report, *Breakthrough Britain*, published in 2007, highlighted numerous social problems.[77] Britain had the highest level of divorce and lone parenthood in Europe. There was a relationship between this and crime with seven out of ten young offenders coming from lone parent families. Approximately 3.5 million people were in receipt of benefits which placed no responsibilities on them to find work. There was significant educational under attainment of white boys. Personal debt had reached new heights and was higher than in the rest of Europe. Finally, there was little charitable giving. Welfare reforms would need to strengthen the family and encourage individual responsibility.

Duncan Smith then served as Secretary of State for Work and Pensions. The main reform was the establishment of Universal Credit, which was intended to be a simplification of the benefits system and to foster a stronger sense of social responsibility. However, the measure has been roundly criticised for its failures. In the contemporary welfare state, the Conservatives are still grappling with the same issues discussed at length throughout this chapter, namely how to foster a stronger sense of social responsibility within the welfare state and how to balance the competing demands of social welfare and economic liberalism.

NOTES

1. M. Oakeshott, 'The Masses in Representative Democracy', in T. Fuller (ed.) *Rationalism in Politics and Other Essays* (Indianapolis: Liberty, 1991).
2. See N. Timmins, *The Five Giants: A Biography of the Welfare State* (London: HarperCollins, 2001).
3. M. Oakeshott, 'Contemporary British Politics', *The Cambridge Journal*, 1/8 (May 1948), p. 476.
4. Ibid.
5. F. Hayek, *The Road to Serfdom* (London: Routledge & Kegan Paul, 1944).
6. F. Hayek, *The Constitution of Liberty* (London: Routledge, 1960).

7. F. Hayek, *Law, Legislation and Liberty—Volume Two: The Mirage of Social Justice* (London: Routledge, 1976).
8. R. Law, *Return from Utopia* (London: Faber and Faber, 1950).
9. Ibid., p. 29.
10. The 5th Marquess of Salisbury, *Post-War Conservative Policy* (London: Murray, 1942).
11. Ibid., p. 10.
12. Ibid.
13. Ibid., p. 11.
14. F. Sykes, *Roads to Recovery* (London: Signpost Booklets, 1944), p. 16.
15. T. E. Utley, *Essays in Conservatism* (London: Conservative Political Centre, 1949).
16. See J. Stapleton, 'T. E. Utley and Renewal of Conservatism in Post-War Britain', *Journal of Political Ideologies*, 19/2 (2014), pp. 207–226.
17. P. Worsthorne, 'Class and Conflict in British Foreign Policy', *Foreign Affairs*, 37/3 (1959), p. 427.
18. P. Worsthorne, *Peregrinations* (London: Weidenfeld and Nicolson, 1980), p. 118.
19. I. Macleod and E. Powell, *Social Services: Needs and Means* (London: Conservative Political Centre, 1954).
20. Ibid., Preface.
21. S. Heffer, *Like the Roman* (London: Weidenfeld and Nicolson, 1998), p. 175.
22. Macleod and Powell, *Social Services*.
23. A. Maude, *The Common Problem* (London: Constable, 1969).
24. Ibid., p. 179.
25. Quoted in B. Pilbeam, 'Social Morality', in K. Hickson (ed.) *The Political Thought of the Conservative Party Since 1945* (Basingstoke: Palgrave, 2005), p. 165.
26. Available at https://www.youtube.com/watch?v=sU_pDM1N7i0, accessed 11 May 2019.
27. M. Thatcher, *The Downing Street Years* (London: HarperCollins, 1993), p. 145.
28. A. Clark, *Diaries: Into Politics* (London: Weidenfeld and Nicolson, 2000).
29. Ibid., p. 239.
30. Ibid.
31. Ibid., p. 242.
32. T. E. Utley, *One Nation One Hundred Years On* (London: Conservative Political Centre, 1981), p. 15.
33. C. Moore, *Margaret Thatcher: The Authorised Biography, Volume One: Not for Turning* (London: Allen Lane, 2013), p. 632.
34. P. Worsthorne, 'Too Much Freedom', in M. Cowling (ed.) *Conservative Essays* (London: Cassell, 1978), p. 147.

35. Ibid., p. 153.
36. P. Worsthorne, *By the Right* (Dublin: Brophy, 1987), p. 28.
37. S. Letwin, *The Anatomy of Thatcherism* (London: Fontana, 1992).
38. Ibid., pp. 32–33.
39. Ibid., p. 33.
40. Ibid.
41. Ibid.
42. Ibid.
43. C. Moore, *Margaret Thatcher: The Authorised Biography, Volume 2— Everything She Wants* (London: Allen Lane, 2015), p. 8.
44. Quoted in ibid., p. 9.
45. C. Murray, *Losing Ground: American Social Policy, 1950–1980* (New York: Basic, 1984); L. Mead, *Beyond Entitlement: The Social Obligations of Citizenship* (New York: Free Press, 1986).
46. C. Murray, *The Emerging British Underclass* (London: IEA Health and Welfare Unit, 1990).
47. M. Thatcher, interview for *Woman's Own*, 23 September 1987, available at https://www.margaretthatcher.org/document/106689, accessed 11 May 2019.
48. F. Hayek, 'The Weasel Word "Social"', in R. Scruton (ed.) *Conservative Thoughts: Essays from the Salisbury Review* (London: Claridge, 1988).
49. D. Cameron speech, 10 November 2009, available at https://conservative-speeches.sayit.mysociety.org/speech/601246, accessed 11 May 2019.
50. R. Scruton, *The Meaning of Conservatism* (Basingstoke: Palgrave, 2001, 3rd edition), p. 91.
51. Cowling (ed.) *Conservative Essays*.
52. R. Scruton, *The Conservative Idea of Community* (London: Conservative 2000 Foundation, 1996).
53. R. Scruton, *How to Be a Conservative* (London: Bloomsbury, 2014), pp. 8–9.
54. M. Thatcher, Speech to General Assembly of the Church of Scotland, 21 May 1988, available at https://www.margaretthatcher.org/document/107246, accessed 11 May 2019.
55. R. Butt, 'The Tension of the 1980s', in M. Alison and D. Edwards (eds.) *Christianity and Conservatism* (London: Hodder and Stoughton, 1990), p. 40.
56. Ibid.
57. Thatcher, Speech to General Assembly of the Church of Scotland.
58. Ibid.
59. See E. Filby, *God and Mrs Thatcher: The Battle for Britain's Soul* (London: Biteback, 2015).

60. B. Griffiths, 'The Conservative Quadrilateral', in Alison and Edwards (eds.) *Christianity and Conservatism*.
61. Ibid., p. 218.
62. Ibid., p. 232.
63. Ibid., p. 241.
64. B. Griffiths, *Monetarism and Morality* (London: Centre for Policy Studies, 1985), p. 8.
65. Ibid., p. 17.
66. Interview with Lord Griffiths, London, 6 April 2017.
67. I. Crowther, 'Mrs Thatcher's Idea of the Good Society', *The Salisbury Review* (Spring 1983), p. 42.
68. I. Crowther, 'Thatcherism and the Good Life', *The Salisbury Review*, 8/1 (September 1989), p. 4.
69. M. Cave, 'Victorian Lessons', *The Salisbury Review* 14/1 (September 1995), p. 54.
70. Crowther, 'Thatcherism and the Good Life', p. 6.
71. Quoted in Filby, *God and Mrs Thatcher*, p. 348.
72. P. Worsthorne, *The Politics of Manners and the Uses of Inequality* (London: Centre for Policy Studies, 1988), p. 9.
73. No Turning Back Group, *Choice and Responsibility in the Welfare State* (London: Conservative Political Centre, 1990), p. 18.
74. Scruton, *The Meaning of Conservatism*, p. 172.
75. Ibid.
76. Scruton, *The Conservative Idea of Community*, p. 15.
77. Centre for Social Justice, *Breakthrough Britain: Ending the Costs of Social Breakdown*, available at https://www.centreforsocialjustice.org. uk/core/wp-content/uploads/2016/08/BBChairmansOverview.pdf, accessed 11 May 2019.

Society

The aim of this chapter is to explore Conservative Right attitudes to social reform. Generally, the Right adopted socially conservative attitudes. This has led them to frequently be critical of their own party when in power. Even during the Thatcher years the extent to which the Conservative Party had adopted social conservatism is open to debate, while at other times the Conservative Party has enthusiastically embraced socially liberal measures.

For the Conservative Right, the period since 1945, and especially since the 1960s had been one of moral decline. Traditional morality had been deliberately undermined by political action. Much of the blame for this was placed, naturally enough, at Labour's door. The Labour governments of 1964–1970 had endorsed a number of measures which directly challenged traditional moral codes, which had stressed individual restraint. Much of this legislation had emerged from individual backbench MP's in the form of Private Members Bills. Such measures stand little chance of passing through the House of Commons, however, and so without the support of Ministers it would not have succeeded. The principal enthusiast for such reform was Roy Jenkins as Home Secretary between 1965 and 1967.[1] Rather than appearing as formal government policy, therefore, the measures were introduced by backbench MP's. Such measures would not therefore divide the two major political parties into two opposing blocks. Moreover, much of this legislation was deemed to be votes of personal conscience and so no whipping was involved. Members of Parliament had free votes. Finally, it meant that

© The Author(s) 2020
K. Hickson, *Britain's Conservative Right since 1945*,
https://doi.org/10.1007/978-3-030-27697-3_9

163

much of this legislation was passed without being subject to the ratification of the people in either a General Election or a referendum. For critics of these reforms they were in effect giving licence for all sorts of behaviour which had previously not been deemed morally acceptable, that its long-term effects were far more serious than anything which the government had carried out in terms of economic policy, and that this was all done without the people even being consulted.

However, a closer inspection reveals that the actions of the Labour governments between 1964 and 1970 had been anticipated by the previous Conservative administration. Both Harold Macmillan (Prime Minister between 1957 and 1963) and R. A. Butler (Home Secretary for much the same period) had initiated liberal social reforms.[2] These measures were quite limited at first given the resistance they faced within their own party but, nonetheless, the sense of direction was clear on a whole range of measures. Butler argued that there was a need to shake off the 'Victorian corsetry' in measures related to the family and censorship while also adopting a more humane approach to law and order. Although later Conservatives were to blame social liberalism and its perceived consequences firmly on the Labour governments of Harold Wilson, the contemporary Conservative Right recognised the direction which the Conservatives had taken and didn't like it. Blame was placed not just on these prominent individuals but also the Bow Group, which had led calls for a more liberal direction in social morality. The Monday Club was established to oppose the liberal direction of the Conservative Party, not just in terms of the enthusiasm for decolonisation, as discussed earlier in this book, but also in terms of the liberal agenda in social morality. From 1961 the Monday Club became a leading exponent of traditional social morality.

Moreover, there had also been a trend towards such reforms within the Labour Party. Revisionists argued that a future Labour government needed to embrace social reform of this kind as socialism was concerned not just with economic matters, which Tony Crosland, for instance, argued, with an optimism he was later to reject, had been largely dealt with, but also the promotion of greater freedom in the moral sphere.

THE CHALLENGE OF SOCIAL LIBERALISM

The theoretical case against the liberal social moral agenda consists of critiques of certain aspects of liberalism. For T. E. Utley the philosophical underpinning of liberal social reform was the distinction made by John

Stuart Mill between self-regarding and other-regarding conduct.[3] Conduct which affected only the individuals concerned should not be subject to legal restraint even if society disapproved of such actions. Only individual conduct which affected the interests of others should be subject to regulation. Action which fell into self-regarding conduct could be subject to moral pressure from the wider community but should not be subject to law. This would allow for the minimisation of coercion and the maximum degree of individual liberty. The application of this theoretical approach to social matters in the 1960s led reformers to argue that things such as homosexual acts between two consenting adults, divorce or the reading/viewing of pornography were private matters which should be no concern of the law of the land. Much of the so-called permissive legislation of the 1960s was promoted using this line of argument Utley believed.

However, for Utley, the approach was deeply flawed. He argued that 'it is part of the state's business to promote morality'.[4] There were numerous problems with Mill's approach and Utley drew on the arguments of Mill's great critic Sir James Fitzjames Stephen, who argued that the distinction between self—and other-regarding conduct did not stand up to scrutiny. Many forms of action which may initially be regarded as self-regarding did in fact have wider implications for society. Divorce may have an impact on the children of the divorced parents. Opponents of reform to laws on censorship and pornography believed that graphic portrayals of sex and violence had a negative impact on those reading or watching it and fuelled sex crimes. The distinction did not therefore hold between the two forms of conduct. Ian Crowther picked up the argument in *The Salisbury Review* three decades later: 'libertarians are fond of invoking Mill's distinction between "self-regarding" and "other regarding" actions as a reason for the state's remaining morally neutral. In fact very few actions are without their social consequences and costs'.[5] As such, society had a legitimate right to restrict matters which may be deemed by some to be ones of private morality. Other matters therefore needed to be taken into account by law makers including the likely harm which may result from a change in the law, the effects of the current law and the possibility of enforcing any change in the law. Such considerations would be likely to result in greater continuity in the established laws than to introduce reforms.

Margaret Thatcher approached these matters as distinct issues. She was personally in favour of the restoration of the death penalty. However, she took a more liberal line on divorce due mainly to the fact that she had married a divorcee.

Writing more as a historian of moral change in Britain than as a contemporary commentator, Christie Davies argued that the liberal underpinning to social reform had been rather different. He claimed that the key influence had been a certain form of utilitarianism, which he called causalism.[6] The basis of utilitarian thought is the maximisation of individual pleasure and the minimisation of harm. Social arrangements should be geared to achieving these objectives and reformed where necessary. Rather than promoting social reform in the 1960s on the explicit basis of rights, reformers argued that their favoured measures would reduce known harm. For instance, divorce law reform would allow failed marriages—perhaps where the wife is subject to domestic abuse at the hands of her aggressive husband—to be ended more easily. Abortion law reform was justified less as a right of the mother—as has since been the main justification for not restricting abortion—but rather to end the known harm which illegal abortion clinics were causing. Moreover, both of these instances were linked to social justice in that the rich wife seeking a divorce could afford legal advice or the wealthy pregnant woman could afford a better performed, if still illegal, abortion than a poorer woman who would have to go to someone who was not trained and likely to cause either physical harm and/or infection.

For Davies causalism was a specific form of utilitarian argument which focused only on harm and not pleasure and which examined only the short-term consequences of action and not the possible longer-term effects. None of the measures which were being advocated concerned pleasure. The long-term effects of measures to ease divorce may well be harmful in much the same way as Utley argued that they may well have an impact on others, namely the offspring of divorced parents. Moreover, it could be argued that the existence of traditional moral codes were less likely to cause harm in the long-run. The opposing mode of thought to causalism was moralism. Davies concluded that many of the reforms which had taken place were, in themselves, beneficial. They had extended individual freedom and created more civilised conditions. However, this had been at the expense of de-moralising society. In place of a community bound together by shared experiences and moral outlook there was now considerable alienation. Community had broken down and been replaced by atomised individualism. While some strong individuals may thrive in such an environment many felt isolated and this sense of isolation would cause more harm than that which reforms had been designed to solve.

A further critique of liberal social reform was that by John Selwyn Gummer.[7] Again, he was not opposed to all reforms. Instead he argued that each should be treated on its own merits. However, what had happened was the polarisation into two camps of those who were pro-reform and those who were anti-reform. As the former claimed to be more enlightened it developed the aura of moral absolutism. Those who opposed any measure of reform were portrayed as reactionary and prejudiced. Reform was therefore 'correct' and conservation was 'incorrect'. A similar point was to be stressed later by opponents of what has been termed 'political correctness'. That only certain ideas, policies and language are acceptable.

For Peregrine Worsthorne, however, the rise of the permissive society did not mean more political freedom but less, since the new issues were harder to resolve and required authoritative political leadership: 'not unemployment but immigration, not poverty but permissiveness, not corporation tax but capital punishment, not S.E.T. but SEX, not the cost of living but the crime rate. It is the moral issues, not the material ones, that increasingly arouse the deepest passions'.[8]

In terms of the specific reforms these can be broken down into two broad areas. The first is punishment, notably the debate over the death penalty. Secondly, what the Right saw as permissive legislation: pro-life issues (especially abortion but also euthanasia and embryo research), homosexuality, divorce and censorship.

PUNISHMENT

Since the end of the Second World War, the Conservative Right has invariably been on the side of defending tougher approaches to law and order. This was most apparent in debates over the abolition of the death penalty.[9] In April 1948 the House of Commons voted in favour of a bill to suspend the death penalty for a period of five years. However, the measure was defeated in the House of Lords. A Royal Commission was established to investigate the matter. This reported in 1953 and paved the way for the 1957 bill. This bill, introduced by Butler, created different categories of murder. Butler was an abolitionist and the measure was a compromise recognising that the majority of Conservative MPs were in favour of retention. The annual party conference became a scene for confrontation between the party hierarchy, which was predominantly liberal in outlook on these issues, and the grassroots. The latter argued for the retention of the death penalty and even for the restoration of corporal punishment. The Act was deemed unworkable and inevitably led to further reform.

A bill to abolish the death penalty was introduced by Sydney Silverman in 1964, coming into law the following year despite some Conservative opposition. There had been a number of highly publicised cases which had undermined public confidence in hanging. The new Act had effect for five years. This became permanent four years later. While not all of the Conservative Right were in favour of retaining the death penalty—Enoch Powell was a notable example of someone who was on the Right of the Conservative Party but favoured abolition—retentionists were largely confined to the Conservative Right. They argued their case on one of two grounds. The first was that there was a moral case for retention of the death penalty based on the belief that life of man was a gift given by God and that it was therefore a mortal sin for an individual to take another person's life. The more common argument, however, was that the death penalty acted as a deterrent. This changing argument of the retentionists reflected the wider shift from moralism to causalism according to Davies for it rested not on the perceived rights and wrongs of the action but the likely consequences of removing the death penalty.

Restorationists have continued to argue that the death penalty should be revived because of the deterrence effect it has. Bill Deedes argued that the abolition of the death penalty had reduced the severity that society attached to murder: 'it follows that when we abolished hanging we also (at least in my mind) altered the status of murder'.[10] Nicholas Winterton, chose to make his maiden speech on the subject of law and order when first elected in 1971.[11] He remained a committed believer in the death penalty on the basis that it acts as a deterrent. The Monday Club was a forum for such opinions (though not all members agreed). Sir Adrian Fitzgerald commented at the time Silverman's bill was passing through the House of Commons that, 'the true purpose of legal punishment is to deter, and not reform the criminal... The abolition of the death penalty would remove the deterrent'.[12] In 1972, Jonathan Guinness argued that, 'the time for the Monday Club to exert real influence is approaching'.[13] This included campaigning for stronger law and order policy, including restoration of the death penalty. The task of the Monday Club should be to persuade the Conservative Party to follow the instincts of the British people. In 1973, Guinness stood in the Lincoln by-election and argued that razor blades should be placed in the cells of all convicted murderers, earning him the nickname 'old razor blades'.[14] C. E. Ashworth also wrote in *Monday World* that there was a risk that Britain would experience a revolution. Things were out of hand, including the rise of violent crime.[15]

Margaret Thatcher was in favour of restoration. She allowed a free vote in 1983.[16] Thatcher was in favour of restoration and there had been pressure put on Conservative MPs by voters and constituency associations. However, Thatcher was aware that the issue would be highly divisive in her Cabinet and among the parliamentary party if it went through so she said that she did not expect to win. The vote on having a death penalty for police murders lost by 81 votes and murder of anyone else by 145. Bernard Ingham was privately very critical since Thatcher had been 'part of the conspiracy to kill the issue'.[17] Ann Widdecombe also advocated restoration of the death penalty.[18] There is a moral case for the death penalty, which is one of deterrence. After abolition the number of capital murders increased. 'I looked at the figures and thought that was it, game, set and match'. However, it is not coming back.[19]

In 2018, John Hayes wrote to the Home Secretary to ask for the death penalty to be restored.[20] A poll of Conservative members found that 54% were in favour of restoration.[21] A significant proportion of the population continue to believe in restoration. In September 2010 51% (compared to 37% against) said they favoured restoration of the death penalty, in 2014, 45% did so (39% against). Moreover, more people in the UK felt that the death penalty was a deterrent than in the US (45–35%).[22] However, successive parliamentary votes have shown that the overwhelming majority of MPs are opposed to its restoration.

More generally, there had been too much emphasis on the social causes of crime and on rehabilitation for figures on the Conservative Right. Crime had increased at the same time that the number of social workers had increased said Rhodes Boyson. There was no alternative to strong law and order policies since human nature was sinful and 'such human tendencies will only be restrained by the threat of firm deterrent'.[23] To be sure, the Thatcher Governments did increase police powers through successive pieces of legislation but this was hardly enough to placate the Conservative Right.[24] Paul Helm argued in 1989 that, 'retribution is the most important single feature of punishment, that which makes it fundamentally intelligible and justifiable as a human activity; it is also the most completely lost sight of in current penal policy'.[25] The timing of this is significant. Thatcher had been in power for a decade, but for the Right there had been no significant shift in policy. Liberal opinion still predominated.

As Home Secretary, Michael Howard believed that prisons worked. When he entered the Home Office, he was told by the civil service that there was nothing that could be done about rising crime levels and the only option was to manage public expectations. He was also resisted by the criminal justice profession.[26] Philip Davies maintains that the primary purpose of prison is punishment and it works as it reduces recidivism. 'When people are in prison we've got an opportunity to get them into a work ethic' he argued.[27] Punishment and rehabilitation go together in this sense. However, those who wish to see a tougher law and order policy face the bias of the criminal justice system. 'There is a massive left-wing bias in the courts, the criminal justice system, the judges and the magistrates. Yes, without a shadow of a doubt'.[28]

For Christie Davies, this emphasis on punishment as a solution to social deviancy was seeing the problem the wrong way around.[29] Law and order dealt only with the consequences of social breakdown. The fact that the Thatcher Governments were emphasising law and order showed only the extent to which society had declined. Britain was experiencing a moral death. If law and order dealt only with the consequences of this moral decay, the causes lay in the breakdown of the family and in education. The level of divorce in the UK rose under the Conservative Governments from 138,706 in 1979 to 146,689 in 1997.[30]

Permissiveness

Pro-Life Issues

The decision to legalise abortion in 1967 was opposed by pro-life groups. While not restricted to the Conservative Right—there was still a significant Catholic representation in the Labour Party at this time—the issue has been one which has attracted most political support from those on the Right-wing of the Conservative Party.

The principal organisation which campaigned against the legalisation of abortion was the Society for the Protection of the Unborn Child (SPUC). This attracted the support of several figures on the Right of the Conservative Party.[31]

There were those who opposed, and continued to oppose after its legalisation, abortion outright. The majority of those who are hostile to abortion, however, have tended to focus more on measures designed to restrict its use rather than to reverse the 1967 Act, believing that this had more chance of success. A key issue here has been the length of term at which an abortion is allowed.

Figures on the Conservative Right have continued to call for restrictions. Writing in 1991 in *The Salisbury Review* E. J. Mishan argued that the costs of abortion law reform in the 1960s had been severe:

A conscience-liberated era during which – owing to moral paralysis and political cowardice – a right to abortion on demand was effectively sanctioned by society so fostering a sexual irresponsibility which, in the event culminated in a remorseless holocaust of human life.[32]

Advances in scientific knowledge raised further issues for campaigners. Enoch Powell—who was far from being a social conservative on many issues—objected to embryo research which he felt undermined the sanctity of human life.[33] In 1985 he tried to get support for his bill which would restrict its use. He argued that there would be scientific gains from such research but at the expense of morality. The bill was brought in to oppose the Warnock Report which called for its more extensive use, primarily on utilitarian grounds. However, the bill caused parliamentary uproar and was eventually to be timed out. The Government refused to support Powell's bill. Legislation was introduced which reduced the term limit for abortion from 28 to 24 weeks in 1990, but this was deemed to little, too late by pro-life campaigners.

A further issue which has raised concern for some of those on the Conservative Right is that of euthanasia. For those of a conservative Christian outlook, euthanasia further erodes the sanctity of life. Just as abortion challenges the belief that each human life is precious so does euthanasia. While advocates of reform in this area argue that people with terminal illnesses have a right to a dignified death, opponents claim that this can be achieved through palliative care. Moreover, they fear that the terminally-ill person will be put under pressure to speed up the ending of their own life or that unscrupulous family members will seek to end it prematurely. No amount of safeguards, they argue, would avoid these situations.

Homosexuality

Measures to legalise homosexuality again predate the so-called 'permissive era' of the 1960s. The Wolfenden Report of 1957 concluded that homosexuality between consenting adults should be legalised. Butler sought to move in this direction, but it was again left to the following Labour government with its Sexual Offences Act (1967). Cyril Osborne spoke in the House of Commons against the measure:

> Those who have preceded me have been experts but I am not. I know nothing about what is called buggery but from what I do know about it I hate it and I dislike it.[34]

Opponents of reform again tended to be on the Right and argued against legalisation on several grounds. The first was that homosexuality was immoral. The Creation demonstrated that it was God's wish for a normal sexual relationship to be between a man and a woman, not least for reasons of procreation. The Bible taught that homosexuality was a sin. For some, the sexual act between two people of the same sex was disgusting. The second was that homosexuality was associated with other forms of sexual conduct which were undesirable. Homosexuals were more likely to engage in predatory and/or promiscuous behaviour. T. E. Utley wrote that, 'there can be very little doubt that there is in this country a strong consensus against homosexuality; the practising homosexual is still regarded with some degree of instinctive horror'.[35] However, the existing law contained numerous anomalies and injustices and it was therefore right to change the law.

The AIDS epidemic in the 1980s posed a challenge for Conservative moralists.[36] For some the crisis was a straight forward medical matter to be dealt with in the same way as any other—research into the causes, development of a suitable vaccine, public education and preventative measures—in this case the provision of condoms. However, for moralists on the Conservative Right the crisis was not a simple medical one but also a moral one. Such measures as greater education equated with the promotion of homosexuality in schools and the provision of condoms as the official sanctioning of same-sex relationships. Instead, they felt, the AIDS crisis had proven their predictions. AIDS was a disease which affected a particular section of society and did so because of their sexual behaviour. Peregrine Worsthorne said that, 'its cause is the promiscuous indulgence in sexual practices which until recently were condemned by both Church and State as perverted and unnatural, not to say grossly unhygienic'.[37] However, Worsthorne was to admit that homosexuality had been a 'close run thing' at school and he could easily have been 'one of them'.[38] He was later to support the proposal for gay marriage.

Walter Walker argued that a particular problem created by the legalisation of homosexuality and the growing tolerance of society towards it was in the armed forces where it should not be permitted. 'There is no place...for homosexuals or lesbians in our armed forces. This country has become inflicted with the prominence of the foul and disgusting sexual orientation of so-called "gay rights" groups'.[39]

A particular concern at this time was the provision of sex education lessons in schools. For some this undermined the role of the family. A cause celebre for the opponents of sex education in schools was Victoria Gillick.[40] She had attempted to remove her teenage daughter from sex education lessons and had taken her Local Education Authority to court to challenge their ruling that her daughter must attend these lessons. The courts ruled in favour of the LEA and the Government agreed. However, sympathisers believed that the traditional Tory belief in the family should have prevailed. If the parents did not wish their child to receive such lessons but rather to educate their offspring in their own way they had a right to do so.

A further issue in terms of sex education emerged in the form of the perceived promotion of same-sex relationships in schools. Particular attention focussed on the decision of several London boroughs to use literature which discussed children living in households with two parents of the same sex. For some on the Conservative Right this showed a deliberate ideological attempt to undermine the nuclear family by promoting homosexuality. Campaigners including MPs Peter Bruinvels and Dame Gill Knight MP campaigned on this issue, eventually leading to an additional clause in the 1988 Education Reform Bill, Clause 28.[41] The clause prohibited the teaching of homosexuality to children. Its supporters believed it marked a significant block on the drift of permissive legislation. However, it became a target for critics on the centre and left of the political spectrum who believed that it demonstrated Thatcher's own intolerance. Labour adopted a policy to reverse this measure, which was quickly done once they returned to power in 1997, a measure which was greeted with the approval of civil liberties campaigners. However, for others on the Conservative Right the measure was ineffective and misguided. While campaigners were right to be concerned with the erosion of the traditional family unit they believed that divorce was much more important, after all homosexuality was limited to a small proportion of the overall population.[42]

Divorce

For Peter Hitchens, the most significant social reform of the 1960s was divorce law.[43] This had a major effect on the nuclear family. Prior to 1969 divorce was legal only on narrowly defined grounds including infidelity, desertion or abuse. However, the establishment of 'no fault' divorce in 1969 made legal separation much easier, being allowed after a physical separation of two years. The result has been a significant increase in the number of divorces since. Added to this was the increased number of children born to unmarried mothers. Defenders of the family, such as Hitchens, argue that this has created a situation where children do not learn the value of relationships. Children born out of wedlock are more likely to underperform educationally and are more likely to commit crime and anti-social behaviour. Julian Brazier and Douglas Carswell spoke of the 'tidal wave' of crime affecting Britain by 2005 and felt that 'the decline in healthy families and communities' was a key reason for this.[44]

This is a good moment at which to discuss the reasons why it is that social conservatives support the family. They see it as the main way in which to pass on established social norms. Children learn to be placed within a hierarchical framework in which authority is given to parents, who in turn accept the duty to instil discipline and order into their children. If the traditional family ceases to be a reality for a growing number of children then all of these things are lost. Writing at the end of the Second World War, Christopher Hollis believed that feminism's concern with the extension of women's rights and interests in peacetime meant that there would be a 'reluctance of women to bear children' and would 'make it harder for them to be content with their traditional relationship to man'.[45]

The Thatcher Governments—despite their pledge to reverse these 'permissive' social trends—did little in this area according to socially conservative critics. The reason for this may well have been the view, which Thatcher shared, that the family was an autonomous social institution which should not be interfered with by legislation. This view was certainly argued by Ferdinand Mount in his book, *The Subversive Family*.[46]

Mount was for a time the Director of Thatcher's Policy Unit. The 1986 Education Act did promote the importance of stable relationships but critics argued that more could have been done, especially in terms of tax changes to encourage marriage.

Censorship

A final area of social reform which can be identified—and for which social conservatives place considerable blame for what they see as ongoing moral decline—is the relaxation of laws on censorship. Previously the state, through the office of the Lord Chamberlain, had exercised some degree of censorship over what literature could be published, plays performed and what radio and television programmes could be broadcast. There was a clear case for reform as it was widely accepted that this policy did not work. The Lord Chamberlain would often err on the side of prohibition, leading to numerous legal challenges of which the most notable was over the decision to refuse publication of D. H. Lawrence's *Lady Chatterley's Lover*. The court case attracted considerable publicity, thus ensuring increased sales once the court ruled in favour of its publication.

A prominent campaigner for restrictions on what could be broadcast was Mary Whitehouse, previously a school teacher and who went on to establish the National Viewers and Listeners Association (NVLA) to 'clean up' television and radio.[47] Although non-aligned politically, Whitehouse had a following among social conservatives. NVLA claimed that the broadcasting of explicit scenes of violence and sexual conduct encouraged the reproduction of such acts in those who had seen it. She challenged what she regarded as the liberal establishment in broadcasting, believing the arguments they made in favour of allowing the individual viewer to exercise responsibility over what they watched were inadequate. Moreover, the liberal attitudes of broadcasters was reproduced by politicians who shared their outlook. The moral discourse of Margaret Thatcher led Whitehouse to support her election in 1979. This apparent alignment between Whitehouse and the Conservatives was, however, to be strained shortly afterwards when the Thatcher government appeared to continue with the same agenda as its predecessors. Although she continued to attract the support of individual parliamentarians on the Right of the Conservative Party her impact on the course of government can be doubted.[48]

FIGHTING PERMISSIVENESS?

Peter Hitchens argued that:

> The favourite social causes of our generation - unrestricted abortion, easy divorce, radical education, sexual equality, homosexual law reform, the end of censorship and the abolition of capital punishment - have all been victorious. In every single case, the warnings of the crustiest and stupidest conservatives now turn out to have been sober and accurate prophecies.[49]

What is striking from the above discussion of social change is not just that the Conservative Party has failed to halt reform but also that they have sometimes driven it. This is not lost on the social conservatives. Margaret Thatcher appeared to offer something different. However, Hitchens' comment was made in 1998. As far as the social conservatives are concerned Thatcher had failed to fight back against permissiveness.

Margaret Thatcher claimed that she would reverse the culture of permissiveness, which she associated directly with the Labour Party. Partly this was for tactical reasons.[50] The electoral challenge of the Social Democratic Party following its formation in 1981 led the Conservative Party to redirect its criticism from the socialism of the Labour Party, which had moved leftwards after its 1979 General Election defeat, towards the new threat of the SDP. Since Roy Jenkins was leading the new party and had been the principal architect behind much of the liberal reforming agenda of the 1960s it made tactical sense for the Conservatives to attack on this front. The reforms had, they argued, created numerous social problems, which they were now trying to solve.

However, a more overtly ideological commitment to social conservatism was made by Norman Tebbit, who argued that the Government was not only trying to address Britain's failing economy but also its failing society.[51] Permissiveness had created numerous social problems and the government would seek to reverse these measures. Another prominent advocate of social conservatism was Rhodes Boyson, former comprehensive school headmaster and advocate of a more disciplinarian education policy. Boyson also argued that the social reforms of the 1960s had deleterious consequences on society which needed to be reversed.[52]

The problem for a number of social conservatives was that the Thatcher governments did little to reverse social liberalism. The difficulty with the political rhetoric of reaction is that it was exactly that, it remained rhetorical and there was little substantive policy development.

For Stuart Millson: 'tragically, successive Tory governments failed to cultivate and foster right-wing and traditionalist sentiments, and paved the way for the widespread dissemination of a liberal left social and cultural morality.'[53] This was in 1997 after 18 years of Conservative Government. Writing at the same time, Ian Crowther argued that:

> We have witnessed, alongside Britain's economic recovery, a continuing rise in violent and sexual crimes in hooliganism, vandalism, drunkenness and sheer bad manners, in rates of illegitimacy, abortion, divorce and child abuse.[54]

None of the permissive legislation of the 1960s was reversed. The consequence was that the social trends continued. Moreover, the Government's response to the AIDS crisis—which focused on safe sex education—showed the continuing bias towards technocratic measures based on utilitarian philosophy according to those who wanted to see a change in direction on matters relating to homosexuality. Peter Bruinvels argued that the campaign had made matters worse and Patrick Cormack said that condom packets should carry a health warning that 'Promiscuity Kills'.[55] The fact that Section 28 became such a notorious case only confirmed in the minds of social conservatives that the Thatcher Government was not really socially conservative at all, since it highlighted that this was the only measure that had upset the social liberals and was a misguided measure in any case if the aim had been to restore the nuclear family.

If the Thatcher governments had disappointed its social conservative observers, then subsequent periods of Conservative rule would openly antagonise it. John Major appeared to move in a socially conservative way by invoking the language of 'back to basics' although he always denied it was a statement of intent on social issues at all.[56] For some this sounded like a fight back against social liberalism, Britain's own 'culture war'. However, not only did this not result in any socially conservative policies but his government became beset with allegations of sleaze and corruption. His own ministers engaged in sexual activities which, on occasion, were decidedly bizarre. One social conservative campaigner, Angela Ellis-Jones, resigned from the Conservative Party and stood (as a UKIP candidate) against Alan Clark, who appeared to personify the licentious behaviour which appeared to characterise this government. She had previously argued that Thatcher's reaction to Cecil Parkinson's extra-marital affair with his secretary, which resulted in her pregnancy was inadequate.[57] Melanie Phillips argued that under the Thatcher and Major Governments, 'the Conservatives became debased liberals and promoted a political culture of atomised and irresponsible individualism which has done untold damage to our society'.[58]

For Ann Widdecombe, the 1960s was a much maligned decade. The 1970s were, in fact, worse. Everyone was their own arbiter. The attitude was: 'I can do whatever I like'. In the 1980s the rise of materialism added the attitude of: 'I can have whatever I like'. Thatcher failed to reduce dependency and family breakdown as she had to focus on the economy, trade unions and so on. However, the pursuit of free-market economics was not the cause. It was happening elsewhere—the culture of entitlement and rights. In the 1990s, Major's Government tried to defend the family and stuck rigidly to Section 28.[59]

In Opposition there emerged a debate between competing wings of the Conservative Party. The debate—termed 'mods versus rockers'—was between those who wanted to embrace social change and adopt a more socially liberal agenda (mods) and those who wanted to maintain (or restore) a socially conservative agenda (rockers). The former included Michael Portillo and Francis Maude, who were concerned with what they saw as the increasingly hostile attitude of sections of the Conservative Party towards modern society, summed up neatly in Theresa May's phrase as the 'nasty party'. The latter were relatively few in number but included Norman Tebbit, Ann Widdecombe and Simon Heffer. Ann Widdecombe thought that the 'mods/rockers' distinction was 'stupid' while May's language of the 'nasty party' was a mistake since it reinforced a stereotype of the party.[60] New Labour was socially liberal and the Conservative Party should oppose it: 'why on earth would voters support imitation liberals when they can have the real thing?' John Hayes asked rhetorically.[61] Although socially liberal views were prevalent in the media and in the capital, social conservative views were dominant in the rest of the country. Not only was social conservatism right in principle but also electorally. Heffer opposed the approach of the social liberals with their focus on minority rights: 'the theme running through this obsession with courting minorities is the orthodoxy of political correctness, a creed that dictates that majorities do not necessarily have rights'.[62] However, even when attempts were made to restore a more socially conservative approach, such as Ann Widdecombe's call at the party conference in 2000 for a 'zero tolerance' approach to illegal drugs it was met with derision and the Party quickly moved away from it.[63]

The eventual triumph of David Cameron as Leader of the Opposition in 2005, and Prime Minister in 2010, sealed the fate of the traditionalists. For Philip Davies, this amounted to a 'detoxification strategy that was never needed', the product of a 'self-flagellating mentality'.[64] Cameron stated that he was a 'liberal conservative' and adopted a number of socially liberal policies.[65] The most notable was the legislating of gay marriage. In this he was assisted by being in Coalition with the Liberal Democrats but opposed by the more traditionalist elements of the Party. Cameron said that he wished to introduce this measure because it would promote stable and loving relationships. It didn't undermine heterosexual marriage, but rather would compliment it. However, writing in 1996 John O'Sullivan had argued that homosexual identities are not complimentary to, but rather antagonistic towards, traditional family structures since alternative cultures see traditions as repressive.[66] While, for John Hayes, marriage is about procreation. Some Conservative MPs did not believe in gay marriage, but they thought they were 'doing right by the Leader' in voting for it—the clear majority were against.[67]

The main internal parliamentary opposition to Cameron from a social conservative direction was the Cornerstone Group, which was founded by Edward Leigh, with prominent support from Hayes. But its impact on policy was limited. For Hayes, writing in 2005, 'the great challenges which now face us are no longer (if they ever were) economic at all—they are social and cultural'.[68] Leigh said that the group stood for 'tradition, family, faith, enterprise and nationhood'[69] against the 'liberal orthodoxy which appears so seductive to much of the political class'.[70] The difficulty was that 'liberalism (was) so dominant that it managed to infect the Conservative Party like a virus'.[71] The Group appeared to have had no impact on the social policy agenda, as the same-sex marriage issue demonstrated.

Overall, the impact of social conservatism on the Conservative Party has been limited. Often, the presence of social conservatives within the Party has been seen as an embarrassing one, stopping the Party from appearing 'modern'. This was certainly true at times when the leadership has moved in a much more socially liberal direction such as in the 1950s under Macmillan and Butler (as Home Secretary) and again more recently under Cameron. However, as this chapter has also demonstrated it would be mistaken to see the 1980s as a revival of social conservatism. Certainly, the socially conservative elements did not regard it as such.

NOTES

1. See C. Davies, *Permissive Britain: Social Change in the Sixties and Seventies* (London: Pitman, 1975) for an avowedly socially conservative viewpoint on this period.
2. M. Jarvis, *Conservative Governments, Morality and Social Change in Affluent Britain, 1957–64* (Manchester: Manchester University Press, 2005).
3. T. E. Utley, 'What Laws May Cure' reprinted in C. Moore and S. Heffer (eds.) *A Tory Seer* (London: Hamish Hamilton, 1989).
4. Ibid., p. 331.
5. I. Crowther, 'Conservatism Ancient and Modern', in *The Salisbury Review*, 11/1 (1992), p. 57.
6. C. Davies, *Permissive Britain*; C. Davies, *The Strange Death of Moral Britain* (London: Transaction, 2007).
7. J. Selwyn-Gummer, *The Permissive Society: Fact or Fantasy* (London: Cassell, 1971). Interview with Lord Deben, London, 4 April 2017.
8. P. Worsthorne, *The Socialist Myth* (London: Cassell, 1971), p. 202.
9. J. Knowles, *The Abolition of the Death penalty in the United Kingdom*, available at https://www.deathpenaltyproject.org/wp-content/uploads/2017/12/DPP-50-Years-on-pp1-68-1.pdf, accessed 12 May 2019.
10. B. Deedes, 'Capital Punishment and After', *Solon*, 1/1 (October 1969), p. 33.
11. S. Winterton, *The Wintertons Unmuzzled* (London: Biteback, 2016), p. 114. Interview with Nicholas and Ann Winterton, Cheshire, 23 September 2016.
12. Sir Adrian Fitzgerald, 'Capital Punishment: Dangers of Abolition', *Force* (Autumn 1965).
13. J. Guinness, 'The Club Today', *Monday World* (Spring 1972), p. 4.
14. D. Rubin, 'Profile: Jonathan Guinness, Lord Moyne—Requiem for an Irish Dynasty', *Independent*, 9 November 1997, https://www.independent.co.uk/news/business/profile-jonathan-guinness-lord-moyne-requiem-for-an-irish-dynasty-1292951.html, accessed 12 May 2019.
15. C. E. Ashworth 'The Coming British Revolution', *Monday World* (Spring 1972).
16. C. Moore, *Margaret Thatcher: The Authorised Biography, Volume Two: Everything She Wants* (London: Allen Lane, 2015), p. 79.
17. Ibid., p. 81.
18. A. Widdecombe, *Strictly Ann: The Autobiography* (London: Weidenfeld & Nicolson, 2013), pp. 119–122.
19. Interview with Ann Widdecombe, London, 11 October 2016.

20. B. Kentish, 'Tory MP Asks Government to Consider Bringing Back Death Penalty', *Independent*, 3 November 2018, https://www.independent. co.uk/news/uk/politics/tory-mp-bring-back-death-penalty-john-hayes-lincolnshire-capital-punishment-a8615731.html, accessed 12 May 2019.
21. L. Buchan, 'More Than Half of Tory Activists Support Death Penalty, Finds Landmark Survey of Grassroots Members', *Independent*, 4 January 2018, https://www.independent.co.uk/news/uk/politics/conserva-tives-death-penalty-poll-grassroots-members-queen-mary-university-lon-don-a8139946.html, accessed 12 May 2019.
22. W. Dahlgreen, '50 Years on Capital Punishment Still Favoured', YouGov, 13 August 2014, https://yougov.co.uk/topics/politics/articles-reports/2014/08/13/capital-punishment-50-years-favoured, accessed 12 May 2019.
23. R. Boyson, *Centre Forward* (London: Temple Smith, 1978), p. 154.
24. B. Pilbeam, 'Social Morality', in K. Hickson (ed.) *The Political Thought of the Conservative Party Since 1945* (Basingstoke: Palgrave, 2005).
25. P. Helm, 'Punishment in the Community' *The Salisbury Review*, 7/4 (June 1989), p. 20.
26. Interview with Lord Howard, London, 12 September 2017.
27. Interview with Philip Davies MP, London, 19 January 2017.
28. Ibid.
29. Pilbeam, 'Social Morality', p. 167.
30. 'Divorce Rates Data, 1858 to Now: How Has It Changed?' *The Guardian*, https://www.theguardian.com/news/datablog/2010/jan/28/divorce-rates-marriage-ons, accessed 12 July 2019.
31. Davies, *The Strange Death of Moral Britain*, pp. 78–90.
32. E. J. Mishan, 'The Quality of Mercy', *The Salisbury Review*, 10/2 (1991), p. 39.
33. S. Heffer, *Like the Roman* (London: Weidenfeld & Nicolson, 1998), pp. 887–891.
34. Quoted in Davies, *The Strange Death of Moral Britain*, p. 172.
35. Utley, 'What Laws May Cure', p. 328.
36. M. Durham, *Sex and Politics* (Basingstoke: Macmillan, 1991), pp. 123–142.
37. P. Worsthorne, *By the Right* (Dublin: Brophy, 1987), p. 147.
38. P. Worsthorne, *Tricks of Memory: An Autobiography* (London: Weidenfeld & Nicolson, 1993).
39. W. Walker, *Right Now* (October–December 1999), p. 8.
40. Durham, *Sex and Politics*, pp. 39–56.
41. Interview with Dame Gill Knight.
42. P. Hitchens, *The Abolition of Britain* (London: Quartet, 1999).
43. Ibid.

182   K. HICKSON

44. J. Brazier and D. Carswell, 'Criminal Justice Gone Mad', in Cornerstone Group, *Being Conservative: A Cornerstone of Policies to Revive Tory Britain* (London: Cornerstone Group, 2005), p. 53.
45. C. Hollis, *Quality or Equality?* (London: Signpost Books, 1944), p. 15.
46. F. Mount, *The Subversive Family* (London: Cape, 1982).
47. M. Whitehouse, *Who Does She Think She Is?* (London: New English Library, 1971).
48. M. Durham, *Sex and Politics*, pp. 76–98.
49. P. Hitchens, 'The Legacy of the Sixties', *Prospect*, 28 (1998), p. 14.
50. Durham, *Sex and Politics*, p. 131.
51. Ibid., p. 132.
52. Ibid.
53. S. Millson, 'New Government, New Danger', *The Salisbury Review*, 16/2 (Winter 1997), p. 33.
54. I. Crowther, 'Thatcherism and the Good Life', *The Salisbury Review*, 8/1 (September 1989), p. 4.
55. Durham, *Sex and Politics*, p. 127.
56. J. Major, *The Autobiography* (London: HarperCollins, 1999).
57. A. Ellis-Jones, 'The Politics of Economics', in R. Scruton (ed.) *Conservative Thoughts: Essays From The Salisbury Review* (London: Claridge, 1989).
58. M. Phillips, *All Must Have Prizes* (London: Little, Brown, 1996), p. 326.
59. Interview with Ann Widdecombe.
60. Ibid.
61. J. Hayes, 'On Being Conservative', in Cornerstone Group, *Being Conservative: A Cornerstone of Policies to Revive Tory Britain* (London: Cornerstone Group, 2005), p. 7.
62. S. Heffer, *What Tories Want* (London: Politeia, 2000), p. 20.
63. Pilbeam, 'Social Morality', p. 169.
64. Interview with Philip Davies MP.
65. See B. Williams, *The Evolution of Conservative Party Social Policy* (Basingstoke: Palgrave, 2015); M. Beech, 'A Tale of Two Liberalisms', in S. Lee and M. Beech (eds.) *The Cameron-Clegg Government: Coalition Politics in an Age of Austerity* (Basingstoke: Palgrave, 2011).
66. J. O'Sullivan, 'Conservatism and Cultural Identity', in K. Minogue (ed.) *Conservative Realism* (London: HarperCollins, 1996).
67. Interview with John Hayes, London, 4 July 2017.
68. J. Hayes, 'Being Conservative', p. 5.
69. E. Leigh, *The Strange Desertion of Tory England: The Conservative Alternative to Liberal Orthodoxy* (London: Cornerstone Group, 2005), p. 4.
70. Ibid.
71. Ibid., p. 13.

CHAPTER 10

Conclusion

We have examined the political thought of the Conservative Right since 1945 across a broad range of thematic issues in order to try to capture its essence as a relatively neglected tradition within British politics. These issues have been: empire, immigration, Europe, constitution, Union, economy, welfare and society. Three debates internal to the Conservative Right were highlighted. These were the debate between imperialists and nationalists; between constitutional radicals, conservatives and reactionaries; and, finally, between those who were more predisposed to economic liberalism and those who were more hostile. The presence of a core set of values, as set out in the Introduction, and also points of tension and contestation means that the Conservative Right can be understood as an ideological tradition. The evolution of the Conservative Right has been placed within three historical periods.

The first was from 1945 to 1979. The end of the Second World War and the election of the first majority Labour Government in the same year posed major challenges to the Right of the Conservative Party. In this period, the Right are best understood as diehards. They opposed the changes which many regarded as inevitable. This included, most notably, the end of the British Empire. There can be no doubt that Britain declined in absolute terms as a world power and for the Conservative Right—which had been defined by its attachment to imperialism for many years—this proved to be a crisis of identity. However, there were not just strains over the Conservative Party's attachment to empire but also growing concerns over the expansion of the central state.

© The Author(s) 2020
K. Hickson, *Britain's Conservative Right since 1945*,
https://doi.org/10.1007/978-3-030-27697-3_10

The Conservative Right opposed what it regarded as the unnecessary and undesirable growth of state activity in the economic and social fields. For some it necessitated constitutional innovation in order to halt the rise of 'socialism' in the UK. But, the Conservative Right also opposed the influence of liberalism in the form of the social changes which were also occurring. Opposition from the Conservative Right came, firstly, in the form of the Suez Group, then the Monday Club, and finally Enoch Powell and his followers. If the first two represented the last gasps of imperialism the last combined rationalist economic liberalism with a romantic nationalism. These two aspects—whatever Powell thought— were never fully reconcilable. There were clearly differences between the imperialists and the Powellites. This shift in the thinking of the Right was one from paternalism to populism, from economic protectionism to economic liberalism, and from empire to nation.

The second period was from 1979 to 1990. This is the shortest time period considered here. But it was highly significant. The Conservative Right may have been deemed to have been more content with the nature of politics in these years. 1979 marked the electoral appeal of a more right-wing form of Conservatism than Britain had seen since before the War. Margaret Thatcher was elected to unravel the postwar consensus which the Conservative Right disliked. There was a clear shift in the approach to the economy with the adoption of free-market policies. There also appeared to be a shift in the direction of a more socially conservative agenda and a more overtly patriotic premiership. I say appeared, since in fact the Conservative Right was sceptical of Margaret Thatcher, at least initially, since she had not been 'one of them'. In the leadership contest following Heath there had been an unwinnable candidate from the Right in both rounds—Hugh Fraser and John Peyton respectively, coming last both times. Thatcher had been a loyal member of Heath's Cabinet. The Conservative Right were wary throughout her time as Leader of the Opposition as she appeared to compromise on numerous issues. Even in the early years of her premiership they remained wary. It was only with the Falklands War that some of them became more active supporters. Others supported her initially and then became more sceptical. Others still opposed what Thatcher did throughout her premiership from the Right. It was not just that the moderates opposed what she did, but some on Right also.

The final period is from 1990. The Conservative Right were critical of John Major's premiership throughout. For them, he was always going to be an inferior substitute for Mrs Thatcher, even though he continued with her broad policy platform. In Opposition after 1997 the Conservative Right remained critical of the leadership. This was despite the fact that William Hague, Iain Duncan Smith and Michael Howard could all be deemed to have a position within the Conservative Party to the right of centre. Certainly the Right had managed to avoid the leadership of Kenneth Clarke, which they were strongly opposed to as the Party became more Eurosceptic. However, the leadership had to manage a divided party and was deemed too willing to compromise. David Cameron then sought to 'modernise' the party, which meant moving decisively in a socially liberal direction. This was given a boost by the formation of the Coalition in 2010. Finding themselves in opposition to its own leadership, the Conservative Right established the Cornerstone Group. The Conservative Right was always likely to be disappointed by the leadership of Theresa May between 2016 and 2019. She had to navigate the torrents of Brexit—from the General Election of 2016 without a parliamentary majority. The compromises this involved were always likely to alienate the Party's right wing, which feared a 'Brexit betrayal'. The Conservative Right have been more willing to support Boris Johnson due to his tougher approach to Brexit, but his socially liberal opinions sit uncomfortably with those of a more traditionalist attitude.

Several issues stand out from this narrative for our purposes. The Right frequently adopts an oppositionist stance whether their party happens to be in government or in opposition. The Conservative Party is rarely deemed to be a conservative force at all. This may well be because of the competing strands of thought and practice within the Conservative Party and the need for any Leader to seek to balance them. As Jonathan Aitken commented, 'pure right-wingery is just not possible' as there is always a need to balance different factions within the Conservative Party.[1] The Right will always be disappointed.

This takes us some way to understanding the Conservative Right's approach to political change. It is likely to feel variously frustrated, angry, pessimistic or betrayed but rarely content. With William F. Buckley Jr, 'it stands athwart history, yelling Stop, at a time when no one is inclined to do so, or to have much patience with those who so urge it'.[2]

This highlights a central tension within the thought of the Conservative Right. According to Michael Oakeshott the conservative disposition is 'to prefer the familiar to the unknown, to prefer the tried to the untried, fact to mystery, the actual to the possible, the limited to the unbounded, the near to the distant, the sufficient to the superabundant.'[3] However, change is inevitable even though the conservative will know that it entails 'certain loss' yet only 'possible gain'.[4] Change will always be painful, though inevitable. The task of the Conservative states-person is to manage that change by making it as limited as possible.

For T. E. Utley, the Conservative politician is characterised by a 'sophisticated timidity'.[5] Politics involves concession to the forces of change and the only thing which can be done by the Conservative is 'to decide what he loves best and then consider how he can preside most ele-gantly and judiciously over its destruction'.[6] For him this was a positive: 'is it not the great merit of English Conservatism that it comes to terms with reality and the great merit of the Tory party that it confines itself to the role of a midwife to history?'[7] However, he also felt that within this approach there was a pitfall, one into which the Party had fallen since 1945 'that if one looks at the facts and considers the circumstances, the only course which it is ever worth following is that of controlled sur-render'.[8] Since 1945, the Conservative Party had been willing to make all sorts of concessions in ways which the Right did not welcome. Lord Coleraine put it thus: 'the danger was not that the Conservative Party would prove too reactionary, but that it would be carried so far along the road of change as to lose the characteristics which would enable it, in due course, to make a distinctive contribution to the creation of the new society. And that is what happened. All that the Party had to offer, in the wasted years, was a reformulation of the fashions of the day'.[9]

For Coleraine, the Party needed to overcome this by moving in the direction of free-market economics. If the concessions had all been made at a time when the Party was too willing to embrace the mixed economy and the welfare state then a free-market programme would restore the values which Tories should hold dear. There was no tension, for him, between economic liberalism and traditional Toryism.[10] Others took a pessimistic view. The free market would undermine the principles of the Conservative Right. Markets are neutral between competing social theories and are likely to be destructive of the things which conservatives seek to defend. Hence, some Conservatives were sceptical of Thatcherism from the outset or became so. The debate between Shirley Letwin and Peregrine Worsthorne over the character of Thatcherism is most relevant here.[11] Whereas Letwin argued that Thatcher was using economic means for moral ends—to restore the lost virtues—Worsthorne argued, with more justification, that all she had done was to encourage greed, selfishness and materialism. We are not required to share his faith in the old ruling class in order to recog-nise the essential truth in his assessment of the Thatcher years.

A further distinctive conservative argument can be made here. Namely, the unintended consequences of radical change. The Thatcher years were certainly radical. For the economic liberal this may well be a good thing, if it furthers their principles. Economic liberalism is just as 'rationalistic' as socialism in the sense that it aims at the restructuring of society. Opponents need to be dealt with. Hence, economic liberalism did not just mean the extension of the free market but also the strengthening of the central state.[12] But, for the traditionalist conservative the consistent pursuit of free markets—just as any other goal—will lead to unintended consequences. Worsthorne argued that in order for Thatcher to implement economic liberal reforms the trade unions needed to be defeated, but in order to do that she had to enlist the support of unconservative forces.[13] These 'ugly passions' were 'spectacularly and horribly destructive of much of what made this country a lovable place'.[14] The things which were destroyed included both the old Labour Party and the old Conservative Party; the sense of working-class solidarity and the traditional ruling class. The new alliances she forged were 'very much a case of out of the frying pan and into the fire'.[15] The language revealed the real nature of Thatcherism. It was a 'profoundly un-English period in British politics'.[16] The ethos of public service was destroyed, in its place came selfishness. This went across all institutions and all professions, public and private, where all that mattered was the making of money.[17] Britain had become a 'ratocracy' where all that mattered was having sharp elbows to nudge others out of the way in the rat run of life.[18]

For Peter Hitchens, also, the 1980s was not a conservative era at all. He argued that, 'the Thatcher Government unwittingly helped to destroy many of things Conservatism once stood for'.[19] The Thatcher years marked the 'undoing' of conservatism.[20] The social forces unleashed by the market led to radical and negative social changes. Since then there has simply been more and more social liberalism piled on top of the situation which she left behind. However, there was nothing new in this in that the Conservative Party had never really been a conservative force in any meaningful sense. If the Thatcher years disappointed, the record of the Conservative Party before and after was never going to gain the support of the right wing. If postwar Conservative leaders conceded too much ground to 'socialism' then more recently the Conservative Party has been too willing to embrace liberalism, according to figures on the Conservative Right.

However, simply because the Conservative Right feels ill-suited to modern times it should not lead on to reaction. Although some thought that it was perfectly possible to turn back the clock,[21] others argued more reasonably that once a moment had passed it was lost since 'for what's done is done and what's won is won/And what's lost is lost and gone for ever'.[22] Even if it appeared that history was repeating itself then it never quite did so. Instead history moved along the lines of Hegel's dialectic.[23] The new would never completely destroy the old, but nor could the old ever be fully revived. So much of what the Conservative Right desired had already been so seriously eroded that revival was not a viable position. Pessimism was therefore a more appropriate tone than bellicosity.[24] In 1977 Margaret Thatcher was heard to say that 'we don't want pessimists in our party'.[25] Consequently she embarked on a course of action which proved to be every bit as destructive of the things the Conservative Right held dear. Those of that persuasion have no option in modern times but to be pessimists.

NOTES

1. Interview with Jonathan Aitken, London, 6 February 2017.
2. William F. Buckley, 'Our Mission Statement', *National Review*, 19 November 1955, https://www.nationalreview.com/1955/11/our-mission-statement-william-f-buckley-jr/, accessed 17 May 2019.
3. M. Oakeshott, 'On Being Conservative', in T. Fuller (ed.) *Rationalism in Politics and Other Essays* (Indianapolis: Liberty, 1991), p. 408.
4. Ibid.
5. T. E. Utley, 'The Art of Tory Politics', *Daily Telegraph*, 14 May 1984, reprinted in C. Moore and S. Heffer (eds.) *A Tory Seer: The Selected Journalism of T. E. Utley* (London: Hamish Hamilton, 1989), p. 72.
6. Ibid.
7. Ibid.
8. Ibid., p. 73.
9. Lord Coleraine, *For Conservatives Only* (London: Tom Stacey, 1970), pp. 62–63.
10. Ibid.
11. See Chapter 8.
12. A. Gamble, *The Free Economy and the Strong State: The Politics of Thatcherism* (Basingstoke: Palgrave, 1994, 2nd edition).
13. P. Worsthorne, Intelligence^2 Debate, London, 2 November 2004, https://www.youtube.com/watch?v=kfeBReJA-0g, accessed 17 May 2019.

14. Ibid.
15. Ibid.
16. Ibid.
17. P. Worsthorne, 'Ship of State in Peril', in G. Dench (ed.) *The Rise and Rise of Meritocracy* (London: Wiley Blackwell, 2007).
18. P. Worsthorne, speech to the Athenaeum, 21 June 2006.
19. P. Hitchens, *The Abolition of Britain* (London: Quartet, 1999), p. 348.
20. J. Gray, 'The Undoing of Conservatism' (London: Social Market Foundation, 1994).
21. Enoch Powell speech, available at https://www.youtube.com/watch?v=Ob6Wv_FPp7w, accessed 17 May 2019.
22. Lyrics taken from the song, 'The Town I Loved so Well'.
23. J. Kersey, speech to the Traditional Britain Group, December 2013, https://johnkersey.org/2013/12/14/traditional-britain-group-conference-2013/, accessed 17 May 2019.
24. R. Scruton, *England: An Elegy* (London: Continuum, 2006).
25. P. Gosh, 'Towards the Verdict of History: Mr Cowling's Doctrine', in M. Bentley (ed.) *Public and Private Doctrine: Essays in British History Presented to Maurice Cowling* (Cambridge: Cambridge University Press, 1993), p. 288.

BIBLIOGRAPHY

A. INTERVIEWS

Jacob Rees-Mogg MP (London), 9th February 2016.
Jesse Norman MP (London), 12th September 2016.
Nicholas Winterton (Cheshire), 23rd September 2016.
Ann Winterton (Cheshire), 23rd September 2016.
Peter Hitchens (London), 11th October 2016.
Anne Widdecombe (London), 11th October 2016.
Lord Salisbury (London), 12th October 2016.
Sir William Cash MP (London), 13th October 2016.
Sir Edward Leigh MP (London), 17th January 2017.
David Burrowes MP (London), 17th January 2017.
Charles Moore (London), 17th January 2017.
Philip Davies MP (London), 19th January 2017.
Sir Gerald Howarth MP (London), 19th January 2017.
Dr. Myles Harris (London), 27th January 2017.
Lord Sudeley (London), 6th February 2017.
Jonathan Aitken (London), 6th February 2017.
David Nicholson (London), 13th February 2017.
Gregory Lauder-Frost (telephone), 23rd February 2017.
Richard Ritchie (London), 8th March 2017.
Tim Janman (London), 27th March 2017.
Lord Deben (London), 4th April 2017.
Lord Griffiths of Fforestfach (London), 6th April 2017.
Lord Tebbit (London), 6th April 2017.
Sir Adrian Fitzgerald (London), 10th April 2017.

© The Editor(s) (if applicable) and The Author(s) 2020
K. Hickson, *Britain's Conservative Right since 1945*,
https://doi.org/10.1007/978-3-030-27697-3

Edward Norman (telephone), 28th April 2017.
Cedric Gunnery (London), 2nd May 2017.
Paul Bristol (London), 3rd May 2017.
Harvey Thomas (London), 3rd May 2017.
Ian Crowther (telephone), 12th May 2017.
Iain Duncan Smith MP (London), 4th July 2017.
Angela Ellis-Jones (London), 4th July 2017.
John Hayes MP (London), 4th July 2017.
Dennis Walker (London), 24th July 2017.
Lord Howard of Lympne (London), 12th September 2017.
Lord Cormack (London), 13th September 2017.

B. ARCHIVES

Julian Amery Papers, Churchill College, Cambridge.
John Biggs-Davison Papers, House of Commons, London.
Monday Club Papers, personal possession of Sir Adrian Fitzgerald.
Enoch Powell Papers, Churchill College, Cambridge.

C. PERIODICALS

Monday World.
Primrose League Gazette.
Right Now.
Solon.
The Salisbury Review.
The Spectator.

D. SELECTED BOOKS AND ARTICLES

Amery, L. S. *Thoughts on the Constitution* (Oxford: Oxford University Press, 1947).
Ashdown, P. *Diaries, Volume 1: 1988–1997* (London: Allen Lane, 2000).
Astor, W. W. *Our Imperial Future* (London: Signpost, 1943).
Atkins, J. '"Strangers in Their Own Country": Epideictic Rhetoric and Communal Definition in Enoch Powell's "Rivers of Blood" Speech' *Political Quarterly* 89/3 (September 2018), pp. 362–369.
Aughey, A. *Under Siege: Ulster Unionism and the Anglo-Irish Agreement* (Belfast: Blackstaff, 1989).
Aughey, A. 'Traditional Toryism' in K. Hickson (ed.) *The Political Thought of the Conservative Party Since 1945* (Basingstoke: Palgrave, 2005).
Aughey, A. *The Politics of Englishness* (Manchester: Manchester University Press, 2007).

Aughey, A. *The Conservative Party and the Nation: Union, England and Europe* (Manchester: Manchester University Press, 2018).

Bacon, R. and W. Eltis, *Britain's Economic Problem: Too Few Producers* (London: Macmillan, 1976).

Baker, D. *Ideology of Obsession: A. K. Chesterton and British Fascism* (London: I.B. Tauris, 2017).

Bale, T. *The Conservatives Since 1945: The Drivers of Party Change* (Oxford: Oxford University Press, 2012).

Bale, T. *The Conservative Party from Thatcher to Cameron* (Cambridge: Polity, 2016, 2nd edition).

Bartlett, B. and T. Roth, *The Supply-Side Solution* (London: Macmillan, 1984).

Bassett, R. *Last Imperialist: A Portrait of Julian Amery* (Settrington: Stone Trough, 2015).

Beech, M. 'A Tale of Two Liberalisms' in S. Lee and M. Beech (eds.) *The Cameron-Clegg Government: Coalition Politics in an Age of Austerity* (Basingstoke: Palgrave, 2011).

Biffen, J. *A Nation in Doubt* (London: Conservative Political Centre, 1976).

Biffen, J. *Political Office or Political Power?* (London: Centre for Policy Studies, 1977).

Biffen, J. *Forward from Conviction* (London: Conservative Political Centre, 1986).

Biggs-Davison, J. *Look to the Foundations: A Tory Restatement* (London: Edinburgh Press, 1949).

Biggs-Davison, J. *Tory Lives* (London: Putnam, 1952).

Biggs-Davison, J. *An Uncertain Ally* (London: Johnson, 1957).

Biggs-Davison, J. *Europe: Faith Not Despair* (London: Monday Club, 1967).

Biggs-Davison, J. *The Centre Cannot Hold: Or Mao, Marcuse and All That Marx* (London: Monday Club, 1969).

Biggs-Davison, J. *Ulster Catholics and the Union* (London: Friends of the Union, 1987).

Blake, R. *The Conservative Party from Peel to Major* (London: Heinemann, 1997).

Blake, Lord and J. Patten (eds.) *The Conservative Opportunity* (London: Macmillan, 1976).

Blond, P. *Red Tory* (London: Faber, 2010).

Body, R. *England for the English* (London: New European Publications, 2001).

Boyson, R. *Centre Forward: A Radical Conservative Programme* (London: Temple Smith, 1978).

Brandon, R. *Suez: Splitting a Nation* (London: Collins, 1973).

Brazier, J. and D. Carswell, 'Criminal Justice Gone Mad' in Cornerstone Group, *Being Conservative: A Cornerstone of Policies to Revive Tory Britain* (London: Cornerstone Group, 2005).

Brittan, S. *The Economic Consequences of Democracy* (London: Holmes & Meier, 1979).

Bruce-Gardyne, J. *Whatever Happened to the Quiet Revolution?* (London: Knight, 1974).

Buchanan, J. and G. Tullock, *The Calculus of Consent* (Ann Arbor: University of Michigan, 1962).

Bulpitt, J. 'Conservative Leaders and the Euro Ratchet: Five Doses of Scepticism' *Political Quarterly* 63/3 (1992), pp. 258–275.

Bulpitt, J. 'The European Question' in D. Marquand and A. Seldon (eds.) *The Ideas That Shaped Postwar Britain* (London: Fontana, 1996).

Burke, E. *Reflections on the Revolution in France* (Harmondsworth: Penguin, 2003).

Butler, R. A. (ed.) *Conservatism, 1945–50* (London: Conservative Political Centre, 1950).

Butt, R. 'The Tension of the 1980s' in M. Alison and D. Edwards (eds.) *Christianity and Conservatism* (London: Hodder & Stoughton, 1990).

Cash, B. 'Rediscovering Conservatism for the British Nation' in Cornerstone Group, *Being Conservative: A Cornerstone of Policies to Revive Tory Britain* (London: Cornerstone Group, 2005).

Cash, B. 'A Better Britain in a Better Europe: Time for a Dose of "Eurorealism"' in D. Davis, B. Binley and J. Baron (eds.) *The Future of Conservatism: Values Revisited* (London: ConservativeHome, 2011).

Chesterton, G. K. *A Short History of England* (London: Chatto & Windus, 1907).

Clark, A. *Diaries* (London: Weidenfeld & Nicolson, 1993).

Clark, A. *Diaries: Into Politics* (London: Weidenfeld & Nicolson, 2000).

Cockett, R. *Thinking the Unthinkable: Think Tanks and the Economic Counter-Revolution, 1931–83* (London: HarperCollins, 1994).

Coleraine, Lord. *For Conservatives Only* (London: Tom Stacey, 1970).

Collings, R. (ed.) *Reflections: Selected Writings and Speeches of Enoch Powell* (London: Bellew, 1992).

Convery, A. *The Territorial Conservative Party: Devolution and Party Change in Scotland and Wales* (Manchester: Manchester University Press, 2016).

Cowling, M. *1867: Disraeli, Gladstone and the Revolution: The Passing of the Second Reform Bill* (Cambridge: Cambridge University Press, 1967).

Cowling, M. *The Impact of Labour* (Cambridge: Cambridge University Press, 1971).

Cowling, M. *The Impact of Hitler* (Cambridge: Cambridge University Press, 1975).

Cowling. M. (ed.) *Conservative Essays* (London: Cassell, 1978).

Cowling. M. 'The Sources of the New Right: Irony, Geniality and Malice' *Encounter* (November 1989).

Cowling, M. 'The Case Against Going to War' *Finest Hour* (70) 1991.

Cox, G. 'The Living Constitution: A Conservative Reply to Liberal Constitutionalism' in D. Davis, B. Binley and J. Baron (eds.) *The Future of Conservatism: Values Revisited* (London: ConservativeHome, 2011).

Cranborne, Lord. *The Chain of Authority* (London: Politeia, 1997).

Cranborne, Lord. *The Renewal of Unionism* (London: Friends of the Union, 1997).

Crowther, I. *Chesterton* (London: Claridge, 1993).

Crowther, I. 'Conservatism' in W. Outhwaite (ed.) *The Blackwell Dictionary of Modern Social Thought* (Oxford: Blackwell, 2002).

Dalrymple, T. *Our Culture: What's Left of It* (Chicago: Ivan R. Dee, 2005).

Davies, C. *Permissive Britain: Social Change in the Sixties and Seventies* (London: Pitman, 1975).

Davies, C. *The Strange Death of Moral Britain* (London: Transaction, 2007).

Dorey, P. *British Conservatism: The Politics and Philosophy of Inequality* (London: I.B. Tauris, 2010).

Durham, M. *Sex and Politics* (Basingstoke: Macmillan, 1991).

Ellis-Jones, A. 'The Politics of Economics' in R. Scruton (ed.) *Conservative Thoughts: Essays from The Salisbury Review* (London: Claridge, 1988).

Elton, Lord. *The Unarmed Invasion: Survey of Afro-Asian Immigration* (London: Collins, 1965).

Ferguson, N. *Empire* (London: Allen Lane, 2003).

Filby, E. *God and Mrs Thatcher: The Battle for Britain's Soul* (London: Biteback, 2015).

Finer, S. (ed.) *Adversary Politics and Electoral Reform* (London: Wigram, 1975).

Foot, P. *The Rise of Enoch Powell* (Harmondsworth: Penguin, 1969).

Forster, A. *Euroscepticism in Contemporary British Politics* (London: Routledge, 2002).

Fraser, H. *A Rebel for the Right Reasons* (Stafford: Stafford and Stone Conservative Association, 1975).

Freeden, M. *Ideologies and Political Theory* (Oxford: Oxford University Press, 1998).

Friedman, M and R. Friedman. *Free to Choose* (Harmondsworth: Penguin, 1970).

Fuller, T. (ed.) *Rationalism in Politics and Other Essays* (Indianapolis: Liberty, 1991).

Galbraith, J. K. *The New Industrial State* (London: Hamilton, 1967).

Gamble, A. *The Conservative Nation* (London: Routledge, 1974).

Gamble, A. *The Free Economy and the Strong State* (Basingstoke: Macmillan, 1988, 1994).

Garnett, M. and K. Hickson. *Conservative Thinkers: The Key Contributors to the Political Thought of the Modern Conservative Party* (Manchester: Manchester University Press, 2009).

George, A. *An Awkward Partner* (Oxford: Oxford University Press, 1998).

Gilmour, I. *Inside Right* (London: Quartet, 1977).

Gilroy, P. *There Ain't No Black in the Union Jack* (London: Routledge, 2002).

Gosh, P. 'Towards the Verdict of History: Mr Cowling's Doctrine' in M. Bentley (ed.) *Public and Private Doctrine: Essays in British History Presented to Maurice Cowling* (Cambridge: Cambridge University Press, 1993).

Gow, I. *Ulster After the Agreement* (London: Friends of the Union, 1986).

Graham, C. and T. Prosser (eds.) *Waiving the Rules: The Constitution Under Thatcher* (Buckingham: Open University Press, 1988).

Gray, J. *The Undoing of Conservatism* (London: Social Market Foundation, 1994).

Griffiths, B. *Monetarism and Morality* (London: Centre for Policy Studies, 1985).

Griffiths, B. 'The Conservative Quadrilateral' in M. Alison and D. Edwards (eds.) *Christianity and Conservatism* (London: Hodder & Stoughton, 1990).

Griffiths, P. *A Question of Colour? The Smethwick Election of 1964* (London: Leslie Frewin, 1966).

Hailsham, Lord. *Dilemma of Democracy* (London: HarperCollins, 1978).

Hailsham, Lord. *On the Constitution* (London: HarperCollins, 1992).

Harwood, J., J. Guinness and J. Biggs-Davison. *Ireland: Our Cuba* (London: Monday Club, 1972).

Hayek, F. *The Road to Serfdom* (London: Routledge, 1944).

Hayek, F. *The Constitution of Liberty* (Chicago: University of Chicago, 1960).

Hayek, F. *Law, Legislation and Liberty: Volume 2—The Mirage of Social Justice* (London: Routledge, 1976).

Hayek, F. *Denationalisation* (London: Institute of Economic Affairs, 1978).

Hayek, F. 'The Weasel Word "Social"' in R. Scruton (ed.) *Conservative Thoughts: Essays from The Salisbury Review* (London: Claridge, 1988).

Hayes, J. 'On Being Conservative' in Cornerstone Group, *Being Conservative: A Cornerstone of Policies to Revive Tory Britain* (London: Cornerstone Group, 2005).

Hazell, R. (ed.) *The English Question* (Manchester: Manchester University Press, 2006).

Heffer, S. *The End of the Peer Show?* (London: Centre for Policy Studies, 1996).

Heffer, S. *Like the Roman* (London: Weidenfeld & Nicolson, 1998).

Heffer, S. *Nor Shall My Sword: The Reinvention of England* (London: Weidenfeld & Nicolson, 1999).

Heffer, S. *What Tories Want* (London: Politeia, 2000).

Heffer, S. 'Traditional Toryism' in K. Hickson (ed.) *The Political Thought of the Conservative Party Since 1945* (Basingstoke: Palgrave, 2005).

Helmer, R. 'Europe: A Conservative Rethink' in Cornerstone Group, *Being Conservative: A Cornerstone of Policies to Revive Tory Britain* (London: Cornerstone Group, 2005).

Hickson, K. *The IMF Crisis of 1976 and British Politics* (London: I.B. Tauris, 2005).

Hickson, K. (ed.) *The Political Thought of the Conservative Party Since 1945* (Basingstoke: Palgrave, 2005).

Hinchingbrooke, Lord. *Full Speed Ahead: Essays in Tory Reform* (London: Simpkin, Marshall, 1944).

Hitchens, P. 'The Legacy of the Sixties' *Prospect* 28 (1998).

Hitchens, P. *The Abolition of Britain* (London: Quartet, 1999).

Hogg, Q. *The Case for Conservatism* (London: Penguin, 1947).

Hollis, C. *Quality or Equality* (London: Signpost Booklets, 1944).

Howe, G. 'Sovereignty and Interdependence: Britain's Place in the World' *International Affairs* 66/4 (October 1990), pp. 675–695.

Hutber, P. *The Decline and Fall of the Middle Class and How It Can Fight Back* (Harmondsworth: Penguin, 1977).

Jago, M. *Rab Butler* (London: Biteback, 2015).

Jarvis, M. *Conservative Governments, Morality and Social Change in Affluent Britain, 1957–64* (Manchester: Manchester University Press, 2005).

Jones, A. *The Pendulum of Politics* (London: Faber, 1946).

Jones, N. 'Enoch Powell: A Personal Insight' *Political Quarterly* 89/3 (September 2018), pp. 358–361.

Joseph, K. *Freedom Under the Law* (London: Conservative Political Centre, 1975).

Joseph, K. *Stranded on the Middle Ground* (London: Centre for Policy Studies, 1976).

Kelly, S. *The Myth of Mr Butskell* (Aldershot: Ashgate, 2002).

Lamont, N. *Sovereign Britain* (London: Duckworth, 1995).

Law, R. *Return from Utopia* (London: Faber and Faber, 1950).

Layton-Henry, Z. *The Politics of Immigration* (Oxford: Blackwell, 1992).

Leigh, E. *The Strange Desertion of Tory England* (London: Cornerstone Group, 2005).

Leruth, B., N. Startin and S. Usherwood (eds.) *The Routledge Handbook of Euroscepticism* (London: Routledge, 2018).

Letwin, S. *The Anatomy of Thatcherism* (London: Fontana, 1992).

Liddle, A. *Ruth Davidson and the Resurgence of the Scottish Tories* (London: Biteback, 2018).

Macleod, I. and E. Powell, *Social Services: Needs and Means* (London: Conservative Political Centre, 1954).

Macmillan, H. *The Middle Way* (London: Macmillan, 1938).

Major, J. *The Autobiography* (London: HarperCollins, 1999).

Marten, N. *The Common Market: No Middle Way* (London: Common Market Safeguard Campaign, 1974).

Maude, A. *The Common Problem* (London: Constable, 1969).

Maude, A. and E. Powell. *Biography of a Nation* (London: Pitman, 1955).

Mead, L. *Beyond Entitlement: The Social Obligations of Citizenship* (New York: Free Press, 1986).

Molyneaux, J. *Sixth Ian Gow Memorial Lecture* (London: Friends of the Union, 1996).

Monday Club Home Group. *You: Your Children, Your Job, Your Home, Your Umbrella* (London: Monday Club, 1962).

Montagu, V. *The Conservative Dilemma* (London: Monday Club, 1970).

Moore, C. *First Ian Gow Memorial Lecture* (London: Friends of the Union, 1991).

Moore, C. *Margaret Thatcher: The Authorised Biography, Volume 1: Not For Turning* (London: Allen Lane, 2013).

Moore, C. *Margaret Thatcher: The Authorised Biography, Volume 2: Everything She Wants* (London: Allen Lane, 2015).

Moore, C. *Margaret Thatcher: The Authorised Biography, Volume 3: Herself Alone* (London: Allen Lane, 2019).

Moore, C. and S. Heffer (eds.) *Tory Seer: The Selected Journalism of T. E. Utley* (London: Hamilton, 1989).

Mount, F. *The Subversive Family* (London: Cape, 1982).

Murray, C. *Losing Ground: American Social Policy, 1950–1980* (New York: Basic, 1984).

Murray, C. *The Emerging British Underclass* (London: IEA Health and Welfare Unit, 1990).

No Turning Back Group. *Choice and Responsibility: The Enabling State* (London: Conservative Political Centre, 1990).

Norton, P. *The Constitution: The Conservative Way Forward* (London: Conservative Political Centre, 1992).

Norton, P. 'The Constitution' in K. Hickson (ed.) *The Political Thought of the Conservative Party Since 1945* (Basingstoke: Palgrave, 2005).

Norton, P. and A. Aughey. *Conservatives and Conservatism* (London: Temple Smith, 1981).

Nozick, R. *Anarchy, State and Utopia* (Oxford: Blackwell, 1974).

Oakeshott, M. 'Contemporary British Politics' *The Cambridge Journal* 1/8 (1948).

Oakeshott, M. *On Human Conduct* (Oxford: Clarendon, 1975).

Oborne, P. *The Triumph of the Political Class* (London: pocket Books, 2008).

O'Brien, Conor Cruise. 'Address to the Friends of the Union' (London: Friends of the Union, 1988).

Onslow, S. 'Unreconstructed Nationalists and a Minor Gunboat Operation: Julian Amery, Neil McLean and the Suez Crisis' *Contemporary British History* 20/1 (2006), pp. 73–99.

Orwell, G. *The Lion and the Unicorn: Socialism and the English Genius* (Harmondsworth: Penguin, 2018).

O'Sullivan, J. 'Conservatism and Cultural Identity' in K. Minogue (ed.) *Conservative Realism* (London: HarperCollins, 1996).

Phillips, M. *All Must Have Prizes* (London: Little, Brown, 1996).

Pickthorn, K. *Principles or Prejudices* (London: Signpost Booklets, 1943).

Pilbeam, B. 'Social Morality' in K. Hickson (ed.) *The Political Thought of the Conservative Party Since 1945* (Basingstoke: Palgrave, 2005).

Pitchford, M. *The Conservative Party and the Extreme Right* (Manchester: Manchester University Press, 2013).

Popper, K. 'The Open Society and Its Enemies' *The Economist* 23 (April 1988).

Porter, B. *The Lion's Share: A Short History of British Imperialism, 1850–1983* (London: Longman, 1984, 2nd edition).

Portillo, M. *A Vision for the 1990s* (London: Conservative Political Centre, 1992).

Powell, E. *A View on Education* (London: Working Men's College, 1964).

Powell, E. and A. Maude (eds.) *Change is Our Ally* (London: Conservative Political Centre, 1954).

Powell, E. and Wallis, K. *The House of Lords in the Middle Ages* (London: Weidenfeld & Nicolson, 1968).

Redwood, J. *Popular Capitalism* (London: Routledge, 1988).

Ritchie, R. (ed.) *A Nation or No Nation? Six Years in British Politics* (London: Elliot Right Way Books, 1979).

Ritchie, R. (ed.) *Enoch Powell on 1992* (London: Anaya, 1989).

Roberts, A. *Salisbury: Victorian Titan* (London: Orion, 1999).

Rossiter, M. *Sink the Belgrano* (London: Batam, 2007).

Salisbury, 5th Marquess. *Post-War Conservative Party Policy* (London: Murray, 1942).

Schofield, C. *Enoch Powell and the Making of Postcolonial Britain* (Cambridge: Cambridge University Press, 2013).

Schumpeter, J. *Capitalism, Socialism and Democracy* (New York: Harper, 1942).

Scruton, R. *The Conservative Idea of Community* (London: Conservative 2000 Foundation, 1996).

Scruton, R. *The Meaning of Conservatism* (Basingstoke: Palgrave, 2001, 3rd edition).

Scruton, R. *England: An Elegy* (London: Continuum, 2006).

Scruton, R. *Our Church* (London: Atlantic, 2012).

Scruton, R. *How to Be a Conservative* (London: Bloomsbury, 2014).

Seeley, J. *The Expansion of England* (London: Macmillan, 1899).

Selwyn-Gummer, J. *The Permissive Society: Fact of Fantasy* (London: Cassell, 1971).

Skidelsky, R. *Oswald Mosley* (London: Macmillan, 1981).

Smith, P. (ed.) *Lord Salisbury on Politics* (Cambridge: Cambridge University Press, 1972).

Smith, S (ed.) *Reassessing Suez 1956: New Perspectives on the Crisis and Its Aftermath* (Aldershot: Ashgate, 2008).

Speed, K. *Sea Change* (London: Ashgrove, 1982).

Spencer, H. *The Man Versus the State* (London: Williams and Norgate, 1884).

Stapleton, J. 'T. E. Utley and Renewal of Conservatism in Post-War Britain' *Journal of Political Ideologies* 19/2 (2014), pp. 207–226.

Storey, D. and T. Taylor. *The Conservative Party and the Common Market* (London: Monday Club, 1983).

Sudeley, Lord. *The Preservation of the House of Lords* (London: Monday Club, 1991).

Sudeley, Lord. *Peers Through the Mists of Time* (London: Diehard, 2018).
Sutherland, C. *The Decline of the Scottish Conservative Party* (Leicester: Book Guild, 2016).
Sykes, F. *The Road to Recovery* (London: Signpost Booklets, 1944).
Taggart, P. 'A Touchstone of Dissent: Euroscepticism in Contemporary Western European Party Systems' *European Journal of Political Research* 33/3 (1988), pp. 363–388.
Taylor, E. *Teddy Boy Blue* (Glasgow: Kennedy & Boyd, 2008).
Taylor, H. '"Rivers of Blood" and Britain's Far Right' *Political Quarterly* 89/3 (September 2018), pp. 385–391.
Tebbit, N. *By Their Fruits Ye Shall Know Them* (London: Friends of the Union, 2002).
Thatcher, M. *The Downing Street Years* (London: HarperCollins, 1993).
Timmins, N. *The Five Giants: A Biography of the Welfare State* (London: HarperCollins, 2001).
Troen, S. and Shamesh, M. *The Suez-Sinai Crisis, 1956: Retrospective and Reappraisal* (London: Cass, 1990).
Utley, T. E. *Essays in Conservatism* (London: Conservative Political Centre, 1949).
Utley, T. E. 'The Mandate' *Cambridge Journal* 3/10 (July 1950).
Utley, T. E. *Not Guilty: The Conservative Reply* (London: MacGibbon and Kee, 1957).
Utley, T. E. 'A Comparison of Parties' in P. Dean, J. Douglas and T. E. Utley (eds.) *Conservative Points of View* (London: Conservative Political Centre, 1964).
Utley, T. E. *Enoch Powell: The Man and His Thinking* (London: HarperCollins, 1968).
Utley, T. E. *Lessons of Ulster* (London: Dent, 1975).
Utley, T. E. *One Nation: One Hundred Years On* (London: Conservative Political Centre, 1981).
Walker-Scott, D. and P. Walker. *A Call to the Commonwealth* (London: Worcester, 1962).
Wheatcroft, G. *The Strange Death of Tory England* (Harmondsworth: Penguin, 2005).
Whitehouse, M. *Who Does She Think She Is?* (London: New English Library, 1971).
Widdecombe, A. *Strictly Ann: The Autobiography* (London: Weidenfeld & Nicolson, 2013).
Wiener, M. *English Culture and the Decline of the Industrial Spirit, 1850–1980* (Cambridge: Cambridge University Press, 1981).
Williams, B. *The Evolution of Conservative Party Social Policy* (Basingstoke: Palgrave, 2015).
Winterton, S. *The Wintertons Unmuzzled* (London: Biteback, 2016).

Wood, J. (ed.) *Freedom and Reality* (Kingswood: Elliot Right Way Books, 1969).

Wood, J. (ed.) *Powell and the 1970 Election* (Kingswood: Elliot Right Way Books, 1970).

Wood, J. (ed.) *Still to Decide* (Kingswood: Elliot Right Way Books, 1972).

Worsthorne, P. 'Class and Conflict in British Foreign Policy' *Foreign Affairs* 37/3 (1959), pp. 419–431.

Worsthorne, P. *The Socialist Myth* (London: Cassell, 1971).

Worsthorne, P. 'F A Hayek: Next Construction for the Giant' in M. Ivens (ed.) *Prophets of Freedom* (London: Aims of Industry, 1975).

Worsthorne, P. 'Too Much Freedom' in M. Cowling (ed.) *Conservative Essays* (London: Cassell, 1978).

Worsthorne, P. *Peregrinations* (London: Weidenfeld & Nicolson, 1980).

Worsthorne, P. *By the Right* (Dublin: Brophy, 1987).

Worsthorne, P. *The Politics of Manners and the Uses of Inequality* (London: Centre for Policy Studies, 1988).

Worsthorne, P. *Tricks of Memory* (London: Weidenfeld & Nicolson, 1993).

Worsthorne, P. *In Defence of Aristocracy* (London: HarperCollins, 2004).

Worsthorne, P. 'Ship of State in Peril' in G. Dench (ed.) *The Rise and Rise of Meritocracy* (London: Wiley Blackwell, 2007).

Young, G. K. *Who Goes Home? Immigration and Repatriation* (London: Monday Club, 1969).

Young, H. *This Blessed Plot* (London: Macmillan, 1999).

INDEX

© The Editor(s) (if applicable) and The Author(s) 2020
K. Hickson, *Britain's Conservative Right since 1945*,
https://doi.org/10.1007/978-3-030-27697-3

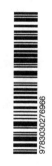